WORLD CITIES

NEW YORK

CONTENTS

Times Square on the eve of the millennium

New York was the quintessential city of the 20th century. Its worldliness, its creativity, the multiple spikes of its skyline – the nearest architecture comes to an act of nature – became in the course of the last century an object of intense desire, not just for the disaffected but for all the world. What follows presents its most significant works of architecture both built and projected, from the past 10 years and 10 years into the future. It is less a record of the imagination of architects and more a document that views architecture as the most permanent residue of the profound culture of a city. Unseen but always present with the multiple activities that are concentrated within the fabric of a great city are deeply rooted structures that sustain the essential ideological nature of its organisation. And beneath all the glitz and grime it must not be forgotten that New York remains the most ideological of cities, created by the Enlightenment. Created to form a ruthless rational order whose reality would forever be in a state of becoming.

This work has two major elements: a series of essays on the past, present and future of the city, and an extensive presentation of the more significant works of architecture, built, projected and dreamt during the last decade of the last century. The essays offer the material evidence of the state of the city at the start of the new millennium. They present a continual concern with the erosion of that order with which the city was reformed at the start of the 19th century. An erosion that not only affects the shape of communities and neighbourhoods but also their political and social order. The gridding of Manhattan, that regulated playing field that allowed the city to become a dominant mercantile power, became softened by the sense and sensibility of late 19th-century civics – a cultural paternalism which enabled the wealthy to build institutions with a permanence surpassing that of Europe. By the century's end New York had both produced and attracted vast extremes of wealth and poverty, all held within the constant egalitarian order of the grid.

Into the first decades of the 20th century population soared as waves of immigrants fled the disassembling of Europe. The city rapidly spread across north, south and east building communities that were formed increasingly by private speculation and cultural difference. The 20th century brought a brutal machine order, carried in the hundreds of miles of highways driven through the city under the direction of Robert Moses and careless of social and political consequences. Though all past orders persist into the present and continue to have influence, a continual absorption of the world's migrants and the unresolved divisions of class and race have created a city of deeply divided ethnic and cultural enclaves, united to the idea of New York by only one common bond: the shared participation in the goods and services of commerce and industry.

Each of my essays draws on quite distinct kinds of evidence. The first, 'Orders', is developed from the rich historical scholarship of recent years – primarily *Gotham* by Edwin G Burrows and Mike Wallace, *The Encyclopedia of New York* edited by Kenneth T Jackson, and Robert Caro's *The Power Broker*, the epic biography of Robert Moses. The essay, 'Boroughs', is shaped by the experience of driving more than 300 miles throughout the five boroughs over a period of several months. 'Architecture' offers a critical assessment of the material received from over 100 architects and was stimulated by the countless discussions that arose in the process of collecting and selecting their contributions. Penultimately, 'Futures' uses the material from the preceding essays to construct a series of imagined futures for the city as a complement to the architects' physical dreams for New York. Adding colour to my words are photo-essays which reinforce two qualities peculiar to the reality of the city. 'Icons' presents evidence of the conscious promotion of key structures, from the Statue of Liberty to the Empire State building, as consumable artefacts. This material is drawn from Dorothy Globus' collection of New York memorabilia, which must be one of the most extensive and deliciously eccentric. Ms Globus, who is the curator of the Gallery of the Fashion Institute of New York, helped with the selection. 'Streets' is an evocation of the distinct character of the streets of Manhattan from a video by June Park.

The five commentaries in 'Perspectives' are by individuals who each in different ways understands, and has influence on, the perception and reconception of the city. Joseph Rose is Chairman of New York City's Planning Commission and Director of the Department of City Planning within the Giuliani administration. Rebecca Robertson was the director of the 42nd Street Development Corporation and was appointed in 2000 to head a development group for the Lincoln Center area. Malcolm Holtzman is a partner in that most New York of architectural practices Hardy Holtzman Pfeiffer Associates. Raymond Gastil is the director of the Van Alen Institute, one of the few foundations in the city that exists solely to imagine its future, and Kenneth Frampton is Ware Professor of Architecture at Columbia University and one of the city's most influential teachers and critics.

The more than 150 projects represented are illustrated with drawings and short descriptive texts supplied by the architects. I must recognise that such a wealth of evidence is open to many more interpretations than are presented here. The material is divided into three sections. 'Buildings' presents work constructed in the last 10 years. 'Projects' are works in progress and 'Dreams' includes projects conceived within realistic programmes and those created to raise the ambitions of the city and the desire for the new. It is within the pursuit of such dreams that New York will discover its ability to continue to compel the imagination of the world into the new millennium.

Alan Balfour

ORDERS 1

MANHATTAN: THE COMMISSIONERS' PLAN

The essential architecture of New York emerges from three distinct structures: the grid, the climacteric of the 18th-century republican enlightenment; the park, the grandest demonstration of bourgeois sentimentalism; and lastly, the highways, bridges, mass transit and mass housing of 20th-century progress. In an exact sense these are products of changing political and social orders as the emerging republic seeks to manage reality.

Imagine three maps superimposed one on the other. At the first level are the patterns of the streets that form the five boroughs of New York: the rigid grid that covers most of Manhattan. Created by a public decree, it imposed itself on the borough through the 19th century until it slowly gave way to the more random orders of streets driven by private speculation. At the next level are the parks: the mothering figure of Central Park and formal parks and cemeteries in all the surrounding boroughs which give way to vast stretches of undeveloped land acquired by the city in the late 19th century, both for recreation and to receive the dead. And lastly, overriding all, are the broad bands of highways that ring the water's edge round all five boroughs and cut latterly through the Bronx and Queens, running the full length of the eastern edge of Queens to divide it from Long Island. Just as the grid forced the levelling of Manhattan, these highways recognise no natural barriers as they bridge rivers and bays and ride high and roughshod through neighbourhoods.

Between 1811 and 1821 a team of men laboured to place 1,647 markers in the earth and rock of Manhattan, at the intersecting points of a precise grid that would give order to the island's future. Their task took them through the extensive wilderness in the interior of the island and on to the many private estates and farms that had grown along the water's edge for 100 years and more. Across the fields and forests they carried, and drove in, 1,549 white marble markers, 3 feet 3 inches long and 3 inches square, engraved with the numbers of the intersecting streets and avenues that would cross these points and define the city. And when they came upon rock they hammered order into the bare stone with 98 iron bolts, the street numbers forged on to the metal. They were led by a young surveyor, John Randel Junior, who was the author of this most radical of city plans.[1]

Imagine the conceptual force of this act. The colonial city with its late medieval street pattern ran barely a mile north of the fortified southern point of the island. By the mid-18th century the city, as it expanded north, became increasingly rational in its form. The 10 miles and more of Manhattan Island north of the colonial town was a mixture of forests and rocky ridges, with ancient farms and small settlements along the shoreline. The hills and dales of the interior formed many small valleys whose streams flowed into ponds and extensive marshes. Forcing a marble and iron trace of order across a rural and wild landscape had to be done with axe and scythe, in the face of persistent hostility from landowners, hunters and squatters.

It is too easily forgotten that this ruthless marking of a new order was the product of the modern world's most successful revolution. The signatories of the Declaration of Independence immediately faced the problem of devising the means to achieve social cohesion in the new republic. They were all children of European monarchies which maintained order from the top down through the structures of rigid class systems, reinforced by standing armies and by a Church that recognised the divine right of kings. The new republic had no such structures. It had to invent arrangements that would be driven, with equality, from the bottom up and expected its citizens to take up arms to defend their country and sacrifice private desire for the public good. Such reliance on the moral virtue of their citizens made republican governments fragile. The only lessons from history came from small republics that were almost continuously in arms; such a model was not inappropriate for this grand mercantile project. The answer would lie in the application of just and neutral law to all things.

The need to plan for the future of the city was recognised in the first decade of the century with the feverish rise in its expectation of commercial growth. In 1804 the New York Common Council gave instructions that a plan be prepared 'for new streets to be laid out and opened'. In 1807 the state legislature appointed a streets commission to propose a plan for laying out 'streets, roads, public squares of such extent and direction as to them shall seem most conducive to public good'. It was to do so in such a manner 'as to unite regularity and order with Public convenience and benefit, and in particular to promote the health of the city' by allowing for the 'free and abundant circulation of air'. The recommendations of the Street Commission, which included Gouverneur Morris and Simeon De Witt, surveyor general of New York State, would have the force of law. In the light of what is to follow, note that 'Public' is an idea of such significance that it must be capitalised; it has replaced the Crown as the ruling authority.

The first task was to carry out an accurate survey of the island. The person chosen to do this, John Randel Junior, was still in his early 20s and had been surveyor to General Simeon De Witt. He aimed not only to produce a survey 'with an accuracy not exceeded by any work of its kind in America', but also one that blended with Manhattan's topography. He wrote, 'I superintended the surveys with a view to ascertain the most eligible grounds for the intended streets and avenues, with reference to the sites least obstructed by rocks, precipices, and steep grades and other obstacles.' This suggests he was initially considering a plan which would sit gently on the rocky landscapes of the island; the results could not have been more different .

Randel reported regularly to the commissioners, for whom the form of the plan was a matter of deep concern. The record reflects their discussion as to 'whether they should confine themselves to rectilinear and rectangular streets, or whether they should adopt some of these supposed improvements, by circles, or ovals, and stars'. Randel's survey was completed in 1810. It provided a scientific mapping of the coastline and a detailed delineation of the topography and water flows of the island. It showed an island essentially unchanged since the Ice Age, a rocky and forested wedge, 4 miles at its widest and 12 miles long. The commissioners determined, with Randel's advice, that a hard and constant grid would be the appropriate order in which to lay out a comprehensive and permanent system of streets on the island. Their reason: 'They could not but bear in mind that a city is to be composed principally of the habitations of men, and that straight sided and right angle houses are the most cheap to build and the most convenient to live in.' They determined that this future city would consist of 12 north–south avenues, each 100 feet wide and, at intervals of 200 feet, 155 cross streets, each 60 feet wide. The Act that had created the commission made its decision 'the final and conclusive law unalterable except by state action'. The grid, though vastly disruptive, was accepted without debate. Thus New York City became bounded by 'one grand permanent plan'.

Randel was requested to engrave this sweeping rational

order on to the plate of his just completed survey. The resulting drawing, 106 inches by 30 inches, was printed in 1811 and henceforth was known as the 'Commissioners' Plan'. In the months that followed its publication each permutation of the 12 by 155 grid was carefully carved into marble posts and forged into the iron bolts that Randel forced into the land to establish the new order. Forcing this abstract order of reason on to the natural skin of the island seems a dramatically modern act. Nature mastered without compromise. Man's intellect dominant – projecting on to the island an utterly rational absolute future. The commissioners' order to stake out the ground with the coordinates is a measure of how firmly they believed that rational order would determine the future, setting the boundaries for freedom within reason. They were not unaware of the force of their proposal. They wrote that the plan provided space enough 'for a greater population than is collected at any spot on this side of China'. Its ruthlessness still shocks. The vast composite structure which fills the island of Manhattan was ordained at the beginning of the 19th century in the absolute conviction that it was right. It continues to exert its compounding intensity and strangeness on the culture of the city.

At the time of the Commissioners' Plan New York had lost all political power, yet even before the clear emergence of the Industrial Revolution in America the city's leaders believed it capable of powerful commercial growth. The increase in the city's foreign trade after 1790 led one newspaper to predict that New York's population could grow to 700,000 by 1850 and reach three million by the end the 19th century. The plan was necessary to control a city that would evolve through commercial enterprise and speculation. It was realised that a city based purely on commerce – a new idea – should be formed free from distortions of political, religious or aristocratic power to provide the appropriate field for commercial action. Indeed, Randel was later to write that his plan heightened opportunities for 'buying, selling and improving real estate'. The commissioners, though, argued that to have taken the grid beyond 155th Street would have led to speculation beyond reason!

Conceptualisation on such a scale has no parallel in the history of cities. In 1803 Joseph Françoise Mangin and Casimer Goerick had developed a plan for the future Manhattan which, unlike the commissioners' plan, proposed clearly distinct densities of grids for the various needs of the emerging city – health, recreation, commerce, community – but the commissioners would have none of this. Like the proposed Erie Canal, the development of Manhattan was seen as 'internal improvements ' that gloried in the supremacy of technique over topography. The same rational determination that drove the building of the canal was present in the grid, the same men and the same revolutionary spirit.

Because the city, had lost political influence the plan made no attempt to anticipate future centres of power. In the new republic neither gods nor kings would command any special place. For the first time a city was conceived as a decentred and univalent field of enterprise. The only power in its future would be commerce. The plan, however, did have two specific designations of use. One plot of land high on the west side was, in enlightened fashion, 'concentrated for the purpose of science'. And the largest clear area in the grid, just north of Greenwich Village, was designated The Parade. This was a nation still under constant military threat from Britain.

In their epic work *Gotham,* historians Edwin G Burrows and Mike Wallace offer engaging insights into the Commissioners' Plan:[2]

> The grid established Republican as well as realtor values in its refusal to privilege particular places or parcels. All plots were equal under the commissioners' regime and the network of parcels and perpendiculars provided a Democratic alternative to the royalist avenues of Baroque European cities. The shift from naming streets to numbering them, beyond promoting efficiency also embodied a lexicographical leveling; no longer would families of rank and fortune memorialize themselves in the cityscape.

The plan asserted republican order over lingering Tory tendencies among the old families, and the royalist landscapes along the river's edge. It forced equality not only by the discipline of the grid but by the small size of the lots. It was the pressure of ambition on the small lots that forced Manhattan into the sky. The plan was a new beginning with all evidence of the past removed.

The configuration of Manhattan Island allowed for a plan that was wholly internal to itself; there were no major roads crossing it and no favoured link to any of the surrounding lands. The attempt to remove the only major historic route north through the island, now named Broadway, failed: usage proved more powerful than the law, but only in this one case. With the increasing pace of street openings Broadway alone resisted submersion beneath the gridiron, and continues to this day to give complexity and texture to the monotonous walls of the grid.

The gridiron has lost none of its control on the reality and on the political, social and economic forces that led to its adoption. These remain embedded in its continual evolution. Place yourself in the minds of those commissioners advocating in public a plan without charm, without centre, without bias. In this, and consciously so, it is the antithesis of the European city: the city as a field of free enterprise and speculation within reason versus the city of power centres and vested interests. The European city reinforcing and flattering the powers of Church and Crown, structured to demonstrate hierarchies of power; structured to resist change. The new American city ordered to allow continual change in a structure of constant order, a neutral field for the public pursuit of commercial enterprise; structured to constrain all ambition in a frame of reason. The neutrality, the lack of emotion are almost painful. This city is a tough place.

Randel engraved the final Commissioners' Plan in 1821. It is beautifully drawn with faint echoes of Piranesi. It depicts three superimposed maps. At the top it is a small map of New York State, across the centre is the great grid plan and across the bottom, in a *trompe l'oeil* effect suggesting an unrolled drawing dropped below the main work, is a small plan of Philadelphia. Randel is not recorded as having any involvement in the survey of that city, but offering its venerable plan as evidence of the historical use of the grid could have been designed to diffuse criticism. Randel would have us see the new Manhattan as a direct descendant of Penn's noble plan for Philadelphia.

The plan has never ceased to be attacked. Clark More, philosopher and author of 'Twas the Night Before Christmas', wrote in 1824 that, 'the great principle which governs these plans is, to reduce the surface of the earth as nearly as possible to dead level. The natural inequities of the ground are destroyed, and the existing watercourses disregarded. These are men – who would have cut down the seven hills of Rome'. He may have resented the plan but he willingly developed his own property within the rules of the grid, to become the area that is now Chelsea. Edgar Allan Poe complained that the grand plan limited the picturesque development of the city because 'streets were already mapped through areas that may have different potential'. All land, irrespective of its formal quality, became town lots. Poe was much concerned with the plan's levelling effect on the society. 'The great uniformity in the breadth and circumstances of the streets' failed to produce a variety 'which is necessary for the adequate habitations of classes, differing extremely in opulence, but must be found united in the population of a great city'. The overly democratic or neutral character of the grid was a persistent concern. Burrows and Wallace quote citizen William Duer who complained that the commissioners, 'had swung the scythe of equality across the island replacing the country estates of the privileged classes with block after democratic block, no one necessarily better than any other, each equally exposed to the ebb and flow of the market.'

The architectural historian Vincent Scully wrote in recent decades that the 'implacable gridiron' created a frame to support the American tendency towards private luxury and public squalor. John Reps, the most passionate recorder of the American city, wrote that, 'the fact that the gridiron served as a model for later cities was a disaster whose consequences have

11

barely been mitigated by recent city planners'. Lewis Mumford, the wise defender of social democracy, wrote that Randel 'with a T square and a triangle – the municipal engineer, without the slightest training as either an architect or a sociologist could "plan" a metropolis'. He summed it up as 'civic folly'. Given the plan's radical egalitarianism, this is a very bourgeois view from such an old lefty. Why does this most substantial observer of the culture of cities not offer more insight into the political force of the proposition – why blame it all on the surveyor?

The grid would provide the frame within which this new democracy would advance commercial enterprise; a neutral field that would protect, but not interfere with, individual rights. The grid would unify ambition within a frame of reason. The grid would manifest Public order. It would bind all ambitions and anxieties and oppositions into a coherent whole. The grid would be both the least and the most public interference with private enterprise. The grid would be in the exact sense the public realm. Such political conceptualisation suggests a desire either for unity or intellectual dictatorship. As the result of a tactic designed to produce uniformity of opportunity, New York has become a city of factions or fiefdoms, each centre of power playing out a highly idiosyncratic game exaggerated by the constraint of the grid.

The Commissioners' Plan was directly paralleled by the national plans that not only determined the boundaries of states but also laid the virtual reality of a grid over thousands of miles of undeveloped heartland, which it subdivided to structure the commercial, educational and civic order of community. Even now, as can be seen from the air over the Midwest, this desire for order marks lines for miles across the cornfields, and most roads are on the Cartesian grid.

With Randel's marble stakes as a guide the geometric pattern of streets was slowly engraved on the land. There was ample compensation for landowners whose property was being brought within city order. They were free to speculate in the development of the newly arranged parcels of land but not to retain any vestige of past order or use. An observer wrote in the 1830s that none of Manhattan's ancient hills, dales, swamps, springs, streams, palms, forests and meadows would be permitted to interrupt the fearful symmetry of the grid. The Common Council, entrusted with establishing the new order, was empowered to demolish and remove any streets that stood in the path of the gridiron. Thus the Bowery village laid out in 1779 on a true north–south grid was slowly removed as Third Avenue cut through the city.

The rule of law did not last long and, predictably in a great commercial city, the development of land became an increasingly competitive commercial enterprise. It was driven by the rapid growth of road and rail links east through the independent cities of Brooklyn and Queens on to Long Island and north into the Bronx. Gradually, the unity that was demanded by the grid faded as the public realm became the commercial realm. This was a gradual shift and, as it evolved, the need to give significance to an American idea of society became more emblematic.

of the City of New York

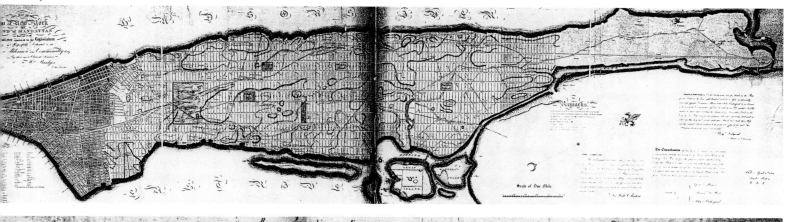

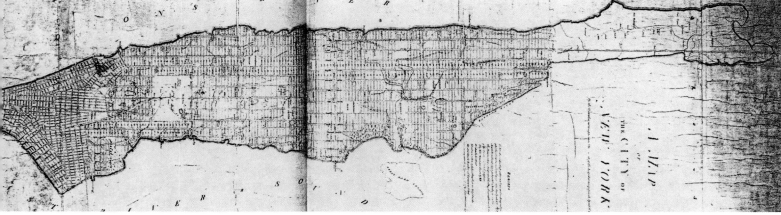

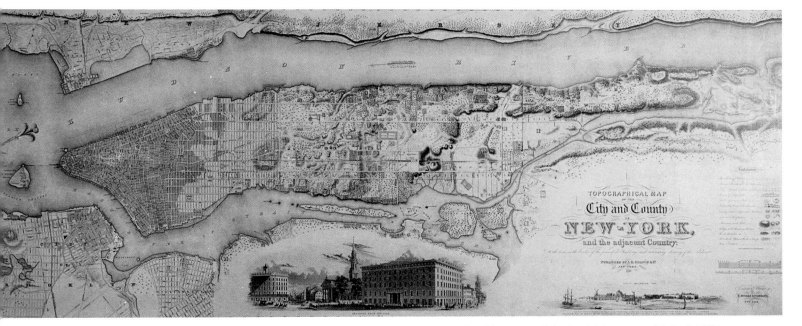

top: The Commissioners' Plan, 1811: a map of the City of New York by the commissioners appointed by an act of the Legislature passed 3 April 1807
pher John Randel, Jr), uncoloured manuscript on paper, 106 x 30 7/16 inches;
Adaptation of the Commissioners' Plan: map of the City of New York and island of Manhattan as laid out by the commissioners (cartographer John Randel, Jr;
Peter Maverick; adapted and published by William Bridges, New York, 16 November 1811), coloured line engraving on copper, 91 3/8 x 24 5/8 inches;
Topographical Map: topographical map of the City and County of New York and the adjacent country (cartographer David H Burr; published by J H Colton and
, New York, 1836), uncoloured engraving, 67 1/8 x 29 3/8 inches.

CENTRAL PARK

Fifty years after embedding the grid into the soil of Manhattan the city forced into it a new element: Central Park. Central Park is a miracle that gains its grandeur from being both a complement, and an opposition, to the grid. Its natural-seeming landscapes are made glorious within an intense and rigid frame. Although the essential difference between grid and park is a product, in some measure, of the random forces of history, it is a beautiful reflection of both, a shift in the politics of order and in the metaphysics of the Western cultural imagination: 18th-century reason, cold and disciplined, ensuring order through the force of law; 19th-century civic society trusting in human nature and sensibility to maintain social harmony – the park would bring out the best in people and can be seen as the most sympathetic stage on which to enhance the natural harmony of society. Both aspects seem present in Thomas Paine's pamphlet *Common Sense* (1776). While government promotes our happiness only 'negatively by restraining our vices, society promotes our happiness positively by uniting our affections'. Grid as government and the park as society are exquisitely thesis and antithesis: one could not have been created without the other.

The first important public expression of a major inadequacy in the Commissioners' Plan came in editorials by William Cullen Bryant in the *New York Evening Post*. Although the matter had been long in his thoughts it was first publicly expressed in July 1844: 'If the public authority who spend so much of our money in laying out the city would do what is in their power, they might give our vast population an extensive pleasure ground for shade and recreation.' The commissioners had admitted that their plan made little provision for public space: 'It may be a matter of surprise that so few vacant spaces had been left [open in the plan] and those so small, for the benefit of fresh air and consequent preservation of health.' The note continued: 'Certainly, if New York had been situated alongside a small stream, such as the Seine or Thames,' it might have needed more ample public space. 'But those large arms of the sea which embrace Manhattan Island render its situation, in regard to health and pleasure, as well as to the convenience of commerce, peculiarly felicitous.' Not so, thought Bryant.

The leaders of mid-19th century New York culture were deeply impressed by the parks of Europe, particularly those in London. Bryant used the *Evening Post* persistently to promote the need for a great public park and landscape architect Andrew Jackson Downing took up the cause in his magazine *The Horticulturist*. The effect of the lobbying in the press was such that in 1850 both candidates for mayor strongly favoured establishing a city park. In April 1851 newly elected Mayor Kingsland presented to the city council a clear and strong concept:[3]

Such a park, well laid out, would become a favoured resort of all classes … There are thousands who pass the day of rest among the idle and dissolute in porter houses, or places more objectionable, who would rejoice in being enabled to breathe the pure air in such a place, while the ride or drive through its avenues, free from the noise, dust and confusion, inseparable from all thoroughfares, would hold out strong inducements for the affluent to make it a place of resort.

It is a statement with a healthy spirit of egalitarianism. Downing, too, encouraged an egalitarian vision for the park. The *New York Times*, however, was not so sure. It loathed the notion of giving the very poor, the Boweryites, free access: 'As long as we are governed by the Five Points [the poorest, roughest part of the city], our best attempts to elegance and grace will bear some resemblance to jewels in the snouts of swine. Rather the park should never be made at all if it is to become the resort of rapscallions.'

Inspiration came from London. Dominating the Great Exhibition of 1851 was the vast and glorious Crystal Palace. It not only presented tangible evidence of the fruits of industry, but created the most compelling artificial destination for all the people of Britain, rich and poor alike. The nationwide network of railways brought to its gardens the greatest cross section of the population ever assembled. The grounds of the exhibition were truly the most egalitarian of landscapes and were expanded into extensive pleasure gardens when the Crystal Palace was moved to south London. Downing seems to have been impelled by visions from the Great Exhibition when, in August 1851, he wrote in *The Horticulturist* of a future where, 'in such a verdant zone would gradually grow up, as the wealth of the city increases … winter gardens of glass like the great Crystal Palace, where the whole people could luxuriate in groves of palms – while at the same moment that sleighing parties glide swiftly and noiselessly over snow covered avenues'.

Locating the park would take several years and much political and legal wrangling. The major competition was between a site on the East River and the central site where the park now lies. All the debates took place against a background of the city growing more rapidly, and with more prosperity, than anyone could have predicted. The strongest opposition came from those who saw such a use of land as limiting the open field of enterprise that the grid provided. In November 1853 the State Supreme Court appointed commissioners to take the land in the central part of the island, much of it rocky ridges above marshes and woodland. The competition to prepare designs for the park was announced in October 1857.

Frederick Law Olmsted had been a farmer and a journalist. The journal recording his travels through the South conveys a dread of slavery and foresees troubles ahead. During a journey

© Museum of the City of New York

15

through England he found great pleasure in the new parks being created by Sir Joseph Paxton: his excited report of a visit to Birkenhead Park near Liverpool delights in the mixing of the classes dashing for shelter from the rain. It was Paxton who conceived of the Crystal Palace and it was Paxton's example that led Olmsted to become America's great landscape architect and artist of civic life. However, although Olmsted overshadows all the others who contributed to making Central Park, it was formed as much by the forces of history and circumstance as by any one imagination. The formative influence on the design was the thorough mapping of the topography and watershed by Lieutenant Egbert Viele who was appointed engineer in chief for the new park in 1854. Olmsted was appointed park superintendent in 1857, just before the competition was announced. Olmsted later claimed that he had no intention of entering the competition until invited to partner the English architect Calvert Vaux. What definitely changed his mind was Viele's attitude: 'I'm completely indifferent whether you enter or not,' Viele told him. On 28 April 1858 the commission determined that Greensward, the submission from Olmsted and Vaux, should receive first prize. The animosity between Viele and Olmsted never faded and Viele subsequently won a lawsuit in which he claimed Olmsted had stolen his design.

In his writings Olmsted conveys the sense of statesmanship and grandeur of vision that he embodied in the park:

The whole island of New York would, but for such a reservation, before many years be occupied by buildings and paved streets; that millions upon millions of men were to live their lives upon this island, millions to go out from it – and that all – would assuredly suffer – from influences engendered by these conditions. The time will come when New York will be built-up, when all the grading and filling will be done, when the picturesquely varied rock formations of the island will have been converted into the foundations for rows of monotonous straight streets, and piles of erect buildings. There will be no suggestion left of its present varied surface, with the single exception of a few acres contained in the park.

At a time when the street grid had barely reached the middle of the island, Olmsted saw clearly in his mind's eye the city that would arise around the great park. In a letter to William Robertson in 1872 he wrote, 'I wish to present to you that it was designed as a park to be situated at the precise central [point] of the city of two million ... There is every reason to believe that the park will [one day] be enclosed by the compact town the borders of which were a mile away when it was laid out.' He foresaw a time when an artificial wall would surround the park, as high he wrote, 'as the Great Wall of China'. Here he gives us a glimpse into his imagination.

He states clearly in his report to the park commissioners that his park would be 'an antithesis of objects of vision to those of the streets and houses' of the grid-bound city. The many picturesque moments offered in the shifting landscapes of the park – these objects of vision – were drawn mainly from the English landscapes of the 18th and 19th centuries, the landscapes of Capability Brown and Joseph Paxton. There is a distinct similarity between the splendid balloonist's view of Central Park and a similar view of the Crystal Palace at Sydenham in London: both landscapes are filled with different events animated by a profusion of movement.

Looking at the plans of a European city it is easy to recognise the centres of power. They present a palimpsest of shifting layers of order as culture moves from the power of the Church to the power of the king, then to merchants and then industry. Then come marked changes in the organic texture of the city as its population expands, dramatising the distance between wealth and poverty. City form and fabric are the direct residue of the political, economic and social project. Manhattan from the air shows none of the conflicts and power plays reflected in the European city. It is marked by one dominant opposition – park and grid – an exquisite juxtaposition in the metaphysics of reality. The grid, formed to govern freedom within reason, frames a great park designed to be a natural enhancement of social harmony. In the park the spiritual has primacy over the material and the expedient. In the grid the streets are continually reformed in expediency and speculation. Yet the juxtaposition is filled with paradox: the naturalness of the park is achieved by the absolute control and manipulation of nature. It is the city that represents nature's more basic forces in the survival of the fittest: God in reason versus the illusion of God in nature.

There is a more profound political dimension in the contrast between these realities, between the mercantile republicanism at the turn of the 19th century and the conservatism at the mid-century. The park is European, a bourgeois infection that reflects a weakening of the egalitarianism of the republic. An attempt at creating a crucible of social harmony, the park in ways served to dramatise difference. In effect, although offering highly intricate events and vistas and the much-celebrated separation of traffic, the Greensward plan was distinctly unfriendly to the working classes. As the authors of *Gotham* point out, recreations like dances and picnics were forbidden, as were the rituals of working-class Republican political culture; military displays were banned, along with civic processions and public oratory. Instead the tree-lined mall was reserved for genteel activity: promenades and polite, but not political, exchange, the middle class in its carriages and the working class on foot.

The creation of Central Park disrupted some of the poor of the city more directly. Over 1,600 residents in shantytowns in the area were displaced including Irish farmers and German gardeners. Seneca village, a black settlement at Eighth Avenue and 82nd Street which had three churches and a school, was levelled. However, well into its second century the park is the great public forum of the city, fostering social harmony within a more complex society than would have been conceivable in the 19th century.

By 1850 rational idealism had been replaced by a belief in the power of social harmony. By 1890 the spirit of egalitarianism was being eroded by harsh competition, and by 1920 the city's growth was merely another manifestation of *laissez-faire* speculation. Until Robert Moses.

16

Central Park, The Bethesda Terrace and the Angel of the Water Fountains, photo by JS Johnston, 1894

© Museum of the City of New York

ROBERT MOSES

No other individual in the 20th century has so changed a city as Robert Moses has New York. For 44 years, from a complex base that rested at its core on a concept of 'public authority', he wielded power, in many ways absolute power, over all the major elements of the city's infrastructure, parks, parkways, highways, bridges and public housing. And those he did not control he diminished.[4]

As the map illustrates, his projects affected every borough. In 1968, when he surrendered his last base of power – chairman of the Triborough Bridge and Tunnel Authority – he had administered the creation of much vaster landscapes than Central Park, forming almost 10,000 acres of new parks including the Lido at Jones Beach on Long Island, and caused more than 416 miles of highway and 13 bridges to be built within the five boroughs. His highways fragmented and eviscerated neighbourhoods in the Bronx and Brooklyn, yet the extensive road and bridge network opened the metropolitan area to unprecedented development. His clearance of the slums on Manhattan strengthened neighbourhoods and created new wealth for the middle classes, yet the displacement of more than 500,000 people who were forced into public housing still seems irrecoverable. In the almost 200 years during which public order was defined only Robert Moses succeeded in subverting the grid of Manhattan. He fused blocks together in many of his smaller developments, but in building Stuyvesant Town he removed the roads from 18 city blocks.

Moses was 36 when he entered public life in 1924, appointed chairman of the State Council of Parks and the Long Island Parks commissioner. He remained the major power in the city until 1968. In 1934 Mayor Fiorello La Guardia made him New York City Parks commissioner and from there Moses moved quickly to expand and consolidate his power base, eventually gaining control of 12 major public offices in the city – an unequalled and quite irregular achievement. Using all his influence and assets he pursued a ruthless paternalistic policy aimed at imposing what he viewed as a progressive transformation on the infrastructure of New York. Appointment to the city's planning commission in 1941 gave him the revenues from the Triborough Bridge and Tunnel Authority to finance his desire to modernise the city. Named the city construction coordinator in 1946, he set out to rebuild New York for the automobile. In quick succession he pushed through the construction of the Brooklyn Queens expressway, the Gowanus parkway, and the Cross-Bronx expressway. Wilfully, it was felt, he planned the paths of these highways through the tenements and apartment buildings in some areas he considered undesirable.

His public posture was as a man with a passionate commitment to progress, to making the city healthy. Yet his actions, more than those of any other, are the root cause of some of its worst slums. He eradicated areas that he saw as diseased tissue, clearing the land for healthy development. The process was applied to many areas of Manhattan and the clearances were often several blocks in extent – Corlears Hook, the Lower East Side, south of Washington Square, the Upper West Side. There were also half a dozen smaller pockets of development. Over time his actions led to the forced removal of tens of thousands of poor black and Puerto Rican residents to public housing projects constructed to receive them in Brooklyn and the Bronx. Manhattan was far less racially polarised before Moses. There were street demonstrations and large-scale public protest but such was the strength of his power that for a while he was unstoppable. Over 15,000 people were removed from Manhattan's Upper West Side and the land was cleared for redevelopment for the white middle class. Public protest was, however, successful in halting his plan to drive a highway across the city through Washington Square – but did not stop the removal of several thousands from south of the square. These actions actively created racial division.

Moses' racism was expressed not as some vague animosity, but as an active project and he used his power to avoid mixing between the races. Some of his actions were remarkably petty. Under his direction, in the late 1930s, the parks commission built 10 new community swimming pools within the city. Moses had been, briefly, a member of the Yale swimming team and remained a powerful swimmer throughout his life. Creating new settings for swimming either by developing beaches or constructing new pools were favoured projects for him and, despite the Depression, he managed to create buildings of the highest quality. Only one of the new pools was in Harlem. However, there was a second pool, the Thomas Jefferson, in East Harlem between 111th & 114th Street. East Harlem was a white neighbourhood and had been home to Mayor La Guardia, but it was only two blocks from Spanish Harlem and within walking distance of the black community. Moses was determined that the pool would remain white. He employed only white lifeguards to staff it and, in addition, as he later confided to a colleague, he gave instructions that its should remain unheated in the belief that Puerto Ricans and blacks avoided cold water. Judging by the memories of those in the neighbourhood the strategy appears to have been effective.

On a grand scale his actions were equally divisive. Jones Beach was a magnificent achievement with splendid facilities including changing rooms for over 50,000 people. Under Moses' direction the bridges over the highways that served it were deliberately built too low for buses and attempts to run rail or subway connections to the park were discouraged, making it accessible only to those with automobiles and inaccessible to the poor, a large percentage of whom were black. He went further, instructing his staff not to issue parking permits to buses carrying blacks that managed to get to the park on local roads. As with the Thomas Jefferson pool, he employed only white lifeguards.

The expensive and extensive highway network he forced through the dense city could not help but bring conflict. In building the Gowanus parkway in 1941 there was total rejection of appeals by the residents of Sunset Park in Brooklyn to change the route to avoid destroying the heart of the community. Sunset Park was a modest neighbourhood, mainly Scandinavian, just south of Greenwood Cemetery. The community pressed to have the parkway run alongside the docks rather than through their main shopping street. Without any clear justification Moses held to the original plan with the result that more than 100 stores were eventually destroyed and 1,300 families were dislocated. Eroding the edge eventually weakened the whole neighbourhood.

Every mile of highway that he forced into the city created similar confrontations, nowhere more so than in the building of the Cross-Bronx expressway. The neighbourhood of East Tremont in the centre of the Bronx was a modest, mainly Jewish, area which by 1950 had a population of 60,000 of which more than 18 per cent were black or Hispanic. By the 1950s the borough was beginning to show signs of those forces that would lead to decades of urban blight, landlord neglect, increasingly poor tenants and abandoned buildings. Though poor, East Tremont was the kind of neighbourhood where a tolerant acceptance, however fragile, of race and class diversity was evolving. To its south Crotona Park protected it from Morrisiana and Melrose, neighbourhoods in rapid decline. East Tremont had the potential to demonstrate that racial and class integration were possible. In 1952 the residents in the area just north off the park received a letter signed by Robert Moses, telling them that their property was in the path of the Cross-Bronx expressway and they had 90 days to vacate. The neighbourhood quickly resolved to fight the plan, and had strong political and legal support from the beginning. As in Sunset Park, there was a simple alternative that would spare the neighbourhood at apparently no cost to the plan. This involved moving the route of the expressway just two blocks south of its proposed path, allowing it to run at the north end of Crotona Park and thus preventing the destruction of 1,530 apartments and the displacement of thousands of people. After fighting their case for many months the community believed they had won approval for the changed route only to be defeated, inexplicably, at the last moment. Later evidence suggested that Moses had some kind of hold over the influential deputy mayor, who had publicly supported the community, and forced him to change his vote. The only explanation for this senseless destruction was that the alternative path would have affected the properties of one of Moses' political cronies.

The Cross-Bronx expressway was pushed through with brilliant engineering, exceptional management and devastating results. Forcing over 6 miles of multilane highway through the dense tissue of neighbourhoods that were themselves in the middle of adjusting to complex ethnic changes resulted in a path of social dislocation much broader than the width of the road. The management of the construction was superb; the treatment of the families affected was abusive. Neighbourhood relocation offices were rarely open and offered little help when they were. Contractors began to strip buildings that had families still living in them. People felt, with justice, persecuted. An anecdote describes Moses touring the edges of the construction and coming upon a protest march against the highway. At its head the marchers carried a stuffed dummy of him which they proceeded to burn. In speeches he was compared to Hitler and Stalin. Moses was said to have enjoyed it all thoroughly. In his book *Public Works: A Dangerous Trade* (McGraw-Hill, 1970) he wrote, 'You can draw any kind of picture you like on a clean slate, and indulge your every whim in the wilderness laying out New Delhi, Canberra, or Brasilia, but when you operate in an overbuilt metropolis you have to hack away with a meat axe.' Moses was convinced that future generations would be grateful. 'You can't,' he frequently said, 'make an omelette without breaking eggs.'

There is evidence that he made occasional attempts to ease the impact of road building on the people affected, but no such evidence in his management of the Title 1 housing programme – slum clearance. This federal programme, introduced in the 1950s, allowed for the condemnation of houses, blocks of houses and even whole neighbourhoods that were seen as irrecoverable slums. These were, in the main, rental properties occupied by the poorest in the city. The process of condemnation was often undertaken with the encouragement of developers and in New York City the major targets were black neighbourhoods, throughout Manhattan and extensively in Harlem. What followed condemnation was a process of forced removal of tenants, many of whom simply disappeared from official records. Many moved into already overcrowded housing with the result that the neighbourhood deteriorated even further. A vivid account of the process is recorded in the report of the Woman's City Club in 1953: 'Manhattantown looked like the cross section of bombed-out Berlin right off the World War II. Some of its tenements were still standing, broken windows gazing sightlessly at the sky, basement doors yawning uncovered on the sidewalks, and surrounding them were acres strewn with bricks and mortar and rubble. The wreckers and bulldozers had been at work.' People were still living in these buildings.

Moses' actions propelled large sections of the poorest neighbourhoods into desolation and abandonment. The most fortunate people were condemned to live in the bleakest of

18

public housing ghettos, developments controlled by Moses and stretching across the five boroughs from Corlears Hook on Manhattan's Lower East Side to the shore of Long Island and into the old towns on the north end of Staten Island. This strategic restructuring of the population required the construction of more than 140,000 public housing apartments. Among many lessons to be learnt from the great model of the five boroughs which Moses had built for the New York World's Fair in 1964 is the vast scale and total penetration of the multiple projects with which he changed the basic order of the city. The model was one of his last and most attractive projects, and it is not unreasonable to presume that he conceived it to demonstrate his achievements. Essentially, every structure in the five boroughs is represented on the model. Within the simple colour-coding system all public housing projects are painted the same colour of brown. It offers graphic evidence that the process of relocation into public housing moved the poor and the black population into marginal neighbourhoods far removed from centres of social or commercial activity.

In the late 1960s, reflecting on the difficulties he had faced in slum clearance, Moses felt that his greatest failure was in not providing enough new apartments for the displaced population. The solution, he concluded, could lie in the construction of large-scale, isolated apartment complexes, such as the 40,000 units of Co-op City. He helped organise and for this development, and one may see in this extensive assembly of undistinguished apartment buildings part of his vision for the city. It is completely encircled by his expressways, the Whitestone Bridge and Bruchner, and flows at its southern end through a tangle of interchanges into the Moses-created Pelham Bay Park. In a discussion, the senior planner in the New York Transit Authority told how his family had been affected by the building of Co-op City, his aunt moving into the new complex from the Grand Concourse to get away from the instability in the area. He said the Cross-Bronx expressway and Co-op City together destroyed many strong neighbourhoods in the Bronx. The first drove people out, the second provided a haven for the most mobile. Why, he asked plaintively, was Co-op City never connected to the subway system?

Public transport generally, and subways and trains in particular, were not only neglected during the Moses years but actively diminished. Around 1952, there was a move in the legislature to have the Triborough Bridge Authority take over the subways with the bridge tolls providing funds for the renewal of the system. The bridge was the one 'public authority' over which Moses had absolute control. He aggressively blocked the move, arguing that the authority could never become involved in a deficit-producing operation. Where his highways directly competed with railways the

railways suffered, none more so than the Long Island railroad. Although never explicit, there is frequently a connection between Moses' opposition to public transit and his attitude to race and poverty. In 1964 he vetoed attempts to strengthen the subway connections to the World's Fair.

His most impressive public projects were the landscapes and structures in his parks and parkways. Jacob Riis, in Queens, and Jones Beach are great works of public theatre. The great curving pavilion at the southern end of Orchard Beach in Pelham Bay would not have seemed out of place in fascist Italy. The landscapes shaped by Moses are totally lacking the metaphysical reflection of nature that guided Olmsted's vision. For Moses, the park was a place to display the largesse of a public authority more concerned with social solidarity than social harmony. The Olmsted landscapes allow the individual to contemplate his or her relationship with the natural; the parks of Robert Moses seem to demand an enforced communality. The vast highway and bridge construction programmes of the 1950s are as brutal and oppressive as the means by which they were established. But nothing is more brutal and oppressive than the public housing apartments. They are out of reach in the forgotten margins and edges of the city, created by the highways and trapping over half a million people in ghettoised structures whose very nature denies enterprise.

It is a troubling reflection on the distance between myth and reality in New York City that this most epic symbol of freedom and democracy should have allowed major parts of its administration to fall under the absolute control of a single individual. Moses began his career as a brilliant lawyer who prepared well for the role of great public servant. His doctoral dissertation at Oxford was a study of the British Civil Service: he was impressed by its continuity and relative freedom from party political influence. As he moved into public life in New York in the 1930s, he realised that few came close to rivalling his knowledge and understanding of it. It became clear to him that new institutions would have to be created to deal effectively with the problems of his great and complex city. He, like others of his generation, would not have been unaware of the prediction in the writings of Nietzsche that this new century would demand the emergence of Lords of the Earth; supermen who alone would have the will, courage and vision to prevent that most dreadful possibility – the collapse of the West.

Moses readied himself well to be the ideal public servant. His grounding in the law and his ability to create legislation were unequalled and no one was ever more thorough in using every aspect of every law and entitlement to the greatest advantage. To become public servant as Lord of the Earth he needed to find a way to corner the market in public power. Two elements would be vital: a base of authority outside any political influence; and access to limitless resources. Moses achieved the first by creating a new public institution, the Triborough Bridge Authority. And resources came from the bridge tolls, which were completely within his control. Moses was a public servant in the mould of JP Rockefeller Senior; his control of the Triborough Bridge was equivalent to Rockefeller's control of the railways.

As Moses increased his power base the city administration became more corrupt. Though this was much less blatant than it had been under Boss Tweed, the majority of public works programmes involved cronyism and kickbacks to the extent that most projects initiated by the city were compromised. The parks department, for example, offered sylvan gifts to the ward healers and their families. Moses discovered that lots of little houses in out-of-the-way corners of the parks were homes for the party faithful. One woman who camped out in a building in Central Park not only decorated the interior to her taste, but had a grand piano moved in. In his formative years he would have had every reason to believe that the scale and character of the power base necessary to manage this great and dreadful city had to be inversely proportional to the depth of corruption and incompetence in its administration – conditions made much worse by the Depression.

Moses was elitist, racist and utterly convinced, without much need for evidence, of the rightness of his actions. He was a vigorous anti-Communist, but otherwise gave little indication of a grander political vision. What choices had he? Had he possessed a different ambition, his exceptional abilities could have given New York a vital and all-embracing public transport system. Instead, his actions have left it with the least effective and distinguished system of any major metropolis. Had he believed that the city's future would be healthier only through tolerance of the disparity between the races and classes, and used the resources and the legal power of his public authority to advance such a cause, New York would be profoundly different today. The divisiveness and conflict caused by his road building, his slum clearances and the harsh pragmatism of the public housing projects are all as painful now as when they were built.

What, then, do the multiple orders of Moses contribute to this elegantly balanced urban play? They are at their best in his parks programme – he secured for posterity thousands of acres of natural land to be reformed to the sensibility of future ages. They are at their worst in the highways and in public housing which, unlike any other aspect of this continually evolving city, cannot change or be changed. The grid and the park are always in a state of becoming; they are open to endless enrichment. The highways and the housing projects seem even now absolute and intolerant, unable to change and weave into the texture of the city.

The republicanism of the commissioners' grid was meant to offer equal power and opportunity to all who chose to operate

within it. The transcendentalism of the Olmsted parks sought to offer, in the experience of nature, a more profound reality than that defined by mercantilism, but like the grid this reality was tolerant and always in a state of becoming. Moses' constructions are in total contrast, even opposition, to the grid and the park in that they are closed instruments which construct an unchangeable reality. Through his 'public authority' he was able to act as the dictator of the state, rising above the incompetence and corruption of the elected process. He is not unlike Mussolini both in his methods and his achievements. After a daylong discussion with Moses about involving him in the development of public works in the Dominican Republic, the island's dictator, Trujillo Molina, concluded that he could not use him. His reason, Moses later reported, was: 'You'd want my job.'

There is a precision and clarity to the sequence of social ordering in New York that must be due, for the most part, to the fact that the republic was able to make Manhattan a clean slate for a new society. It is hard now to appreciate the extent of the dilemma facing the initiators of what was a dangerous experiment at the end of the 18th century: the formation of a democratic republic, of a scale and ambition unequalled in history. By what means would this new government establish and maintain public order? Structures covering all aspects of social performance had to be rapidly devised and put into effect, not only to govern future behaviour, but to neutralise the persistent power structures of the colonial aristocracy. The new republic took from Greece the concept of an individual's right to bear arms as one key mechanism to achieve this, but it was through the all-embracing power of a just law that it sought to establish control. The gridding of Manhattan was the most complete application of the rule of law to the physical structure of the city. Its ruthlessness matches the revolutionary zeal of the first decades of the republic.

However, by the mid-19th century it was widely felt in both Europe and America that cultivating civic sensibility in the citizenry could develop a social harmony that would maintain control while enriching the culture. It is within this context that Central Park must be seen, as a precisely formed gathering place where the many different strands of race and wealth that were forming the new republic could be woven into a meaningful cloth. The belief led to the emergence, for over half a century, of powerful centralising institutions formed from the convergence of the intellectual and cultural ambitions of New York's citizens: museums, opera houses, cemeteries, botanical gardens, libraries – all housed in, or housing, temple-like structures and built to last for ever.

In the 20th century civil society gave way to Modernism and mechanisation. The sprawling accretion of grids that order the towns and neighbourhoods of the five boroughs is forcibly united in a linked network of highways that brings the speed

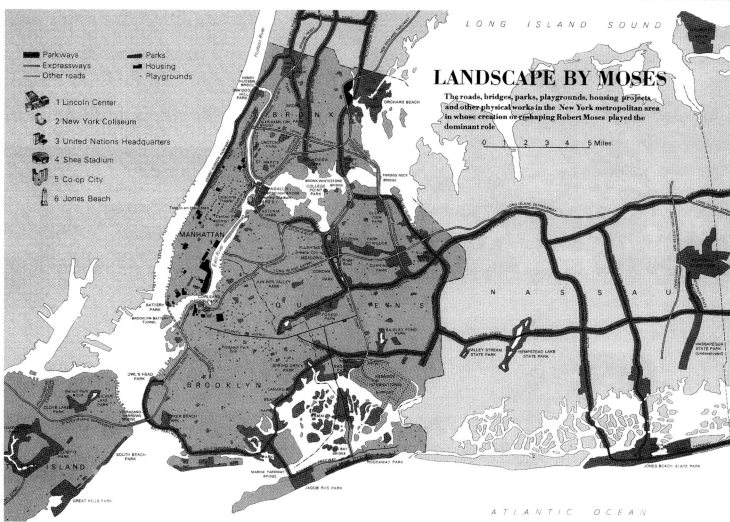

Parkways
Expressways
Other roads
Parks
Housing
Playgrounds

1 Lincoln Center
2 New York Coliseum
3 United Nations Headquarters
4 Shea Stadium
5 Co-op City
6 Jones Beach

LANDSCAPE BY MOSES

The roads, bridges, parks, playgrounds, housing projects and other physical works in the New York metropolitan area in whose creation or reshaping Robert Moses played the dominant role

0   1   2   3   4   5 Miles

and freedom of the automobile to the structure of the city. Orders in reason, followed by order in nature, followed by the intrusive order of the machine are all compounded into the fabric of New York. It is still a city governed by the rule of law, but since the 1920s the unifying ethos of civic sensibility has faded, hastened by corruption and dictatorship. With its passing the role of architecture, and indeed the character of the city, have become increasingly diffuse and uncertain. Today, what is replacing reason, nature and the machine, not only in maintaining social control but in creating the context for shared democratic ideals? In all the diverse towns and neighbourhoods that make up New York's five boroughs it would seem that two forces control and maintain order. The first is consumerism, the second is the factionalism in the city's countless divisions of wealth and ethnicity. It is against these forces that the architectural project should be judged. Architecture presents the most resolved fragments of cultural desire.

NOTES

This is a most fortunate time for anyone studying the history of New York. Two books published in the last two year offer immensely rich and exhaustive histories of all aspects of the city: Kenneth Jackson's *Encyclopedia* and Burrows and Wallace's *Gotham*. These are the result of many years of scholarly work – Burrows and Wallace have considered the subject for over 20 years. This chapter attempts to measure the physical quality of the city and is wholly indebted to the following texts:

The Iconography of Manhattan Island 1498–1909, compiled by Isaac Newton Phelps Stokes, published between 1915 and 1928 in 6 volumes. Republished by New Jersey Legal Printers (1999).

Kenneth T Jackson, ed, *The Encyclopedia of New York*, Yale University Press (New Haven and London) and the New York Historical Society (New York), 1998.

Edwin G. Burrows and Mike Wallace, *Gotham: A History of New York City*, Oxford University Press (New York and Oxford), 1999.

Paul E Cohen and Robert T Augustyn, *Manhattan in Maps 1537–1995*, Rizzoli (New York), 1997.

Eric Homburger with Alice Hudson, cartographic consultant, *The Historical Atlas of New York City*. An Owl book. Henry Holt & Company (New York), 1994.

Ric Burns and James Sanders with Lisa Aedis, *NEW YORK: An Illustrated History*. A Borzoi book, Alfred A Knopf (New York), 1999.

Robert A Caro, *The Power Broker: Robert Moses and the Fall of New York*, Vintage Books (New York), 1974.

1 Paul E Cohen and Robert Augustyn, op cit., p104
2 Burrows and Wallace, op cit., pp419-422
3 Ibid, pp790-795
4 Robert A Caro, op cit. All the material that follows is drawn from this monumental biography of Robert Moses, reproduced by permission of Alfred A Knopf, a division of Random House. The full impact of Caro's dramatic subtitle is only now being fully appreciated.

ICONS 2

The idea of New York was formed in the world's imagination between 1883 with the opening of the Brooklyn Bridge and the early 1930s with the building of Rockefeller Center, a time when the city became the world's most desirable destination for all who were restless and in despair. The creation of artificial destinations was fed by the rise in travel for pleasure made possible by railways and steamships. Elements of cities – ancient ruins, great cathedrals, spectacular scenery – were all commodified and packaged for increasingly affluent and mobile societies. The trains and ships would bring the travellers. Hotels would grow in scale and luxury to house them. Histories would be written to substantiate the significance of the destinations, guides – written and in person – would enhance the experience of visiting them and industries would grow on the provision of mementos: souvenirs, keepsakes and postcards. By the second half of the 20th century great cities were expected to have identifiable features that could be photographed for mass consumption.

 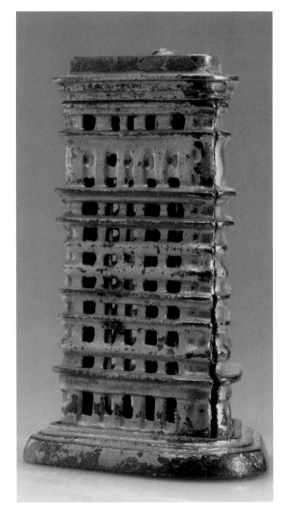

Left: Empire State building, and lower Manhattan. From watercolour study by Marcus van der Hope, 1930s; Right: Flat Iron building, cast iron penny bank, 1920s, Kenton Toy Company, 1920.

The Brooklyn Bridge is a supremely powerful demonstration of America's mechanical strengths and ambition. Walt Whitman saw it as part of the mission to weave the world together that had started with Columbus. The 13 years of struggle to complete the bridge was in marked contrast to the rapidity with which the huge granite structure on Bedloe's Island south of the tip of Manhattan in Upper New York Bay was constructed; the Statue of Liberty was a gift from the French to celebrate the friendship between France and the United States and to mark the centennial of the two great 18th-century revolutions. 'The New Colossus' as Emma Lazarus titled her poem, was clearly capable of touching the imaginations of the world.

'Keep, ancient lands, your storied pomp!' cries she
With silent lips. 'Give me your tired, your poor,
Your huddled masses yearning to breathe free,
The wretched refuse of your teeming shore.
Send these, the homeless, tempest-tossed, to me;
I lift my lamp beside the golden door.

It was conceived to be fabulous, a female Helios, closely echoing the Colossus of Rhodes; the work of the French sculptor Frédéric-Auguste Bartholdi, the statue had to be seen to be believed. The presence of this great figure achieves an anthropomorphic effect that insinuates itself into the subsequent architecture of the city. (The figure is supported by a highly eccentric structure from the imagination of Gustave Eiffel before he began work on the tower that was to bear his name.)

These two monumental entrances to the city were followed by buildings which emerged out of intense competition between a mix of developers and new industrialists, a highly selfish process that took place with barely a glance at what the world might think, and certainly with utter disinterest in the poor and huddled masses desperately trying to become American. The bridge and statue embody the features that have made New York identifiable – they are dynamic, spectacular and strangely personal; not just physical but somehow familiar and sexually appealing.

The most important buildings were, in chronological order, first the newspaper buildings clustering along Park Row: the Tribune, the upstart New York Times and Joseph Pulitzer's World building which stood immediately south of the entrance to the Brooklyn Bridge. It was the readers of the World who had contributed $100,000 to provide a base for the statue. Dominating all was the 30-storey Park Row building designed by RH Robertson and completed in 1899. By the mid-1990s the papers began to move uptown and the buildings came down. The Flatiron building, designed by DH Burnham and Company, was completed in 1903 and although it has only 21 storeys its

extremely slender prow gives a powerful impression of height. It became one of the most celebrated places in the city's imagination, giving rise to every conceivable souvenir from penny banks to beer steins. Songs were written about it and the winds that swept its corner and photographers dramatised the impression of a monstrous prow preparing to sail up Fifth Avenue.

In 1904 the New York Times opened the Times tower on what would quickly be renamed Times Square. In 1908 Ernest Flagg completed the Singer tower which, at 47 storeys, was the tallest structure in the city for a year. In 1909 it was topped by the completed Met Life building, designed by Napoleon Lebrun and Sons and modelled on the campanile in St Mark's Square, Venice. As each building opened its image was memorialised in postcards and in a continual readjustment of the city panorama as it appeared on plates and spoons. Buildings that caught the public imagination generated artefacts of their own, some crude and some, like the silver pencil in the Met Life tower, delicate and elegant.

The climax of the first wave of construction came with Cass Gilbert's Woolworth building which opened in 1913 at a height of 60 storeys and remained the world's tallest structure until it was surpassed in 1929 by the Chrysler building. Conceived as a cathedral of commerce, it gains great energy from a veneer of neo-Gothic detail throughout its soaring height, and established the figural dynamism that gives such pleasure in its more streamlined descendants of the 1930s. The building became a central part of the marketing of the Woolworth stores but, for all its commercial hype, it remains a distinguished yet brooding presence in the city.

Zoning laws introduced in 1916 sought to prevent New York becoming dark with the shadows cast by skyscrapers. They still allow the city to be dense up to 12 storeys and controlled the space around towers that rose above that height. Three buildings, all conceived before Wall Street crashed in October 1929, sealed the world's image of the city. The Chrysler building, designed by William Van Alen, started as a speculative venture and the whole project was taken over in 1927 by industrialist Walter P Chrysler for whom it was restyled in brilliantly inventive automobile Gothic. It has lost none of its thrill and surprise, yet it is so discreet. Nothing else in the world could even hint at the raw soaring power of this reality. With hindsight, all the artefacts of Europe's modern worlds look structures of false hope and thin idealism in contrast to the Chrysler. At 1,046 feet it was the tallest building in the world until it was beaten by its rival the Empire State building only months after it had been completed. Opening in May 1931, the Empire State strained to reach 1,250 feet with the help of its vast spire – 16 storeys tall this was a mooring mast for dirigibles and was used successfully only once. The Empire State remained the world's tallest building until the 1970s.

Clockwise from the top left: Chrysler building postcard 1930s; Chrysler building; The RCA building at Rockefeller Center as a bar of soap, package and contents from the late1930s; Metropolitan Building at Night, postcard from the 1920s.

Designed by Shreve, Lamb and Harmon and the engineers Starrett Brothers and Eken, it was conceived without romance and for one reason: to generate the largest return on investment. Yet it quickly assumed a majestic dominance in the panorama, a gracious presence seemingly part of all the lives of the city.

The last of the trio, Rockefeller Center, seeks not height as much as place. Although the thin cascading elevation of the RCA building (opened in 1932 and now the General Electrical building) as seen from Fifth Avenue is the most powerful of any structure in the city, what John D Rockefeller Junior achieved in this complex was a living room for the city – a village green – a stage for the play of community in this field of speculation. With the collapse of Wall Street and of plans to relocate the Metropolitan Opera on to the site, Rockefeller acquired control of more land than any other single developer. This he shaped with a peculiarly New York blend of private and public agendas. In the depths of the Depression he was able to lease the space by undercutting the competition and buying existing leases while at the same time he choreographed the activities within the public spaces to entertain and educate the citizenry. His most ambitious act was the attempt to bring together the mercantile nations of the world – Britain, France, Italy and Germany – in a series of pavilions along Fifth Avenue, in the belief that commercial enterprise could avert war. Of all the artefacts that are illustrated here, the strangest is the great mass of the RCA building, reproduced in a cake of soap.

All the material illustrated in this section is from the wonderful Globus collection of New York memorabilia. Dorothy Twining Globus, formerly a curator of exhibitions at the Cooper-Hewitt National Design Museum and former director of the Gallery at the Fashion Institute of New York, has over the years collected with passion all those objects that epitomise, each in its peculiar way, the fascination and almost metaphysical aura that lurks within the idea of Manhattan.

25

Clockwise from top left:
Cover of the brochure for the opening of the Empire State building; Municipal and Woolworth buildings seen from the East River, postcard 1920s; RCA building, Rockefeller Center at night, postcard from the 1930s; Silver spoons from the turn of the century showing, top, the Statue of Liberty, middle and bottom, views of the Brooklyn bridge and the Manhattan skyline.

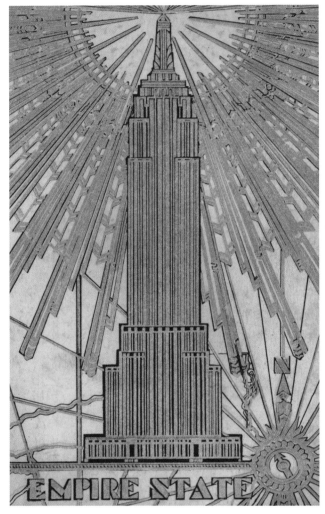

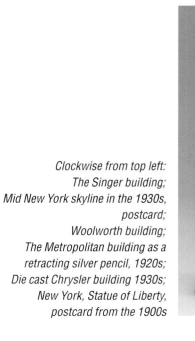

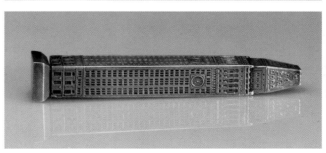

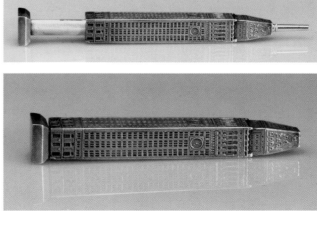

Clockwise from top left:
The Singer building;
Mid New York skyline in the 1930s,
postcard;
Woolworth building;
The Metropolitan building as a
retracting silver pencil, 1920s;
Die cast Chrysler building 1930s;
New York, Statue of Liberty,
postcard from the 1900s

BOROUGHS 3

**STATEN ISLAND
QUEENS
BROOKLYN
BRONX**

STATEN ISLAND

The five boroughs of New York – Manhattan, Staten Island, Queens, Brooklyn and the Bronx – were formed by act of consolidation in 1898. Each has distinct histories and characteristics, and each influences the city and its future in different ways. What follows is an evocation of the history of the settlements and communities that have shaped the four boroughs that surround Manhattan. It presents the range and complexity of the realities that make up New York, and provides a context within which to consider the nature and uses of its architecture. In preparing this work I drove almost 300 miles within the city. It was a journey constructed through long sections – north, south, east and west – that allowed me to experience many different communities and towns, and their changing structure. They continue to absorb immigrants from across the world and tolerate greater extremes of wealth and poverty than is willingly acknowledged. It must be added that most of the neighbourhoods that form the city of New York are of interest only to those who live in them, and touch few imaginations.

The clearest impression, in driving the length and breadth of the city, is of a measurable decline in the need for architecture. New York has changed from the time when its total order could be mandated by commission to a complex, ever-shifting organism formed from a million transactions. Few visitors to the city venture into the unpredictable confusion of neighbourhoods and communities that surround Manhattan. Their immigrant population is growing, yet there is no evidence that this will drive the creation of new architectures. Music, religion and food offer a more satisfying definition of cultural identity than architecture. The small percentage of new Americans who do melt in the pot of culture assume the anonymity of suburban tract housing, where notions of cultural differences are obscured.

Opposite, top: Grand Concourse in the Bronx; Bottom: the Beach Pavilion on Hunters Island, Pelham Bay Park, Bronx.

The 60 square miles of Staten Island are the furthest removed from the centre of New York City. Lying southwest of Manhattan Island across Upper New York Bay, it is much more closely linked in character and history to New Jersey than New York. A ferry to the tip of Manhattan has linked the two islands since the 18th century. Population remained small throughout much of the 19th century, but rose strongly in the 20th: it was 13,000 in 1880, rising to 175,000 in 1940 and more than doubling to 400,000 by 1990.

The coastline north, east and south forms an almost continuous succession of settlements, from the public housing projects on the north shore to the remote charm of 19th-century Tottenville in the south. It is a passage through old towns and villages, past fragments of 19th-century resort architecture, large fading institutions, abandoned industrial parks and naval yards. The heart of the island was opened up after the Depression with the initiation of a series of public works projects designed to stimulate the economy. This led to over 30 years of public investment in infrastructure throughout the island – building roads, highways and bridges as well as an extensive system of parks. Much of this was under the direction of Robert Moses and it was Moses who drove the construction of the Verrazano Narrows Bridge linking the island with Brooklyn. It remains the island's only physical connection to the other boroughs. Though the bridge forced the removal of over 6,000 people from the Bay Ridge community in Brooklyn it opened the way for a process of suburbanisation that continues into the present. The expansive carpet of modest tract housing, garden apartments and town houses has turned the body of Staten Island into a nondescript place: anonymous streets of neat houses and gardens and occasional strip malls, all unfocused and without a larger sense of order, but comfortable nonetheless. The west side of the island is dominated by Fresh Kills, the only active landfill in the city. The world's largest garbage dump, it is scheduled to be closed in 2000.

Yet this is a troubled island, with a large number of its relatively young populace commuting daily to public sector jobs in Brooklyn and Manhattan. It is a population dissatisfied with uncontrolled development, inadequate transport, pollution from the refineries and petrochemical plants in New Jersey and the continual dumping of New York's garbage into Fresh Kills. The deliberate weakening of the borough's administration by the office of the mayor of the city of New York, diminishing the office of the borough president and abolishing the board of estimates, led in 1990 to a commission to consider secession from the city. The draft charter for an independent Staten Island was supported by over 65 per cent of the borough population, but fiercely opposed by the New York City administration. This wish for independence has been muted, but has not disappeared.

29

QUEENS

Significant architecture exists in a number of the old towns and is a faded reminder of the splendour of town life in mid-19th century America. The largesse of 19th-century philanthropy can be seen in the monumental Sailors Snug Harbor home for seamen, which dates from the 1830s. The most curious reflection on history is the village of Richmond, established in 1729 as the county seat for Richmond County, as the British called Staten Island. It sits on high ground in the centre of the island, appropriately crowned by the county court house and adjoining administrative buildings. Almost all the other structures including stores, houses and New York's oldest schoolhouse are a romantic assembly of buildings moved to Richmond from across the island: one of the few places with a sense of place and focus is actually a confection. The nostalgic charm of the buildings is in total contrast to all that surrounds them. Though small, this is a pleasant fiction, much more interesting than the anonymity of suburbia. It is, however, a sanitised version of an aristocratic order in which all were subject to the greater and absent power of the British Crown; this architecture was meant to impress. It can be argued that the absence of similar satisfying place-making elsewhere on the island can be seen as a virtue. The citizens, unlike the subjects of the British Crown, are free within the market to define their own realm. The pain is in the ebb and flow, in destruction and reconstruction, in matching settlement with productivity.

A notable development is the plan for the extensive reconstruction of the Staten Island Ferry Terminal and surrounding area. The architects of the master plan are Hellmuth, Obata + Kassabaum. The project as planned will probably include two museums and a minor league baseball stadium as well as the terminal. The most spectacular proposal is the museum designed by Peter Eisenman. It will be the first major New York project for Eisenman – still a most radical force in New York's conservative architectural culture.

Queens is the largest of the five boroughs – roughly 120 miles square. At the beginning of the 19th century, the landscape of century-old farms and villages was changed as neighbourhoods formed along the main turnpike routes east and west. The first railway reached the area in 1836 and to attract customers the company developed a racetrack at the end of the line. Other railway companies followed suit and this in turn led to the development of coastal resorts. A law passed in 1830 banning burials in downtown Manhattan had the unexpected effects in the decades that followed of increasing business for the railways and the development of vast cemeteries across the centre of Brooklyn and Queens, which continue to be a dominant element in the landscape. By mid-century the rural character of Queens was rapidly disappearing beneath waves of new immigrants. Irish fleeing the potato famine settled around Astoria; Germans moving west from Brooklyn established businesses and factories along the major east–west avenues. The 17th-century town of Flushing, which had been a centre of British life even in the Dutch colony, remained British well into the1840s, but such was the force of change that by 1860 it had become wholly German. In the years after the Civil War Queens developed around industries shaped by the skills and business cultures of the different immigrant groups.

With the opening of the Brooklyn Bridge in 1896 trolley routes linked Queens to Manhattan, cutting travel time and opening up the land for commuter suburbs. Despite the pressures on growth, neighbourhoods continued to maintain strong ethnic distinctions. Even into the first decades of the 20th century the Chinese owned and operated farms in central Queens, growing vegetables for the Chinese community and supplying the increasingly popular Chinese restaurants on Manhattan. It was a community that retained a Chinese way of life and kept very much to itself. German farms supplied Manhattan with flowers for its German restaurants and hotels. With consolidation at the turn of the century, Queens was formed from over 100 separate towns and villages, old and new, and had no coherent identity.

The neighbourhoods of Queens have three distinct characteristics. First are the towns and villages of the colonial and postcolonial farmers, second the linear commercial and industrial neighbourhoods spawned by turnpikes, railways and then highways. Last is an extensive pattern of redevelopment, particularly at the edges of existing neighbourhoods, which has been particularly attractive to new immigrants.

From Jamaica Bay, directly north through numerous communities in central Queens into Flushing Meadows and ending in the isolated town of College Point, is a journey through the most suburban and settled neighbourhoods of Queens. Jamaica Bay is a vast protected body of water between Brooklyn and the western end of Long Island. It forms

*Neglected but still surviving,
Philip Johnson's New York
State Pavilion from the 1964
Worlds Fair in Flushing
Meadows*

David H Balfour

the heart of the Gateway National Park, an area of 26,000 acres of preserved natural land. Anyone looking out across the bay from the Rockaway Inlet on a summer day will see hundreds of small boats busy about the creeks and estuary. The air will be alive with sea birds and the continual roar of planes landing and departing from Kennedy airport. The park is part of the Moses progressive project, as is Jacob Riis Park on its southwestern edge. The bathing pavilions in Jacob Riis carry a rigidly formal order that still communicates the authority with which Moses sought to make the city stronger and more healthy. On a sunny day the beaches and all the surrounding areas are crowded. They teem with people out to relax, mainly black and Hispanic families picnicking and playing on every accessible scrap of land. Even beneath the highways and along the sides of the road smoke rises from a thousand barbecues. Just beyond the park is the town of Rockaway, with its neat houses and trimmed and manicured lawns on short streets that lead to the Atlantic Ocean. Further east, Rockaway declines into dilapidation and neglect, ending in the bleak ranks of a low-income apartment complex, Hammels Houses, where once stood grand hotels. There is a relationship between the stark utility of housing projects and the gridding of Manhattan. Both resist any attempt to put a kind face on the surface of necessity, yet the grid is open to continual interpretation while the residents of these apartments have to live with their charmless discipline for as long as the buildings stand.

Stranded in the centre of Jamaica Bay is the island village of Broad Channel. Though a busy road runs down its centre the few streets on either side form a community that seems both misplaced and isolated. Encompassed by boats, the scale and mood of the streets would not be out of place in the rural South. Little cottages surround deep channels cut into the island on the west side which provide shelter for pleasure and fishing boats. The residents are mainly of Irish descent and are said to be suspicious of outsiders.

Travelling north out of the village, the road hops from island to island across the wildlife refuge: Black Bank Marsh, Pumpkin Patan Marsh, Elders Point Marsh. On across the Congressman Joseph Addabbo Bridge which runs by the western edge of the John F Kennedy International Airport, and into Howard's Beach. Both Broad Channel and Howard's Beach live beneath the persistent noise of the flight paths – planes landing or taking off every 15 seconds – yet both seem unaware of it. Shell Bank Basin runs the length of Howard's Beach and is busy with pleasure boats in this mainly Italian-American community. Howard's Beach is just as much an island as Broad Channel, cut off by the highway on the north and waterbound on the other three sides. Like so many other neighbourhoods in Queens, its architecture is modest, almost indistinct, and the expression of community is muted.

Community is a private affair, with no need to be recognised by architecture, no need to attract the attention of outsiders. The neighbourhood is still remembered for the vicious attack on three African-American youths who were passing through on an evening in 1986.

To the north is Ozone Park, home of the Aqueduct racetrack, the last surviving artificial destination developed by the railway companies and now the last venue for racing within the five boroughs. Like much of Queens Ozone Park is made up of consistently modest developments of one- and two-family frame houses. It remains mainly Irish and German, though new immigrants are moving into neighbouring Woodhaven, an early industrial town founded in the 1870s around a factory that specialised in tin-stamping. The factory closed in 1955 with the community intact but changing, increasingly attracting immigrants from the Caribbean and Latin American. Further north there is a monotonous sameness. Only the names on the map identify the neighbourhoods as different until the road crosses into Forest Hills – at the eastern end of the great city of dead – with its dense walls of redbrick apartments and into the fantasy of Forest Hills Gardens.

Forest Hills Gardens was developed by Margaret Slocum Sage, the benefactor of the Russell Sage Foundation, and was the most extravagant – and expensive – development for the new commuter. It was laid out by the Olmsted Company between 1908 and 1910, re-creating the spirit of medieval England. The company was led by Frederick Law Olmsted Junior, the son of Olmsted Senior who died in 1903 after ailing for many years. The new commuter, affluent, ambitious, would

32

arrive from Manhattan – 30 minutes away – and descend from the station down an elegant stair into a most charming courtyard. Immediately facing the station a stylish medievalised hotel adjoins equally romanticised apartments. The brick structure that carries the elevated railway is made to seem like a city wall pierced by two great arches. From this village centre an extensive tissue of winding lanes and culs-de-sac creates exquisite landscapes sheltering a wonderful array of rustic cottages. The winding lanes still discourage through traffic and give an intimacy and tranquillity to the houses and gardens. Away from the station the medieval veneer becomes thinner and finally fades into the unadorned walls of Forest Hills. In every sense, Forest Hills Gardens has maintained the spirit of its founding concept. This may be due to the romantic use of architecture, but it is mostly the product of its ability to attract wealth. Adjoining the village is the West Side Tennis Club, formed in 1915 and the home of the United States Open Tennis Championships until 1990. While the communities of Forest Hills and Forest Hill Gardens have remained predominantly Jewish, they are not untouched by the complex movement of peoples into the city. Since 1980 the largest group of new arrivals has been from Iran, followed closely by immigrants from India, the Soviet Union and Israel. Many are Jewish but there is a spreading Chinese presence on the eastern edge.

A detour leads to the adjoining neighbourhood of Rego Park,

a town developed after 1920 by the Real Good Construction Company on land bought from Chinese farmers. Unlike Forest Hills, Rego Park has continually altered and adjusted the character of its development to suit changing markets. This climaxed in the development of Lefrac City. The largest private apartment complex in the borough, it has a self-contained population of 14,000 on 40 acres and includes recreational, shopping and office development. With each successive phase in the growth of the city, development has become increasingly driven by private property and has moved from being shaped by public consensus into general packaging for a wide range of markets.

Across Queens Boulevard the road comes to the southern reaches of Flushing Meadows. Queens Boulevard is the product of the automobile; there is a hint of Los Angeles in the untidy mix of apartments and high-rise offices and large strips of drive-in retail. Though the adjoining neighbourhoods are quiet and prosperous, Flushing Meadows was transformed by Robert Moses from one of the largest garbage dumps in the United States to become the site of the 1939/41 and 1964/65 world fairs. The fairground is one of the few places in Queens where architecture still has some significance. The remnant from the first world fair, the New York City Building of 1939, became the temporary headquarters of the United Nations from 1946 to 1950 and is now the Queens Museum of Art.

The museum is of importance to architects because it

Main Street, Flushing, Queens – the centre of Asian New York

houses the splendid 'Panorama of the City of New York'. Constructed for the 1964 fair, it is claimed to be the world's largest scale-model of any city. It occupies 935 square feet and reproduces more than 800,000 buildings with streets, parks and bridges. Nothing prepares one for its scale and complexity. Although not strictly true, it seems as if every building in the city from bungalow to skyscraper is there. The setting is theatrical. An elegant ramp winds its way round the dark walls that enclose the model; at points the floor becomes glass and occasionally allows one to move into space above the city. It is a document that is open to endless interpretation. For example, the public housing is all the same neat brick colour giving immediate evidence of the scale of the programme and the strategic links both to highways and areas of least resistance. The grain and logic of the organism can be read: shifting grids, the green areas and highways. The scale of the buildings on Manhattan Island appears to be exaggerated, yet the model demonstrates the utter dominance of Manhattan and the force of land speculation in shaping the five boroughs. One would have expected to see small clusters of tall buildings arising from a circle of satellite towns bordering the great city but the model shows that Manhattan has managed to hold all power for itself, allowing none of its energy to escape, save for two small leaks – across the East River on to Hunters Point and across the Hudson into Jersey City. Commissioning this model was surely Robert Moses' most benign project. It was also one of his last. It was remodelled between 1992 and 1994 and is continually updated.

Other remnants of the fair have survived less well. The most tragic – yet strangely satisfying – is the New York State Pavilion, briefly used in the closing scenes of the movie *Men in Black*. Its visible decay, if left unattended, will present a poignant memorial to its architect Philip Johnson. The 1964 fair came to the water's edge and left behind the marina and Shea Stadium. This hub of sports and recreation was joined in 1990 by the National Tennis Center, new home of the United States Open Tennis Championships. If Moses and his colleagues had not forced the development of the world's fair, Queens would not be marked by any major public building. In this continually shifting field, the infusion of huge sums of public money into highways and world fairs creates explicit lines of physical difference as the projects of public investment cross the uneven edges of private speculation. At its most destructive, in the aftermath of urban renewal, it is still riven with unclaimed seams of land beneath or adjoining highways and elevated rails: collecting points for the city's detritus of garbage, graffiti, burnt-out cars, the homeless and drug addicted.

Crossing the Meadows and approaching the old town of Flushing from the southern end of Main Street is to experience the emergence of ethnocentric market-driven reality at its most robust. One of the oldest settlements on Long Island, Flushing was established by the British in 1654. There are still some wonderful survivors from the period: the Bowne House built in 1661 and still used for Quaker meetings and the Kingsland farm house of 1785 are both just off Main Street. Direct rail to Manhattan was established in 1854 and the town has been changed by every wave of immigration that has moved through Queens in the last 100 years, as single-family frame houses gave way to garden apartments and are now giving way to high-rise condominiums. Flushing today is an Asian town. Unlike other Asian enclaves in the city – Chinatown or Little Tokyo – it is formed from the most extravagant and energetic blending of many major Asian cultures. Two-fifths of the Asian population of New York City live in Queens. Although the Chinese form the majority there are large numbers of Koreans, Filipinos, Cambodians, Vietnamese and Indians. There are Asian neighbourhoods from Jackson Heights to Elmhurst to Corona, but all are centred on Flushing. It has become one of the major Asian cities in North America. Its Main Street has the vitality of Nathan Road in Kowloon, but with a more complex blending of cultures: in religions – Korean churches, Hindu temples and Buddhist shrines – in foods and in entertainments from Bollywood to kung fu movies. But most compelling is the convergence of ambitions. Banks and all kinds of businesses cluster along Main Street – many without translation into English. There is the sense of a new community emerging from the fusion of cultures and ambitions. At Flushing's centre, on the triangle formed at the intersection of Main and Kissena, is the new Queens Public Library. From the office of James Stewart Polshek, it is one of the very few new works of public architecture in the borough. It is a quiet, thoughtful building which conveys the order, clarity and generosity of public institutions. The library has one of the largest business sections in the five boroughs and the new citizens of Flushing are often waiting for the doors open.

Queens has other equally powerful ethnic concentrations. Half the Latino population of New York City – from every country in Central and South America – lives here. Haitians tend to congregate in south Queens. New arrivals from the Caribbean are swelling the population of the well-established black neighbourhoods in the southeast of the borough.

North from Flushing is College Point. Totally walled off by the highway, it offers an intact example of mid-19th-century industrial development. It was built by the German industrialist Conrad Popenhusen (the library and several major streets still carry his name) to house the workers employed in his hard rubber factory. With great care he supervised the development of the streets, houses, businesses and schools to serve his newly arrived German workforce. Today it does not seem

33

BROOKLYN

particularly German, but it is one of many very American small towns surviving in the fabric of the great city. By the end of the century the town's river edge was lined with beer halls, dance pavilions and pleasure parks aimed at the German community. Now all that's left is a view across it to La Guardia airport.

From College Point east and south to Hunters Point, the most western tip on Queens immediately opposite midtown Manhattan, is a journey through a succession of neighbourhoods that move back in time to the desolate residue of the 19th-century industry that once lined the East River. On the other side of La Guardia airport from College Point is the community of Steinway, also cut off by the highway. William Steinway established it in the 1870s to house the German workforce employed in his piano factory. The factory is still there, still making the most majestic of the world's grand pianos, and craftsmen and descendants of craftsmen still live in the neighbourhood. Astoria is reached through an endless succession of small houses on tree-lined streets. Only the major commercial street, which runs for over 2 miles, continues to give the sense of being stretched eastward by roads and rails. It is a surprise to find stores that are the mainstay of the malls – the Gap, Victoria's Secret – sharing this quite narrow road with local hairdressers and pizza parlours. Unlike Main Street in Flushing, the many modest ethnic restaurants reveal a cultural diversity that is not expressed in the architecture. Elmhurst, immediately to the south, is the most ethnically diverse community in the city with 118 different nations represented in its population.

The road goes through Ravenwood and into the remains of 19th-century industrial towns, then on through Long Island City, which now exists in a half-life between abandoned and impoverished occupations, with a mixture of tenement apartments and row houses. Isamu Naguchi, the Japanese-American sculptor, moved his studio to Long Island City in 1950. It has been preserved exactly as he left it among the many small factories and workshops that occupy the shells of earlier industry. In these same semi-industrial lands is the heroic Public School 1. PS1 is a crusty, end-of-the-last-century school building which has been converted into a charming uncertain art gallery by the Californian architect Fred Fisher. This brings a strangely unreal life back to an area that feels deserted. Lastly, in the most westerly tip of Queens – Hunters Point, in the shadow of the Queensborough Bridge – sits the City Corps Building, the tallest structure outside Manhattan and a tentative indication of the potential for new development along the roads and rails that run east.

Brooklyn is the most populous of the boroughs. Its 2.5 million people occupy 210 square miles. At the time of consolidation in 1898 it was the nation's third largest city. It had been chartered in 1834 and, following Manhattan's lead, a state commission proposed mapping the streets and public squares. Although the resulting plan of 1839 had none of the republican absolutism of the commissioners' grid it did establish a dominant grid that matched in part the orientation of Manhattan's. Yet, unlike Manhattan's, the plan contained an overlay of diagonal boulevards that moved eastward as the city developed. The shifting grids that were laid down graphically reveal the changing character of the community, from order ordained by the state to its gradual dissolution by private speculation.

In the 20th century three structural changes transformed Brooklyn. First, was the continual decline of its industrial base. Second, the loss of jobs that caused the relatively affluent to move, leaving behind neighbourhoods of increasing poverty and unemployment. Third, was the Moses highway programme which linked all the boroughs in an extensive network of highways and bridges. This led to a rapid rise in automobile ownership, giving unprecedented freedom in choosing where to live. Highways swept through the borough, eastward to the new suburbs in Queens and westward across the Verrazano Narrows Bridge to Staten Island. The bridge was not just an engineering triumph; in spanning the distance between Brooklyn and the new suburbs being built on Staten Island it engineered a change in the former's population. Prosperous Brooklynites left the old streets for new housing on Long Island, Staten Island and New Jersey, a process of dispersal that continued well into the 1970s, leaving much of central Brooklyn devastated. In recent years the continual arrival of new immigrants into the borough has increased the ethnic richness of some neighbourhoods while creating divisions in others. An estimated 40 per cent of the population of central Brooklyn consist of first-generation Americans. Affluent neighbourhoods such as Brooklyn Heights and Park Slope are well clear of public housing ghettos with their chronic unemployment and drug-based crime. More recently, the downtown business district and the government centre are being renewed. The city is asserting some independence from the control of Manhattan.

Two paths were driven through Brooklyn. The first runs north to south from the Manhattan Bridge on to Flatbush Avenue, cuts diagonally through the original grid of the city to Prospect Park, then continues on down Olmsted's Grand Ocean Boulevard to Coney Island and the sea.

Flatbush Avenue cuts through the historic centre of the city and runs past the classical facade of the City Hall, built in 1849 when the idea of Brooklyn was a grave and powerful thing. It goes on to the Fulton Market – a public investment of 1971 in the renewal of the city's shopping streets – to Metrotec Center,

The junction of Eastern Parkway Kingston Road in Brooklyn looking towards the Lubavitch World Headquarters on a high holiday

8 million square feet of development, begun in 1986, which houses both the research facilities of the Brooklyn Polytechnic Institute and extensive areas of so-called 'back office space' – cheap space to house low-level support staff for Manhattan's corporations. Metrotec has been the major employer of architects including Davis Brody Bond, Swanke Hayden Connell, and Skidmore, Owings & Merrill. Although it has been successful it does little to enhance the city: it is a hard cold place with raw edges.

The middle- and upper-middle-class neighbourhoods west of Flatbush Avenue are formed in rows of confident 19th-century brownstones. Fort Greene on the east consists of shingle, clapboard, brick, limestone and brownstone houses. It is an integrated neighbourhood with a strong black middle class, and several large public housing projects from the Robert Moses programme. These were built close to the navy yard, a source of work. The yard closed in 1966. South of Fort Greene on Lafayette, the Brooklyn Academy of Music, BAM as it is known, has become the city's most ambitious supporter of the avant-garde in dance, music and theatre. It remains in its original 1908 location. Though the interiors have been enthusiastically reinvented by Hardy Holtzman Pfeiffer & Associates and additional performance space has been added, the exterior remains unchanged in an area that is physically and socially much less certain than it was. It is this unease – not knowing what kind of streets these are – that discourages people from visiting Brooklyn.

Past Lafayette, Flatbush Avenue runs on to Prospect Park. Beginning in 1865, Olmsted and Vaux prepared designs for a grand park that included a comprehensive development plan to extend the influence of its landscape along boulevards to its south and east. It has many of the same features as Central Park – a rolling lawn, the long meadow, the rocky heavily wooded area overlooking the picturesque Prospect Lake – and, as with Central Park, various forms of traffic were allowed to pass through the landscape. It opened in 1868 and by 1870 was attracting two million visitors annually. Unfettered by the grid, and perhaps believing that the leading citizens of Brooklyn had more ambition than the city fathers in Manhattan, Olmsted sought to make Prospect Park affect the whole borough. He lobbied with passion to make it the climax of a link between Brooklyn and Manhattan, between Central Park and Prospect Park. In his mind's eye he could see a grand tree-lined boulevard running through Brooklyn and Manhattan and becoming the central avenue of public life, the Champs Elysées of New York City. Though he failed in this, he did create two grand boulevards: Eastern Parkway running east from Grand Army Plaza, and Ocean Parkway which runs south from the park to the sea.

The climax of Flatbush Avenue is Olmsted's Grand Army Plaza. Its promise of magnificence must have been designed to mark the grand arrival from Manhattan. Remaining incomplete, the oval lacks the enclosure of a wall of buildings which would have given it a European grandeur. The last length of Flatbush

*Brooklyn Museum with the
grand entry stair removed*

David H Balfour

Avenue divides Prospect Park from the Brooklyn Museum and the Botanical Gardens. The Brooklyn Institute had become the centre of the city's cultural life by 1850, and out of it grew the Brooklyn Institute of Arts and Sciences, which led to the foundation of the Brooklyn Museum as well as the botanical gardens and the academy of music. The master plan for the museum was developed by McKim, Mead and White, the pre-eminent New York architects at the turn of the century. They proposed organising its extensive and diverse collection around the classification system devised by the French rationalist JNL Durant. This would have produced a vast inhabitable encyclopedia containing all the objects of human culture. However, only one pavilion was completed. It lies within the grand classical facade, the magnification of the civic ideal for which McKim, Mead and White were masterly stage managers. A new master plan is being prepared by James Stewart Polshek and Arata Isozaki.

One curious result of the conflict between 19th-century civics and the rise of American socialism in the 1930s (much influenced by the new immigrants) was the alteration to the facade of the Brooklyn Museum. The museum director of that time removed the grand stairway from the front of the building believing this would make the museum more accessible and less autocratic. The result can be seen as either democratising or weakening the public presence of his grand building; perhaps they are one and the same thing. The struggle between public and private values was played out in a very revealing episode in 1999 when the mayor of New York City, Rudolf Giuliani, took action to withdraw city funds from the museum as a protest at their showing the Saatchi exhibit *Sensation* because there was some faecal matter on a portrait of the Madonna. The museum responded by suing the mayor for interfering with the first amendment: the right to free speech. The exhibition went ahead.

The areas around Prospect Park were developed for an emerging class of affluent commuters. The most splendid, Park Slope, is the largest landmarked district in Brooklyn with rows of tree-lined streets, gently sloping away from the northwest edge of the park. Its apartments and row houses in dark brick are slightly mysterious behind Romanesque and neo-classical facades. It has never suffered decline. On the other hand, by the mid-1960s Prospect Heights to the east had become predominantly Afro-American and poor. It was the site of severe racial tension, leading to rioting and arson which left much of the area ruined. In recent years extensive renovation and renewal projects have attracted the middle class and working class, home owners and renters, many of them new immigrants from the West Indies.

The east side of Prospect Park leads to Ocean Parkway, the great boulevard conceived by Olmsted in the spirit of Haussmann's Paris. Heading south to the sea, it cuts through a perfect sampler of the many worlds of Brooklyn: Prospect Park South, developed with the park, which has remained wealthy and grand, then on through integrated Kensington, Jewish and Italian Lakeville, Jewish Mapleton. These ethnic attributions identify the majority population, but all these neighbourhoods are experiencing an increasing Asian presence. The boulevard goes on down to Gravesend, settled by the British in the 17th century and now very Italian. Its neighbour to the east, Homecrest, is a rich mix of Indian, Chinese and Guyanan. This is not only a journey through ethnic neighbourhoods but through fundamental shifts in the fabric of community.

The journey began in the formal row houses of mid-19th century Brooklyn, which were built not only to represent the status of their occupants but also to reflect the unity of civic life. This was eroded by the end of the century as communities were increasingly formed by private speculation linked to the train and trolley systems. In the first half of the 20th century the ever-expanding roads and highways drove large-scale speculation in housing development. The forms of the houses and garden apartments were defined by developers who responded to the tastes of the market and over the years made less and less use of the imagination of architects. And over the years the buildings became more modest and were built more cheaply. They achieved an almost conscious anonymity – subdued, undemanding and conformist – for a docile working class. They seem as fragile as the ambitions of those who live in them.

Ocean Parkway ends at the sea amongst the strangest mixture of neighbourhoods including Coney Island and Brighton Beach. At the turn of the century New Yorkers travelled to Coney Island to gamble, watch races and boxing matches, visit whorehouses and lose themselves in the fantasies of Steeplechase Park, Luna Park and Dreamland. These were the most exuberant amusement parks in the

David H Balfour

The elevated railroad running down the centre of Brighton Beach Avenue, the heart of Russian New York

nation, precursors in every way to Disney and Six Flags. They offered a dense assortment of rides, amusements and restaurants, all housed within splendidly theatrical buildings, brilliantly lit at night. Inspired by Chicago's great exhibition of 1896, they combined the grandeur of the White City and the random thrill of the Midway. Dreamland was destroyed by fire in 1911. Luna Park was enduringly successful until it too burnt down, in 1944. But Steeplechase continued to attract the crowds until it closed in 1964. The sensuous and raucous history of Coney Island still lingers in the remaining sleazy strip of shops and amusement arcades. A few modest rides sit in the shadow of the abandoned ruins of Steeplechase. The wooden roller coaster and the tower that once held the parachute jump are abandoned behind high fences, artefacts of lost desires, majestic and grave in the trashy streets that still draw floods of people on summer weekends.

The brash youthful crowds that swarm the streets of Coney

Island are in marked contrast to the melancholic mood of Brighton Beach. A Jewish neighbourhood of neat brick apartments, it began to attract Russian immigrants in the early 1960s, long before Gorbachev. Since the collapse of Communism it has become the most intensely Russian part of America. The main street, always in the lattice shadow of the elevated railway, supplies all the Russian desires for food, fashion and fiction. Odessa seems to appear frequently in shop windows and on signs. But it is the faces of the elderly, staring sadly out to sea, that carry the suffering of Mother Russia.

The second path that was driven through Brooklyn runs east to west from Broadway Junction at the eastern edge of the borough, then almost due west to Red Hook. It begins in the most desolate part of the city. To go from Broadway Junction down Granville Payne Avenue into East New York is to experience the scale of destruction the city suffered in the 1960s and 1970s. Detours on either side of the avenue lead into streets that are still devastated, streets so dead that they resist attempts to bring them back to life. At its worst a block may have only one house still standing. Next to it children, some on bicycles, play around a surviving corner store. However, many blocks are the sites of new construction, simple terraces of two- and three-storey town houses, clean and light and orderly. There is a need for much more construction and more investment to return the streets to normal.

Under the elevated rail tracks, down Livonia Avenue into Brownsville, there are similar landscapes on either side but they have much more life. In this extensive African and Afro-American heart of Brooklyn, from East New York to the edges of Prospect Park, more than a third of the population are new Americans. It is they who are renewing these communities, but they are doing so on their own terms. It is as if they are being allowed to farm in the wilderness. Up Remsen Avenue leads to Eastern Parkway past Wingate, which defines the lower edge between the Jewish and the Caribbean communities.

Eastern Parkway retains on its surface the dignity and authority that Olmsted believed enhanced civic style. It was lined with a grand mixture of housing from the 1870s through to the 1930s. Over most of its 3 miles it is a Caribbean community. The apartment buildings, town houses, churches and civic buildings are maintained but not well; yet there is no sense of abandonment. People enjoy the streets and the institutional buildings, built for one culture and easily adapted to serve another. At its midpoint this Caribbean neighbourhood must coexist with the most private and possessive culture of Jewish Orthodoxy. Crown Heights is east of Prospect Park and, though physically similar to Prospect Heights, is the most ethnically separate community in the city. Imagine the scene on the parkway at Yom Kippur. A restless surging crowd of men unified beneath a waving field of shawls flickering in black and white. The feeling of fervour is palpable and to the Caribbean families across the street, dressed up in their church-going clothes, utterly foreign. The Lubavitchers, an orthodox Hassidic community, began arriving in New York in small groups from the Soviet Union in the 1940s and consolidated their community in Crown Heights. The neighbourhood is now their world headquarters and attracts continual immigration to the area. The edge between Crown Heights and the predominantly Caribbean community is never less than tense. In 1991 the death of a black child in a car accident led to riots which caused the death of a member of the Hassidic community. The community is actively trying to extend its boundaries and move its neighbours out, and makes no pretence at seeking integration. New apartment developments advertised as kosher appear on billboards only in Hebrew. The orthodox community is planning to build a children's museum on Eastern Parkway – it is unclear whether this is in the interest of

being a good neighbour. In contrast, Leffert Heights, the neighbourhood to the south of Crown Heights Prospect, has been well maintained over the years and is as fully integrated across the races as anywhere in Brooklyn. These two distinct conditions present the dilemma for the future of New York, a city formed from a mosaic of changing communities, some open and mobile, others ghettoised by religion, race or poverty.

Crossing Grand Army Plaza and down through Park Slope leads to the Greenwood Cemetery, inspired, as were many American cemeteries, by Mount Auburn in Cambridge, Massachusetts. It was formed as a civic stage 'for the contemplation of death and as a reconciliation with nature'. Commissioned in 1838 and laid out by David Bates Douglas, it was the pleasure of its landscapes that drove the park movement in New York City. It is the Père Lachaise of the city, still sublimely romantic, the last repose of many great Americans from William George to Leonard Bernstein. Melancholy yet substantial, it is a civic city in miniature with its hundreds of carefully formed monuments on promenades. They have a confidence and permanence absent in the real city. The pleasure of outings from Manhattan to the Greenwood in the 1840s helped build the desire for a great park.

Out across modest Italian Gowanis and under the Gowanis expressway leads into Red Hook. Barely a mile separates it from Park Slope yet they exist in realms utterly different. Always a tough harbour town yet a close-knit neighbourhood, it was portrayed in both Arthur Miller's *View From the Bridge*, and Elia Kazan's film *On the Waterfront*. It was destroyed by the construction of the expressway, the Belt parkway and the Brooklyn Battery Tunnel which separated it from the city, and by the loss of jobs when the harbour became a container port. This is a desolate place, 90 per cent black and Latino, dominated by the earliest, and one of the largest, public housing projects: Red Hook Housing. Unlike other projects in the Moses years, this housed people from the community who had been displaced by the highway construction. The public housing starts immediately after the elevated road.

These highways remain alien to city life. The brutality of the surgery runs their full length and the wounds have not healed. Their undersides are dangerous and hostile places, homes for the homeless and for a wide array of gypsy industries that feed on the automobile. It is through such an unwelcome gate that one enters Red Hook. The Hanrahan + Meyers community building puts a rather too tasteful face on an old brick shed. Its elegance is slightly ill at ease but it seems an open and generous place. The grocery store on the next corner is much more at home. Red Hook Housing shares a sameness with public housing across the city. Basic brick apartment buildings are thoughtfully planned with playgrounds and well-maintained gardens ordered around a central area. Yet for all those forced to live in Red Hook and elsewhere there is a sense

THE BRONX

of isolation, a sense of being outside city life. Children play around cars, mothers push perambulators, but nothing seems connected.

Public housing covers much of the southern part of the neighbourhood. Elsewhere, in marked contrast, there are fragments of the old brick row houses that formed the Italian town. Interspersed with seemingly abandoned industrial buildings, they are prettily painted and maintained in total disregard to the fractured world around them. At the north end a great stone church holds the corner of a quiet park and, with careful editing, it is possible to see the remains of a strong community. The Atlantic edge of Red Hook is lost behind the industrial structures that for a century and more maintained the economy and the community. Ancient brick buildings with elegant forms, and towering concrete structures, are all capable of being transformed to tempt the young upwardly mobile. The need is to conceive of projects that overcome not just the decay but the desolation, poverty and racial division; but it is difficult to conceive of a future for Red Hook that will not be divided. Nothing has happened in 40 years to assimilate the public housing into the battered but proud streets of the old town. A ribbon of gentrification along the shore will just add another division.

The 42 square miles of the Bronx is the only part of New York City on the mainland of the United States. It is surrounded on three sides by water: the Hudson on the west, the East River on the south and, to the east, Long Island Sound. The population, in decline for a number of years, was 1.2 million in 1990. The borough's communities are formed in a confused mix of grids and meandering streets dictated by topography and the shifting character of development. It has the greatest extremes of wealth and poverty of any of the five boroughs. The affluent neighbourhoods that make up Riverdale, immediately north of Manhattan, contain some of the grandest homes in the city; those in south and central Bronx have suffered the greatest extremes of decay.

The first path travels up Grand Concourse to Fordham University and then south on to the Bronx's Third Avenue to the Hub, cutting two very different sections – south and north – through the borough. Grand Concourse was laid out between 1902 and 1909 and is a broad, tree-lined boulevard, with side lanes for slower traffic, inspired by the Champs Elysées. In the first half of the century it became the institutional and business spine of the Bronx. It emerges out of the desolate river's edge through a tangle of highways and elevated railways, but quickly comes to order as it passes the utilitarian walls of the Hostos Community College, and is grandest as it passes the Mario Merola Bronx County Building. This monumental civic presence from the 1920s is quite different in its effect to the classicism of the turn of the century, more autocratic and detached. It faces Lou Gehrig Plaza and Joyce Kilmer Park. Here the stage is set for Grand Concourse. The park and concourse are defined by simple elegant apartment buildings with a gentle Art Deco inflection. This is an urbane handsome area and it continues almost uninterrupted as the concourse runs for over four miles north to Fordham. There is some monotony, but this wall of apartment buildings of eight storeys and more is a strong piece of urban fabric.

Built for an emerging white Jewish middle class and now dominantly black and Latino, the area is changing with newly arriving Koreans and Cambodians at its northern end. This is not a wealthy street but neither is it poor or neglected. As on the Eastern parkway, the resilience of the city fabric appears to have allowed it to adjust to significant changes in cultures and prosperity, with little evidence on the surface of neglect or abandonment. The few institutional buildings built for one culture seem to have found new users and new uses. Synagogues have been converted into churches and one has become the Bronx Museum of Art. The street holds as much promise for its new occupants as it did for those who chose to move there in the 1950s and 1960s. When such places as Grand Concourse are removed from the use of those for whom they were created, there can be years of uncertainty as the new players adjust to their culture. However, the present

39

residents of the concourse enjoy it as much as those who have moved on. An autonomous, if mild, social power is embedded in some architecture, sometimes for good, as here, sometimes for ill as in the housing projects.

Only 35 years separates the civic vision that created the Grand Concourse and the beginning of large-scale experiments in integrated apartment development. Parkchester, which houses 40,000 people, was developed by Met Life in 1942 and incorporated all the shopping, cinemas and recreation areas required for self-contained commitment. This was the model that led to the development of Co-op City close to the eastern shore of the Bronx. Completed in 1970, it has more than 15,000 apartments and 60,000 residents, provided with all the

facilities they might need. These private islands of high-rise development seem to reject explicitly the open and shared trust in civic order that was part of the concept for the Grand Concourse. In consciously creating the security of a tightly controlled private community, they weaken trust in the public realm.

The much more modest Third Avenue runs parallel to Grand Concourse, to its east. South of Fordham it is an area of broad streets lined with modest apartments, with occasional stores and automobile shops. As it descends through Morrisania and Melrose the streets on either side are lined with broken and abandoned buildings. At 161st the road divides and at its apex is the vast ruin of the Bronx Night Court, once a firm figure of

David H Balfour

The abandoned Bronx Night Court, Melrose and Third Avenue

40

David H Balfour

The old cemetery on City Island looking towards Hart Island

authority and now a grim shadow. Law was equally a casualty of whatever forces led to the Bronx's devastation. They were similar to those that destroyed Brooklyn, but were more directly the result of the public programmes of Robert Moses and the impact of the highway system, both in destroying neighbourhoods and encouraging flight. In addition, the rapid rise in automobile ownership and the temptation of the new housing estates meant that the large number of people who could afford to move, did.

As noted earlier, the building of the Cross-Bronx expressway was particularly destructive to the Bronx's neighbourhoods, but much less so than it was to the thousands of Afro-Americans and Puerto Ricans who were moved out of Manhattan into public housing in the south and central Bronx – Hunts Point, Morrisania and Tremont – areas that had been identified by social workers in the 1950s as already suffering from enduring poverty. These forced migrations were into areas where rent control was already discouraging landlords from maintaining property. Many landlords instigated the deliberate, widespread wrecking and burning of property to collect on insurance and this systematic destruction affected over 100 city blocks in the Bronx. Many buildings that were not set on fire were abandoned, leaving behind rubble-filled lots and isolating the public housing projects. The degeneration of the neighbourhoods continued long after the decline of their physical structure: massive unemployment, ghettoisation, the rise in a culture of drugs and violence and random crime.

These areas have been recovering slowly since the late 1980s. The buildings that remain are being restored, with new developments filling in the gaps left by the destruction, but it is a poor and dangerous place. However, just a few blocks south of the night court, where Third Avenue crosses Westchester, the Hub, former heart of the city, has recovered in spectacular style. Though it may be in bad shape, on a Saturday afternoon the intersection is as hectic a scene of shopping as anywhere in New York.

In the 1990s the Bronx was once again gaining population. The racial mix is one-third black, one-third Latino and one-third Asian and white. Puerto Ricans account for more than 25 per cent of the population but, as with Queens and Brooklyn, the communities and neighbourhoods are under continual and changing influence from new immigrants. Koreans, Vietnamese, Indians, Pakistanis, Cambodians, Greeks and Russians are all moving into the Bronx in significant numbers. This persistent flow of migrants is warped and compounded by the physical structure of New York. It is a process of complex infiltration in which an ethnic group establishes a foothold in a neighbourhood, thus forming a conduit for its other members until they gain strength and develop businesses. Slowly the group gains increasing control over segments of real estate and commerce. The logic of the process is more serendipitous than rational. How to explain Albanians choosing to settle in Belmont, while Cambodians choose to be close to Fordham? The neighbourhoods that are formed are self-consciously ethnocentric, with little identification with New York City and almost none with the idea of the Bronx. These new arrivals have no need to be concerned with ideas such as the 'public realm', and certainly, at this time, no need for architecture significant or otherwise. Yet they are renewing many of the toughest areas of the city with an ambition and energy and desire known only to themselves.

A second path runs from west to east across the broadest section of the Bronx, from the terraced heights above the Hudson River in Riverdale to Pelham Bay and the island village appropriately named City Island. It begins in narrow twisting lanes among the trees and grand houses that hide away on the steep banks of the Hudson. Riverdale is exceptionally pleasant, with little need to be concerned with other worlds. Travelling east it transforms into the streets of brick apartments that marked so much development in the 1920s and 1930s. Then comes Fieldstone, privately owned and the wealthiest and most splendid suburb in the city; large elegant houses, all slightly different, sit in perfect gardens on tree shaded-streets. By what means could the people of Fieldstone speak to the people of Melrose? Van Cortland Park, once the estate of the Van Cortland family, is next, the house and landscapes very much as they were left by the family in the early part of the 20th century. The extensive stretch of park has retained a natural quality that makes one aware of the artificiality of the Olmsted landscape.

To the east is Woodlawn Cemetery, judged the most noble of all American cemeteries when it was laid out in 1863 by James C Sidney in what was known as a rural style. It contains a collection of structures shaped by the aesthetics of New York culture in 1900 – exquisite objects by, among many others, Stanford White, Louis Comfort Tiffany and John Russell Pope. Yet in contrast to Greenwood it seems cold with a more classical view of death and immortality. The journey from the poverty of Melrose to the sublime unreality of Woodlawn is a journey through the distortions of the American imagination. Woodlawn connects to the most pleasurable of Bronx institutions: the New York Botanical Gardens, developed on land that was purchased in the 1880s as part of an official programme to preserve the natural landscapes within the city. It was chosen as a site for both the botanical gardens and the Bronx Zoo in 1890, and laid out by a team of landscape gardeners that included Calvert Vaux. There is an extensive and varied specimen collection, and species gardens. The major architectural presence is the Enid Haupt Conservatory, recently restored by the architects Beyer Blinder Belle, which is modelled after the greenhouses in London's Kew Gardens. The cultivated land surrounds a large swathe of unmanaged forest, at the edge of which the Bronx River runs through scenes unchanged since before colonisation.

The east side of the gardens leads on to Gun Hill Road and through Olinville and Baychester, neat and tidy neighbourhoods with streets of detached houses and lively businesses. Familiar, comfortable and middle class, they are are totally Afro-American. The forbidding mass of Co-op City is visible from Gun Hill Road behind the mall at Bay Plaza and the New England freeway. This enclave even now gives the impression of being privately conceived to capitalise on the feeling that the public life of the city is getting out of control. It has evolved into an integrated population, predominantly Afro-American and Hispanic, and is considered a very desirable place to live.

A tangle of Moses highways runs across the entrance to Pelham Bay Park. This vast tract of land, three times the area of Central Park, was purchased in the 1880s as part of the programme that held the land for the botanical gardens. It has all the New Deal instruments for the orchestration of public recreation: highways, mass car parks, a boardwalk and a sweeping stretch of white beach. The architecture is at its most modern at Orchard Beach which was laid out in the 1930s. There is still joy in the floating canopy at the bus station and in the great curving colonnade for public assembly.

Orchard Beach also offers passage to the most remote fishing village in the city: City Island. Developed around the shipping industries in the late 18th century it is still a centre for sailing. Ships' chandlers and one sailmaker remain. As with Fieldstone, its placid contentment forces comparison with the urban desolation to the west. City Island has all the self-sufficiency of a small town: tree-lined contented streets of substantial houses and a main street with curio and antiques shops and some overassertive fish restaurants. On one summer afternoon the great fish places at its southern tip catered to hundreds of people, the vast majority of whom were black and Latino.

City Island adjoins the most tragic place in all the five boroughs: Hart Island. For over a century it has been the 'potters field' of New York City, where almost one million of the poor and disgraced lie, three deep, in mostly unmarked graves. The bodies are carried by boat from a closed berth on City Island and the graves are dug by prisoners, volunteers from the correctional facility on Riker's Island.

The journey that began on an island ends on an island. New York is a city which has the virtue of accommodating most nationalities of the world in extremes of wealth and poverty. A question for the future: to what degree does democracy depend on some measure of shared public values and desires, and how are these to be cultivated in such a diverse population?

The commissioners' plan continues to compel future orders to obey its logic and political agenda, yet the changing orders in the 20th-century city have become increasingly devoid of civic content as land speculation has become free from public control. A line drawn on the map of the five boroughs will show the difference between the time when community order was dictated by state and city government and when it was released to private speculation. And the increasing influence of speculation in the development of community is paralleled by a corresponding decrease in the use of architecture to mark significant places.

The boroughs are sustained by three distinct, yet mutually exclusive, ideas. First, the persistence of the 19th-century concept of a civic society and of the boroughs as meaningful political entities. Second, a tolerant and productive society gaining an ambition for power from its multiculturalism. Third, and contemporary with the second, the emergence of ethnic enclaves that increasingly maintain their separateness, by force if necessary and certainly by controlling boundaries.

What are the consequences when a culture divides into so many subcultures that it loses the will to speak with a unified voice and has no way of representing the myriad desires of all the people? It will seek unity in whatever is shared in common. This will increasingly strengthen the influence and control of the media and producers of goods and services. Their products are the only things many of us have in common. The producers of goods and services will control the most powerful tools for bringing the city within public order.

Many immigrants from around the world are from cultures that are emerging from pre-industrial economies. They come to America with the dream of earning enough to transform the fortunes of their family. They keep New York a young raw place, or perhaps a middle-aged raw place. Yet nowhere in this process is there the paternalistic social engineering that attempts to control migration in Europe. Nowhere is there any attempt to educate these new arrivals to respect and use the cultural institutions of the city and the nation. Nowhere is there any attempt to anticipate the long-term implications of this generous and capricious process on the idea of the city.

The journey described here produced evidence of two new orders to add to the city of grids and parks and progressive infrastructure: it is increasingly a city of factions, and a city unified only through consumerism and self-interest.

NOTES

My constant companion through these many days of crossing and recrossing the city was *The Encyclopedia of New York*, edited by Kenneth T Jackson and published by Yale University Press (New Haven and London) and by the New York Historical Society (New York), 1998, which exhaustively documents the people, places, politics and history of this most complex city. I started every visit to a new neighbourhood by consulting the *Encyclopedia,* and it was able to answer almost every question raised in the journey, from the most arcane to the most legal.

Material supplied by the public agencies of the city was also helpful, and the 'Metropolitan' section of the *New York Times* maintains an almost daily engagement with all the turbulent subplots and plays that the city produces.

STREETS 4

The grid has had the effect of choreographing performance on the streets of the island in a way that is unmistakably Manhattan. The experience is dominated by traffic. Because all servicing is from the streets, mainly the cross streets, it is impossible at any time of day, or even night, to avoid delivery trucks and carts and trolleys and produce – vegetables, dresses, filing cabinets. All the equipment of life seems to be in constant motion around the city. Every journey involves stepping around the delivery man, always into the path of cabs and limos. Throughout the midtown the dry oily air is softened by the sour steam rising from the street vents, adding piquancy to the sugared candies and roast kebabs on the pans and grills of the street vendors.

Architecture struggles for position in the great walls of buildings formed by the grid. It is not a subject of much interest and the grid is a great leveller – as it was intended to be. Subtle differences in style become insignificant in the dense sandwich of the city block. There is an awareness of entrances and shop windows and a pleasant sense that, although public life is here on the street, all buildings are in some way accessible. At ground level the presence of architecture is most keenly felt at the entrance lobbies to buildings grand and grim. They establish the type of life and activity within each property. Yet the grid enforces not just conformity but a grudging egalitarianism. From boutiques and the department stores that line Fifth Avenue to the sleaze joints that have been forced to the edges of Eighth and Ninth, and even to the raunch among the meat packers, some peculiar metaphysics makes them all part of the same play.

The city is a complex stage which shapes behaviour in its own way. The bicycle messengers of New York are the most soulful players on its most dangerous stage. They embody the continual struggle that drives the city, seeming to have no race or culture separate from the role they have chosen to play. Dressed in stylish helmets and filthy jackets; unsmiling, always on the verge of anger; risking their lives, with total disregard, in the waves of traffic. They cannot be paid enough to be exposed to such continual danger – they must do it for the sport. They are the gladiators in this city of unceasing conflict, dying young, among the garbage and street furniture and fenders, for all of us.

Scenes from a video by Jane Jinhee Park

ARCHITECTURE 5

New York City is for the most part an art-less place. Art-less for good reason because, apart from the cost of making architecture, using it to reflect symbols and signs of significance in communities that are in constant flux is simply misplaced. In a more compound sense, there is no relation between creating the physical shells that embody a refined set of values enjoyed by a cultural elite – which is the way in which architecture increasingly defines its experimental role – and the needs of neighbourhoods and communities under the strain of relentless cultural adjustment. The results would be at best foolish, at worst an interference with the necessary open-mindedness that such a social transition requires. This transition would seem to be best served by an architecture of modesty and anonymity, one that is light on the ground, able to adjust. Seeking permanence through architecture is simply inappropriate in the culture which thrives on continual change, in which migrant groups seek to establish cultural identity through means that are just as rich as architecture – music and food, rituals and religion – but much less permanent. The European roots of the uses of architecture in America are far removed from the Latino or Afro-American experience. Added to this, most new migrants have little or no cultural connection to the uses and semantic subtleties that infect bourgeois architecture.

Architecture increases the way in which the past weakens and distorts the present. The decay of a neighbourhood is much more painful when the once noble illusions embodied in its architecture are seen to be destroyed. The evidence is everywhere of the folly of attempting to create the illusion of permanence and civic dignity in a society that, with the formation of new communities, is not simply in continuous devolution but is in a state of continual experimentation. It is too seldom acknowledged that America's pluralistic democracy and openness to immigration forces society into a perpetual experiment with the form and structure of community. As waves of migrations move into Brooklyn, the Bronx and Queens no attempt is made to manage their impact on existing communities, to actively direct the process of cultural reformation, and no serious consideration is given to the social and cultural clash inherent in this process. Tolerance of open and unconstrained migration makes the United States utterly distinct, makes America appealing to the world, but the role for architecture within this process has yet to emerge.

Architecture in New York occurs in only three areas of cultural production: the corporations that build to enhance their image; wealthy patrons who glorify their family names by endowing public institutions; and the agencies of government – city, state, federal – that seek ways of signifying public order. The nature of that production divides, as it does in the pages of the *New York Times*, into two quite distinct worlds: the art section and the real estate section. In the art section the critic, often with wit and imagination, explores the architectural issues that emerge from what is essentially art practice. This fashionable and ever changing world exists simply to refresh and stimulate interest in the possibilities of property. The real estate section deals with architecture as a much more stable element in the continual construction of that most serious, and by necessity conservative, project: Manhattan.

TIMES SQUARE

Manhattan in all its untidy energy is a continuous field of widely diverse property speculation. All buildings with the exception of the publicly owned must remain financially viable and must produce revenue to justify their upkeep. This is formative in determining the nature of the city beyond any theories on space, form or architecture. Being forced to account financially for every aspect of built structure gives the architecture of the city a leanness, an ascetic toughness. It is this that creates a hostile mood in so many of the city streets. Controlling all architecture is the structure of the grid; the walls of buildings stretching for many miles up and across the island diminish whatever elegance a single facade might possess. There is power and strength on these great avenues, but little comfort. Comfort comes from consumption – of fashion, of food, of sports, of movies. It makes us all captive, eager yet always dissatisfied, waiting for the next sensation.

New York is a city formed from a myriad speculations, desires, time frames. It is given character by the conceit of individuals large and small, all struggling to gain advantage from any circumstance, avoiding failure and the places of failure and weaving around any interference. Zoning, community interests and public causes are all to be fine-tuned to private advantage. This is not an environment calling out for subtlety, refinement or significance; in the brittle friction that surrounds all development a disciplined architecture emerges as the unmistakable product of the city.

The development of 42nd Street represents all the above forces at play in one dense game. It is the largest commercial urban renewal project ever undertaken in the state of New York. When it is completed in the year 2000 it will enclose more than 7 million square feet of space and house four restored theatres, 39 movie screens, two hotels, various themed restaurants, retail stores, live and virtual amusement arcades and that most compelling of artificial destinations: Madame Tussauds. Within this mix will be the headquarters of the media companies Reuters and Condé Nast. The most visible part of the project will be in the choreography of the

View down Seventh Avenue to Skidmore, Owings & Merrill's project for Times Square

multimedia advertising that will wrap around all the buildings on a continual 100-foot-high band. What appears on the surface to be a dynamic creation of a city devoted to private speculation, is instead the carefully manipulated product of a public development company established by the state of New York: the 42nd Street Development Project Inc, which was directed by Rebecca Robertson for most of the years between 1987 and 1997. And behind all the glitzy trademarks is a substantial amount of public sector investment.

The company was charged with revitalising 42nd Street between Broadway and Eighth Avenue (Rebecca Robertson gives a detailed account of the process in Chapter 7). The decline of 42nd Street had at first been gradual; it was noticeable in the 1950s and by the mid-1970s 42nd was the saddest street in the midtown. The blinking marquees of the movie houses and peepshows offered a wide variety of basic sexual activities, casting a sickly, grimy yellow light on the hustling and dealing and the anxious tourists passing beneath them. At the vital heart of this epic city was a patch of diseased tissue.

In 1984 Philip Johnson gave form to the proposal to transform the area into a sober business centre by cleaning up the untidy activity that had always fed on the theatre district. The new order would be held by four matched multistorey towers, designed by Johnson in a manner that reflects either his cynicism or his ability. They were green and distinct only in their sameness. They failed to raise much enthusiasm and in the subsequent integration each tower was infected with a series of small motifs in a manner that subsequently became known as 'deconstructivism'. Johnson cleverly reduced this portentous theory to a fashion accessory. (This was happening at about the same time that he was co-opting young intellectuals with enthusiasm for such theatres to create an exhibition at MoMA devoted to the subject.) With or without Johnson's vision, the plan continued to evolve until the collapse of the real estate market in the early 1990s froze all development. This chance event allowed 42nd Street to assume a much richer, and indeed stranger, form than otherwise could have been predicted, a form defined by the new state-appointed development team.

The 42nd Street Development Project Inc brought together financial and entertainment consultants, real estate market analysts, designers and a powerful public relations firm. The talented mix of designers formed a highly accessible vision of a new Times Square aimed at preserving its raucous energy while removing the danger. The plan had to be substantial enough, and tempting enough, to attract investment. It was illustrated with appropriately comic drawings by that otherwise most conservative gentleman, architect Robert AM Stern, helped by witty graphics from the late Tabor Kalman. Stern's

most critical influence, however, came from a source more powerful than his drawings. He had served on the board of the Disney Corporation for many years and was one of their favoured architects. He learnt that the corporation was interested in developing productions on Broadway and needed a good theatre. This enabled him to draw Disney chairman Michael Eisner into the development.

Several years passed before all the pieces could be assembled and the architectural elements formed, but to manage this evolution the development group created highly original design guidelines directly aimed at controlling architectural effects. They comprise six principles: aesthetics, chaos, layers, un-planning, juxtapositions and, lastly, icon. The guidelines are aimed at creating a theatrical sensation, building Times Square into a stage set that will satisfy the dreams and expectations of tourists. They emerged apparently without much reflection on the deeper significance of such constructed illusions or the implications of giving the heart of the city over to the manipulative visions of the corporate world, but that's the nature of New York. The basic principle of the plan resembles that most entertaining idea from the 1970s, or was it the 1980s? The postmodern collage – 42nd Street as collage city, without the humbug of too much history and little theory.

Several distinct architectures are collaged on to 42nd Street. Florida architects Arquitectonica have created a massive landmark, a tower hotel, which they won in competition with Michael Graves and Zaha Hadid. The most obvious effect of the guidelines was to make all the entries very similar. Architects Beyer Blinder Belle made a layered box that houses Madame Tussauds and assorted retailers. They had to fit a full-scale hotel somewhere on the roof when it was realised that the site could be exploited to the full. State property is not bound by city zoning regulations.

As the project has moved into construction the devices for achieving layering and complexity have been increasingly refined by employing several architects and subdividing the elements of the building. The extreme case is the staging of Madame Tussauds. The interior of the waxworks museum is designed by David Rockwell and the commercial shell is designed and choreographed by Beyer Blinder Belle with one architect, Rolf Ohlhausen, coordinating all the pieces. In addition there are the designers for the various concessions and the designers of the media subsystems, the theatrical lighting and the sound systems. The enclosure, that object seen from the street, is an empty shell open to carry into the future whatever changing demands its tenants and advertisers make on it. Architecture becomes submerged in a fusion of reality-manipulation driven by media technologies. The armature will carry variable time frames with the walls of

51

Arquitectonica: the hotel on 42nd Street

advertising changing continually, the theme restaurant will rotate at the most every two years and even the most powerful retailers will continually revise their image. These operations will be maintained only for as long as they create wealth, the creation of wealth in this case depending wholly on sustaining our desire in ways sensual, even sexual. The glowing talking walls will become the world's most competitive arena for advertisers, forcing them to stretch the limits of their imagination to satisfy our sensual hunger, forcing them to exploit sensation in ways much more ingenious and outrageous than would ever have been allowed in the old 42nd Street.

The Arquitectonica hotel will be the central figure of the development, responding to the requirement that there is an object to rival the Statue of Liberty somewhere on the street. Designed by Lorinda Spear, it is essentially a box with great curving lines on its surface, marked with both materials and light. The hotel sits on an elegant base that will become an insignificant backdrop to the great wall of advertising, as indeed may the hotel itself.

The most complete architecture comes from the partnership of Fox & Fowle and is the headquarters for Reuters and Condé Nast. This is strong, witty corporate architecture. The machined skins of the towers adjust to the changing context on all four sides and at street level, pushing out to the street edge of the lower levels. It is a layered curving structure which provides a muscular platform for the advertising. The Condé Nast building will dominate the new Times Square and will carry on its roof four screens, intended to carry moving messages across New York, that will run the full extent of the building mass. An 80-foot-high drum pushes out of the corner of the building onto Times Square, completely covered in light-emitting diodes (LEDs), that is able to carry every form of electronic media. It not only dissolves the building structure but eclipses all competing photomurals and small digital screens. Very soon all of Times Square must become a continuous surface of LEDs. This may create a synthetic unity but will certainly increase the de-materialisation of the Times Square experience.

The last distinct architecture is in the extensive restoration of the major surviving theatres on the street. In some cases this task has involved cutting and pasting old theatres together into new configurations but in every case the interiors have been lovingly restored to a gilded brilliance that seems richer than they could have been originally. The result, in the work of such as Hardy Holtzman Pfeiffer Associates, is a most satisfying recollection of lost imaginations, lost fantasies and forgotten senses. The Ford Motor Company underwrote the restoration of the new Ford Theatre. The public-supported youth theatre will perform in the restored Empire and Disney found their new theatre in the recreation of the New Amsterdam

The aim has to been to sanitise 42nd Street and in this the

Courtesy: Arquitectonica/Tishman Realty & Construction Co., Inc

redevelopment will be successful – and in this something will be lost. Removing the sins and dangers of the street flattens the experience of the city. Great cities tolerate extremes of desire. The power of New York is sexual, a power that drives ambition, conceit and arrogance. It is charged with a sense of danger; the opportunity to flirt with the illicit makes people feel more alive. Replacing this sad but memorable street with the bright theatrics of trademarked reality is to trivialise it and, with it, the experience of the city. Marginal areas are important because they tolerate misfortune. Crusading for the good city, and the safe city, leads to an intolerance of even minor deviation and so to a deadening conformity. Vast areas of New York are viewed as being too dangerous to visit, and the flow of immigrants is channelled increasingly into ghettos and enclaves simply so that their differences can be tolerated. The real danger is in the increasing divisiveness and separation of race, of poverty, of difference. The staging of the new 42nd Street has pushed its former unfortunate players further into the shadows.

Yet in reality the reconstruction of 42nd Street is above all a re-invention, an extravagant enlargement on the myth of the city, a much-improved product to capture the world's imagination. It also will create a concentration of the world's desires. Structuring the new 42nd Street and its surroundings to carry the machinery for continually changing media images – vast surfaces that will demand the visual heroics of a thousand Titians – will transform the focus of the world's attention into a virtual reality. What extravagant visions will play across the surfaces? Imagine how this theatre of the most intense competition will drive advertisers to shock or outrage to maintain our interest – co-opting narratives from every culture, allowing walls to carry the most seductive and capricious theories of being.

For well over 100 years the cluster of theatres that formed the entertainment district has been slowly moving north. Rather than allowing it to continue to move uptown, consolidation around 42nd Street indicates that New York City is well into middle age. This consolidation is the grandest example of a process of conservation and preservation that is increasingly of concern to all who influence the shape of the city. New cinema complexes are also being developed – elegant, neutral and precise instruments for the most efficient delivery of movies and related food pleasures.

New York is a place of multiple performances with music and theatre at its heart. The grid removes depth from the city, and the great walls that line the avenues are composed in an intricate sequence of small theatrical moments. Beyond 42nd Street, performance halls are being restored across New York, some converted to television studios, some reworked to improve performances. Carnegie Hall has undergone a decade of restoration and extension under the direction of James

Stewart Polshek, and the acoustics of the Metropolitan Opera House in Lincoln Center were redesigned in the late 1990s with the help of electronic amplification. The demands of restoration are leading to the formation of expert teams, from acousticians to painters and sculptors and experts on wallpaper and 19th-century carpets. Hardy Holtzman Pfeiffer Associates, HHPA, formed just such a team for the restoration of Radio City Music Hall, which resulted in the remanufacture of all the materials that had dressed the building in 1930. Over the last decade a much more inventive process of renovation has revitalised and extended the several halls that make up the Brooklyn Academy of Music. Under the direction of Harvey Lichtenstein, HHPA have carefully restored the Majestic Theater as a setting for BAM's most extravagant experiments. The interior has been stripped of all its applied surfaces leaving a raw shell to carry whatever reality a performance demands.

One of the most interesting new performance spaces is the work of Gluckman Mayner Architects in association with Rem Koolhaas. It re-occupies an old bank building on the corner of 42nd Street and Ninth Avenue and large windows on to the street will allow the city to form a backdrop to the play. The enthusiasm in the press when it opened was for the flashy feel of the seat covers chosen by the client. In the design of the space's many galleries and fashion stores Richard Gluckman has found the most gently elegant minimalism with which to renew the city's interior world.

No grand ideals infect, confuse or distort these restorations. The realities of New York are formed and reformed to remain enduringly tempting to the consumer: every act in the city is essentially an act of consumption. Yet most of this activity seems to operate at very similar levels of convention and invention, resulting in a busy monotony that lacks surprises or the dangers of real temptations. There are dangers aplenty in New York but they're not for consumption. This process of renewal increasingly creates a city that is always experienced from its past, free from objects that promise change. This is as much the result of the grid constraining significant change as of the driving force of consumption. Look closely at the hundreds of photographs that record the great shopping streets of the 1870s, particularly around Lower Broadway. They are places that even now can be entered with complete familiarity.

Throughout midtown old hotels have been transformed into the city's most fashionable places by the imaginations of designers such as André Putnam at the Morgan and Philippe Starck at the Paramount and the Royalton. The grand stairway in the Paramount offers a sensation of weightlessness; the lounge in the deep blue lobby of the Royalton was briefly the only place to be seen. These are small but delicious sensual and strange pleasures. Many shades of white colour the health-conscious walls of Rafael Viñoly's Roger Williams Hotel

53

and its companion with the enigmatic 'W'. The Mercer is the height of minimalist chic and English architect David Chipperfield will challenge this in his refashioning of that most wonderful 1920s tower: the American Radiator building by Raymond Hood, the subject of a haunting night painting by Georgia O'Keefe.

Within the gaunt shells of 19th-century commerce new stages are being created for buying and selling, offering highly refined theatrics in the elegance and arrogance of new life styles. The life of a fashionable interior can be short and notions of a progressively changing reality are confused by equal pleasure in all. Past reality is pleasure in retro. There is nothing new in using styles to sell commodities. What has changed is the detachment of styles from notions of identity or signification; a choice of interiors is as likely to offer a stage from science fiction – Comme des Garçons – as a touch of domestic life in the 18th century in the ABC store.

Signs of restoring and reinventing the past take several forms, from scholarly restorations that, in recent examples, often heighten the quality of the original to renewing the interiors of turn-of-the-century commercial buildings with carefully restored facades by restructuring them to carry the

appropriate fashion for any and every kind of use. This is to be seen at its most ambitious in what was once called Ladies' Mile, at Sixth Avenue in the 1920s. In the first decades of the century a sequence of great department stores lined this most fashionable shopping street and after 50 years of being forgotten they are now being renewed. However, the process of rejuvenating the past means that all objects of cultural production, be they religious, political or tribal, are being reduced to equivalent commodities.

Such a dissolution of coherent reality is certainly not new. Rome has reformed and reoccupied its ancient structures for 2,000 years. What is new for New York is that the desire to restore has become much stronger than the will to destroy and build again. The culture of the city at the end of the 20th century is one which finds it inconceivable that the old Pennsylvania Station could have been torn down and cannot begin to fathom the political climate in which Robert Moses was able to acquire so much power and cause such disruption.

Skidmore, Owings & Merrill
Times Square Project

Yoshio Taniguchi: photomontage of his winning entry for the redevelopment of the Museum of Modern Art

MOMA

the skyline. There are echoes of Eric Mendelsohn's Columbus Haus, just completed in the centre of Berlin. In 1954 Philip Johnson expanded the building east and west and added his most majestic work of public art: the sculpture garden. The major reconstruction came with the celebration of the museum's 50th anniversary. The Argentine architect Cesar Pelli led a team which grandly reordered the interior and added a multistorey tower housing luxury apartments. The decision to add the tower, which would have shocked the civic-minded in Europe, was justified by the trustees as a way of raising money to pay for the improvements. (Imagine a tower rising above the great museums of London or Paris. However, in New York, as all objects become subject to the grid, tall buildings cause little disruption at street level.) Pelli's extensive reworking of the museum only solved immediate problems and failed to anticipate future needs.

Since then, motivated by the need to accommodate the museum's growing collections and above all, in the words of its director Glen D Lowery, 'to explore the intellectual pragmatic and physical possibilities of the museum in the next century', the decision was made to hold a major competition. The first decisive step was to acquire properties on both 53rd and 54th Streets, including the Dorset Hotel on 54th Street. The competition, planned by Terry Riley, the curator for design, was in several phases and began in January 1997 with a charette, an intense design process derived from the French Ecole des Beaux Arts. Ten architects were invited to take part: Wiel Arets of the Netherlands; Herzog & de Meuron from Switzerland; Steven Holl, New York; Toyo Ito, Tokyo; Rem Koolhaas, the Netherlands; Dominique Perrault, France; Yoshio Taniguchi, Tokyo; Bernard Tschumi, New York; Rafael Viñoly, New York and Tod Williams and Billie Tsien from New York. After an intense, several-day briefing at the museum the invitees were given four and a half weeks to develop their presentations. The rules emphasised that conceptual ideas rather than specific plans for development were required. The presentations should illustrate the many different ways of approaching the problem. The drawings should evoke character. The submissions were to be informal, and could include sketchbooks, notebooks – whatever seemed appropriate – provided all the material fitted into a box 11 inches by 17 inches by 3 inches. The boxes were covered in elegant green cloth and one was supplied to each of the entrants.

It is disappointing that in almost every case the submissions lacked the unconstrained invention and conceptual exploration that the process had promised. Most of the studies were architectural and specific: all save the one in the Koolhaas box, which was filled with thrills and slightly rude and naughty suggestions. One can imagine the trustees bemusement at Koolhaas's little golden tower carrying a large sign MoMA Inc, which was explained in the notes as housing the fund-raisers.

55

I move now from invented and self-conscious heterogeneity – the multiple synthetic realities of Times Square – to the plans to expand and enhance the Museum of Modern Art. In fact, when preparing for this new development the trustees at one point considered whether it would be more interesting to employ many architects rather than one, to add to the existing heterogeneity. As things turned out, the architects of the new museum attempted to have MoMA re-emerge as a single building pure enough to cleanse the bourgeois palate.

The museum has been in process of expansion since it came to 53rd Street in 1939. From its temporary quarters on Fifth Avenue it moved briefly into the newly completed Rockefeller Center before being given land that had belonged to JD Rockefeller Junior. (In the 1940s the ties to the Rockefeller family led to a proposal that would have created a grand cultural passage from the museum to Rockefeller Center. This was the kind of self-aggrandisement the commissioners' plan sought to inhibit.) The museum Edward D Stone and Philip Goodwin designed in 1939 was a strong modern object that rivalled the best in Europe. It carries an expansive glass facade floating above a recess base. The expansive canopy over the roof terrace is pierced with circular lights, which give a thrill to

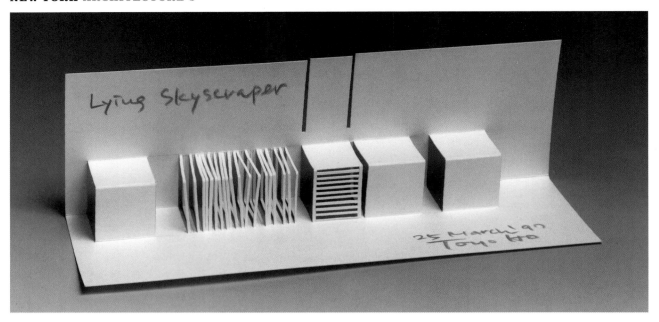

Toyo Ito: Lying Skyscraper,
conceptual study for the new
MoMA

He proposed reorganising the museum as a totally computerised information system where, at a keystroke, any major or minor work could be retrieved for individual delight. His grandest proposition was for a gallery-sized elevator that moved diagonally and vertically through the complex. (The effect would have been not unlike the great moving floor at the centre of his recent house in Bordeaux.)

Toyo Ito's view of the museum as a 'horizontal skyscraper' derived from the fact that the horizontal space made available by the recent land acquisition was as long as the Pelli tower was tall. He illustrated a metaphorical elevation in which the image of marble and brick floats on a weightless surface. Riley saw in this drawing an anticipation of a 'dematerialisation cyberworld'. However, it could be argued that the cyberworld is more likely to be found on the walls of 42nd Street than in the overly tasteful inventions of architects.

Arets used Mondrian's painting *Broadway Boogie Woogie* which seemed to stifle his imagination. Holl offered sketchbooks filled with charming watercolours which examined, in his words, 'cutting and bracketing'. Cutting produced the most forceful effects as galleries were carved out of a mass that would rise to the centre of the museum. Perrault would have formed a new development on the building's east–west spine in three versions: 'aside', 'along' and 'above'. None of the propositions was conceptually strong and produced architecture without much character. Viñoly illustrated several sensitive explorations of future forms of the museum and their relation to the area. One charming and fragile watercolour indicates, in a few brush strokes, his idea of enclosing the garden beneath a massive sliding roof. In another the garden evolves into terraces of hanging gardens that rise above 54th Street. Tod Williams and Billie Tsien conveyed the character they would have sought for the museum in a series of richly textured collages. The effect is strong, the architecture too picturesque, too familiar.

In June 1997, three entries were invited to prepare final submissions – those of Bernard Tschumi, Herzog & de Meuron, and Yoshio Taniguchi. The decision was very much internal to the museum community, trustees and curators. The Koolhaas entry must have seemed too flippant, too irreverent for this reputation-conscious institution. He certainly would have given

the museum a strong, even visionary, character that would have compelled the imagination of the world. More surprising was the failure of Toyo Ito to be chosen as one of the finalists. His ideas were perhaps too conceptually lean and exquisite, but he has an exceptional body of built work. The problem for the jury was possibly the feeling that two Japanese finalists was one too many.

The final competition was to elicit proposals for a new Museum of Modern Art that 'would be boldly conceived, and creatively define an aesthetic vision beyond pragmatic, technical, and financial requirements'. The finalists all stretched painfully to please the 'beyond'. Herzog & de Meuron are able architects, remarkably effective in simplifying complexity. Their submission offered an orderly reorganisation save for the addition, at the western end, of a strange tower. In the form of an asymmetrical polygon, it was to house the administrative and curatorial staff. The accompanying notes explained that this complex figure had nothing to do with 'deconstructive, neo-expressive, or symbolic clichés, rather,' they wrote quoting Giacometti, its form would present a 'see-saw between abstraction and configuration'. Their drawings are more persuasive than their rhetoric. 'Why is it that art keeps asserting itself, keeps arousing curiosity and confronting us with such fundamental questions as, who am I, why am I, where are we going?' they ask. The answers perhaps lie somewhere in asymmetrical polygons?

Bernard Tschumi saw the new MoMA as an urban museum, and sought to remake it as 'heterotopia'. Along with his drawings he offered a manifesto. He would create a museum that preserved and reinforced MoMA's unique character as 1) the repository of an incomparable collection of modern and contemporary art; 2) a pioneer of museums of modern art with unique historical inheritance; 3) an urban institution in a midtown Manhattan location; 4) ' … by seizing the opportunities presented by these aspects of its character, it is possible to transform MoMA into a bold new museum while maintaining its historical, cultural, and social context.' Despite the graphic power of the Tschumi presentation the content seems as vague as the statements. 'Such a museum,' he wrote, would 'combine three distinct types on its site: 1) a received type, the twenty-five-foot square column grid, and the double bay of the historic MoMA; 2) a borrowed type, the almost factory type, for its temporary exhibitions; [and] 3) a new type, a proposal for fixed spaces, variable spaces, and interspace, for the permanent collection'. It must be said that this new type does not emerge clearly from the drawings.

The most curious element in his concept was for a raised garden. In the concluding statements in the manifesto he wrote:

> The garden is usually viewed as an oasis of nature within the urban culture of New York. While acknowledging this important perspective, we also call attention to the garden's often less acknowledged attribute as a space of remarkable range and flexibility … We feel the quality of pragmatic flexibility and social space provides places for activities and art forms that are not easily contained within conventional exhibition galleries. Our concept extends this quality throughout the museum in the form of multiple courts.

The upper garden court that results from his concept is, judging from the drawing, the least appealing addition Tchumi would have given the new museum. His built work is marked by brilliant formal strategy and technical invention but it appears that the context of MoMA failed to stimulate his conceptual invention, which seems to emerge with ease in France.

The board of trustees decided to award the commission for the new museum to Yoshio Taniguchi. Born in 1937 and educated in Kyoto and at Harvard, Taniguchi has a body of work marked by constraint and elegance. His stated goal for the new museum was, 'to create an ideal environment for art and people through the imagination and disciplined use of light, materials and … space'. 'To be', he wrote, 'a most complete and balanced organisation.' In the Taniguchi proposal the garden continues to occupy the centre and is expanded east, west and south into the museum. The enclosing structure is sombrely distinct in honed slate. The main entrance to the new museum will be on 54th Street beneath a sober band of slate, allowing the building to present a unified public facade along most of the block. Taniguchi also maintains the collage of styles from every stage of the museum's existence, including the present, along 53rd Street. Here the Stone Goodwin facade, which for so long symbolised MoMA, will become the entrance to the video and film theatres. The new entrance leads into the grand atrium which is animated by views of many levels of galleries.

This is a reserved yet tough piece of work, and it has the clarity and precision of an instrument. It offers an unselfconscious order of structures and space and material in such apparent harmony that the drawings seem too silent. There is no seesawing between abstraction and figuration here, no fashionable lapses; this new museum will be formed as a confident, neutral Modernist composition at ease with itself and with the city.

There is no indication of the jury process that led to the selection, but it is clear that all was conducted under the intelligent guidance of Terry Riley. In grappling with the subtleties of content in architecture he uses the phrase 'lucus a non incende', which translates as 'a place where it is shining not'. The lucus, in this case derived from the word for light, ends up by meaning its negative. He uses this paradoxical transformation of the word for light into its negative to illustrate 'the illogic that a word with a specific meaning might have embedded within it the opposite meaning'. With sheer bravado he transfers this compounding of meaning to architecture. 'Do we assume,' he writes, 'that a city [explicitly Manhattan] populated by endless re-formations of very few basic building types would be the creation of an obsessively formal society. This is the paradox of many dense urban cultures particularly Manhattan. Embedded in a restrictive formal language is a potential for its opposite – nearly infinite expressiveness.' As illustrations, he uses the drawings of Agnes Martin which comprise varying grids finely drawn on uniform sheets of paper. Then in the same essay he confesses, 'the best architect for the new Museum of Modern Art is one who understands this paradox [the potential for opposite meanings] and who sees the midtown Manhattan landscape as one of inherent possibilities rather than defeating limitations'. For Terry Riley this understanding exists in the architecture of Yoshio Taniguchi.

I have no disagreement with the conclusion, though Riley's proposition seems slightly defensive. The grid was intended to control, and give unity to, society and to produce conformity, to offer freedom within reason. MoMA will reflect the opposite of its new and minimalist order only in the art it chooses to exhibit. Whether the infinite potential in the harmonics of the Taniguchi space will limit or expand the experience of art remains to be seen. If the discomfort with the lack of complexity in the Taniguchi work stems in part from the success of Frank Gehry's Guggenheim in Bilbao, or from the continual goading by such as Peter Eisenman, a much clearer defence would lie in the desire to make a building that was subservient to the art. The only weakness in the Taniguchi project could be over-refinement.

In reviewing all the materials gathered for the competition as a collection from the most engaging imaginations of this time it becomes apparent that they fail to represent the compelling 'defining the aesthetic' vision for the museum of the next century. Nothing comes close to the freshness and originality with which founding director Alfred Barr viewed the modern age. In a collection of essays presenting the competition Kirk Varindoes, chief curator for painting and sculpture, recalls that, 'of all the great premises that [Alfred] Barr had when he [became founding director of] the museum, was … that there was something called the modern spirit, and that there was a common story that united ball bearings and paintings, and made them both belong in the same museum with film and photography'. He concludes, 'that potential is yet to be exploited by this museum in its fullest fashion.'

Nowhere in all the deliberations is there a phrase as memorable as 'uniting ball bearings and paintings'. It would be too harsh to suggest that the new museum is modern more in form than in spirit, yet it is devoid of any ambiguity or risk, any acknowledgement of what Riley called 'cyberworld'. There is nothing to quicken the pulse and raise expectations as Koolhaas's building would have done.

There is a necessary gravity to museum activity, as practised by MoMA and present in the Taniguchi project. Art may be just another branch of the entertainment business/industry, just another context for establishing values, but its contemplation and the pleasure this gives co-exist with its necessary commercial nature. Gravity in manner and in architecture is appropriate to certain cultural performances. Yet it must be asked: which will consume the greatest amount of artistic vision and energy, and have most effect on the future of artistic culture – the curators at MoMA or the managers of the multiplicity of advertisers that will cover 42nd Street? Where will the artistic imagination be most extended – in the neat white galleries of the museum or on the extravagant untidy walls of Times Square? Which will demand most from the illusions of reality? Despite the complete integration of art production into all aspects of consumption – everything is part of fashion – the museum continues to treat art as a home accessory.

Walking the newly fashion-filled streets of SoHo there is no distinction between art gallery, dress shop, garden supplier, restaurant. The task for the new MoMA will be to find the appropriate contexts for the contemplation of art, despite the fact that artistic production, particularly in the visual arts, is influenced by the same market forces that govern all commercial production.

In the midst of a series of so-called 'conversations' with a number of major figures in the arts, which MoMA staged to discuss 'the idea of the museum', Terry Riley said, 'If the Dia Gallery had been a new building it would have been panned, but as a warehouse renovation it was a great success'. He went on to ask plaintively: 'How do I justify this vast rebuilding programme when the competition [rival galleries] find unreasonable success with low-cost renovation?' The reply from the panel was that success comes from what you choose to exhibit, not from architecture. The Dia Gallery is a bare-bones renovation on both sides of 22nd Street by Gluckman Mayner Architects.

Galleries and museums other than MoMA are being formed and refurbished across the city. In the last ten years the Metropolitan Museum of Art has undergone a process of renewal under the unobtrusive guidance of Kevin Roche John

Dinkeloo and Associates. The most recent is the transformation of the gallery of Greek art. This was one of the grander halls from the design by McKim, Mead and White whose great skylights had been covered over for the last half century. The resulting restoration makes the Met more splendid than ever. The most curious and frankly difficult work is the Jewish Heritage Museum by Roche Dinkeloo. Located on the water, it sits as a freestanding pavilion on the edge of Battery Park, a site of dramatic prominence which demands a significant presence. Pentagonal in plan, crowned by a stepped pyramidical roof and formed in a soft limestone, it is neither meaningful nor interesting. It is made more difficult to understand by the approach, through a capricious landscape by the conceptual artist Mary Miss. Even a substantial knowledge of the signs and symbols of architecture doesn't help in the interpretation of this curious work. Internally a continuous passage running through three floors presents European Jewish history before, through and after the Holocaust. The artefacts exhibited are poignant; the architecture adds little. The major Jewish museum in the city has been formed by renovating the great mansion at the corner of Fifth Avenue, designed for Felix M Warburg by CPH Gilbert. It is a splendid and secure place for the presentation of Jewish culture. Elsewhere there is the fragile charm of Maya Lin in the design of the Museum of African Art and the spatial informal elegance of the work of Tod Williams and Billie Tsien has transformed the Museum of American Folk Art.

Gwathmey Siegel are one of a small group of practices whose work contains a distinctly New York voice. Their complicated addition to Frank Lloyd Wright's Guggenheim Museum has been the subject of much sniping, but the results seem convincing. The experience of this obsessively Wrightian play is not diminished and as a backdrop to the public face the addition seems, in use, to fade from view. There can be few burdens more heavy to a family or an institution than inheriting a building designed by Wright. The messianic devotion of his followers and his own megalomania infect his works with a poetic madness. Like it or not, they radiate their passions daily like a sickness. American architecture should not be so subjective or wilful. Gwathmey Siegel are also the architects of the American Museum of the Moving Image in Queens, too far from Manhattan, some say. They used a lean budget to make a clear strong modern building.

The great rival to the Metropolitan Museum for status at the end of the 19th century was the American Museum of Natural History. One can imagine that the patrons of natural history sought to have their museum rise, like the Metropolitan, in Central Park, but they had to be content with a site opposite the park on the Upper West Side. This great classical lump always seems rather forbidding and isolated but all will be changed by the Polshek office's spectacular addition to the museum. To

58

Frank Gehry: conceptual model for a proposed new Guggenheim Museum on the East River south of South Street

create an enclosure for the elaborate planetarium Polshek has constructed a seemingly perfect metal-wrapped sphere which appears to be suspended in a cube of glass. Here architecture with technical skill conveys a seesaw of elemental forces. This crystalline cube houses the Hayden Planetarium, the most visible part of the Frederick Phineas and Sandra Priest Rose Center for Earth and Space. Sandra Priest Rose and Frederick P Rose are among the city's most generous patrons; it was they who in 1997 funded the restoration of the Reading Room in the New York Public Library, in honour of their children. To know the names of the people whose imaginations really shaped New York, read the lists of donors in the entrance halls of new and old institutions.

Thomas Krens, the director of the Solomon R Guggenheim Foundation, made wildly ambitious by the massive impact of the Guggenheim in Bilbao, has invited Frank Gehry to create a new Guggenheim for Manhattan. Guggenheim 2 which sits on the hottest fashion corner in the city, at Prince Street and Broadway, is a very subdued work from the Japanese architect Irata Isosaki, and is in the process of closing down. Gehry's work is compellingly impressive, yet may have too little content to sustain interest. The only content it seems to have is boundless energy – if only the muscles were real. But the Guggenheim is determined to bring this energy to New York

and unveiled in the summer of 2000 a Gehry proposal for a new museum: a brilliant and explosive object and by far the most subjective and radical idea of place ever conceived for the city – it is so untamable that it has to be kept outside the grid of the Hudson River. A highly controlled fragment of the Gehry imagination is animating the walls of the staff cafeteria in the Condé Nast building.

It is a fond wish that a proposal to build a Museum of Sex in the shadow of the Empire State building will produce the museum most likely to undermine the bourgeois conceits of both MoMA and the Guggenheim. It has been designed by a gifted group of young architects who practise under the name SHoP (Sharples Holden Pasquarelli). The seductive slice of a building will be skinned in body-forming curves transformed into glass and steel, its multilevel galleries riven with erotic passage. The highly complex geometry of the facade has what might be called a Columbia complex. A combination of complexity theory and the limitless potential of computer-generated graphics has allowed Columbia's School of Architecture to produce a competent cadre of graduates able to transform the geometry of all and any objects. To recall once again Herzog on Giacometti, this work will be an elegant seesaw between the abstract and the figural.

The grid has been continually successful in limiting the ability

THE COLUMBUS CENTER

of any individual or organisation to create an excessive presence within the city. There are exceptions, Rockefeller Center being the most overpowering. In 1929 JD Rockefeller Junior assumed control of the several blocks in midtown that had been set aside for the development of a new Metropolitan Opera House. After the Wall Street Crash he personally took command of the project, which he believed would provide a civic and moral lesson to the developers of the city. Though he controlled several blocks Rockefeller at no time considered closing or diminishing the order of the grid. The greatest weakening came with the Robert Moses led development of Stuyvesant Town. In his zealous drive to rid the city of slums Moses gained control of 18 city blocks between 14th and 20th Streets on the East River and removed all signs of the grid in the construction of an extensive public housing project. The 42nd Street development, even with the exceptional powers given by the state control of land, at no point considered closing streets or interfering with the grid, and nowhere in the present state of reality is there any desire for the isolated hostile order of the World Trade Center. Developer Donald Trump is freed from the grid in his grim apartment developments along the railways on the Upper West Side.

All such concerns come into play in the proposed development of the Coliseum site at Columbus Circle. Smaller in area than the 42nd Street project – 2.5 million square feet compared with 7 million – the Coliseum was built in the 1950s and made obsolete with the opening of the Jacob K Javits Convention Centre in 1986. Covering two blocks at the southwest corner of Central Park, the development is once again the result of a Moses attack on slums that had occupied the site. The land is still owned by the authority that became his main power base: the Triborough Bridge and Tunnel Authority.

After many years of false starts a project has finally been given initial approval in an intricate waltz between public and private interests. Some knowledge of the process gives an insight not only into the forces that constrain development in the city, but also into the specific way they shape the architecture. Boston Properties were the first to attempt to develop the area with designs from the Canadian architect Moshe Safdie. These failed to find approval because they were seen as failing to respect zoning constraints – the developers proposed a volume 18 times the area of the site, while zoning allowed only 15. Greed was mentioned in turning down the application. However, it was also felt that the mass of the building would have cast lengthy shadows across Central Park and that it was therefore unacceptable. The architecture of the Safdie proposal can be seen as a mannered work of Modernism that gains its character through crystalline forms. At this point Boston Properties switched architects, from Safdie to David Childs of Skidmore, Owings & Merrill (SOM). Childs

produced a more conventional development that respected the limits of zoning. However, weakness in the New York economy at the end of the 1980s, and persistent opposition on environmental grounds, put the project on hold. Boston Properties finally withdrew in 1994.

The following two years were marked by a power struggle between the public owners of the site and the new city administration under Mayor Giuliani and Joseph Rose. In July 1996 the authority issued a public request for proposals to develop the site. There were specific design guidelines, not

Skidmore, Owings & Merrill: conceptual computer model for the Columbus Center Development

© Jock Pottle/Esto

*Skidmore, Owings & Merrill:
model, Columbus Center
development, view across
Central Park*

unlike those developed for 42nd Street, but the desire here was for unity. One instruction was very clear: the street Moses had closed over should be visually reopened and 'a view corridor' that would follow the line of Central Park South through the site was required. Gaining the maximum usable space from the site mandated two towers whose height the guidelines limited to 750 feet. The proposal process led to a two-phase competition with five submissions in the final stage. (To give some insight into the relative significance of architects versus developers, each designed submission was illustrated in a half-page article in the *New York Times* with no mention of the architects.) The architects who prepared the final five submissions were Kohn Pedersen Fox, Helmut Jahn, Robert AM Stern, David Childs of SOM and James Stewart Polshek. The architecture was varied. Some dressed the buildings in the range of mannered geometries that had characterised the Safdie designs. Polshek, Stern and David Childs offered varying degrees of what might be called historicised contextualism, though in quite a mild form, the effect of which would maintain the character of the streets surrounding Columbus Circle.

The struggles that followed between developers and the agencies of the city presented what is perhaps an extreme example of the unpredictability, the almost Darwinian character, of the city's evolution, but one that is typical. In 1997 many felt that the project would go to the developer who already had several successful ventures in the area. The mayor's office was not happy, partly, it was said, because of the developer's overriding wish for profit, but also because, in the mayor's view, the project lacked a suitable public element. Specifically – the development lacked a public theatre. Commissioner Rose commented, 'We were never trying to design the buildings for the architects, we were trying to incorporate values into the project.' The public element, it was quickly agreed, would be a new home for Jazz@Lincoln Center, a popular performance programme directed by trumpeter Wynton Marsalis. All this evolved as the many interested parties pushed to gain the most for their agendas. At

this time Columbus Center Partners went looking for a major tenant who could add a strong name, and at best a brand name, to their package and after a chance or planned introduction to the president of Time Warner invited the company's participation. After several months of reflection Time Warner agreed to join with Columbus Center Partners in developing the site. The partners offered the mayor's office a proposal that would house the world headquarters of *People* magazine and *Sports Illustrated* – and, in a jewel-like setting high above the circle, the stage for Jazz@Lincoln Center. The city's decision to go with Columbus Center Partners was made in July 1998. David Childs directs a team that involves many designers, including Rafael Viñoly who is creating the performance space for Jazz@Lincoln Center.

The evolution of the project illustrates the resiliency necessary both to practise and configure architecture in New York City. All the major elements of the building were predetermined. The massing was a product of an exacting relationship between the zoning ordinances and guidelines added by the city and the developer's need to maximise profitability in all parts of the project. This includes the success of the retail stores, the attractiveness of the performance spaces and the ability to attract powerful tenants. The retail areas on the street level will complete the curve of Columbus Circle and the building will be entered through a grand atrium, on an axis with Central Park South, that carries high above the street the performance space for Jazz@Lincoln Center. The continuation of the grid through the site makes the cut between the two towers, which are held well back on the site to avoid overshadowing the park and to maintain the scale of the buildings around Columbus Circle. Their geometry is created from the trapezium formed between the city grid and the diagonal path of Broadway. The focus of the view down Central Park South will be the cascading glass roof of Jazz@Lincoln Center.

Though a singular and united composition, the Columbus Center is arranged with elegant artifice. The dramatic scenography takes advantage of a site that gains great spatial freedom by being at the circle and on the park. The crowds on the streets will be aware of layer upon receding layer, shifting from the circle through several planes to the crested towers whose final form, brilliantly lit according to Mr Childs, will owe some debt to the Chrysler building. The design makes no direct use of historical elements in its general accommodation to the existing form of the city, and its subtle modulations give it a presence sympathetic to the great work of the 1920s Rockefeller Center. In *Space, Time, and Architecture* the German theorist Siegfried Gideon saw in the patterns of the buildings that surround the RCA tower a natural representation of the dynamics of space and time that he felt would mark the 20th century. Similarly, the effect of the rhythmic modulations

61

to the mass of Columbus Center is to create an implied vortex spinning around the figure of Jazz@Lincoln Center, but this is more apparent than real. There are no reflections of uncertainty, no flirting with fashionable chaos here. Columbus Circle in the new century will present confidence and clear order.

If we consider buildings as bodies and their surfaces as dress one might find fashion equivalents for the various styles assumed by new buildings in the city. The SOM project for Columbus Center might be viewed as being in the culture of, say, Brooks Brothers or Talbot's, MoMA in the spirit of Armani or Prada and Times Square explicitly Disney with a touch of K Mart. It is possible to recognise a convergence between the increasing influence of corporate design on all life-style artefacts so that trademarked reality is displacing individual imaginations. Objects shaped by individuals have an authenticity, if only because subjectivity is absent in objects and places defined by corporations. Such dressings are merely comforting masks on the face of the city, gently seducing with empty promises.

There are several other new towers close to Columbus Circle. Helmut Jahn, whose work over the years has been marked by strong clear forms and order, struggles to give coherence to the City Spire development. This appears to be an example, and there are others, in which the developer's need to maximise every square foot of space makes the formation of coherent architecture impossible. Immediately to the west, the development of luxury apartments above Carnegie Hall illustrates the difference when the architecture is guided by formal principle and not by optimal use. Cesar Pelli has formed an exquisitely elegant wafer of a building, its brick facade textured to be in sympathy with Carnegie Hall. It rises above the complex bulk of the hall forming an elegant curtain that floats within the city. The effect is of an almost tapestry-like backdrop to the great mass of the hall and its simplicity and equanimity give it an authority that diminishes all its neighbours.

All these are products of client desire and the need for profit. A work by Kevin Roche, 750 Seventh Avenue, chooses to be wrapped in shiny black glass and its ungainly bulk overwhelms any attempt at architecture. The crowning spire attracts too much attention to a building that would have been best left to lose itself to the messy collage that is the perceived city. In comparison the Regal Hotel design by Roche and Dinkeloo, close to the United Nations building, has a simple form wrapped in an elegant curtain of glass. Roche and his partner John Dinkeloo designed what still remains one of the great works of Manhattan architecture: the Ford Foundation building. The comparison with 750 Seventh Avenue is obvious. The Ford Foundation required a work of architecture that would embody the distinction and public character of the foundation. This

public dimension led to the creation of an internal garden and the internal relationship between the activities of the foundation and the city has never been repeated. That the same architects are unable to give so little to a task that is explicitly concerned with optimal exploitation of space reflects the constraints of Manhattan, not the limitations of the architects.

For an observable evolution in the design of facades compare the SOM Bertelsmann tower of 1989 with several recent and proposed projects. Each particular volume that forms the Bertelsmann building is given a distinct surface treatment, there is rather crude patterning of windows and panels and the elevation on to Seventh Avenue is given a prow which is capped with a spire that rivals that on the Roche building to the north. In recent projects this kind of piecemeal, rather graphic, formulation has evolved into much more refined public presence and manufacture. The soaring, almost freestanding, tower designed by SOM for Times Square will overwhelm the buildings at the apex of Broadway and Seventh Avenue, its southern facade carrying advertising more than 1,500 feet above the square. Compared with the Bertelsmann building the surfaces comprise a fine weave of softly muted green glass shot through with diagonal patterns that define the angle of the roof edge. Over 700 feet high, it will share with its neighbours 100 feet of advertising space at its base as well as a vertical billboard.

The subtle diagonal inflections on the surface of the Times Square project become embedded in the complex of three-dimensional geometries that defines the shell of the addition to 350 Madison Avenue, from SOM with a team led by Roger Duffy. By far the most experimental project in the commercial centre (and one untouched by Columbia's complexity theories), it is formed to a geometrically complex box that rises from the masonry of the existing building. Its surface, initially a dense mesh, is now an exquisitely modulated curtain wall, its harmonics influenced by the poetic structures of Ellsworth Kelly. It creates the effect of a tense metal plane shafting out to the existing building and projecting back across a 20-foot gap in the block before surrounding the glass volume of the new office space. The most striking effect will be at the entrance into the glowing mass of space formed in the gap and sustained by a combination of light and steam reaching the full height of the building. The way this effect penetrates the block is quite new in the city. Alone among recent commercial constructions, 350 Madison Avenue suggests that there are possibilities for new orders to be explored, and new pleasures to be enjoyed, by developing effect within the depth of the block. The subtlety and complexity of this work suggest that theoretical practice stimulates mainstream practice, but architects will not acknowledge this.

This increasing refinement in the design and technology of

© Nicolas Borel

countless iterations. It is a process in which the technology must match the effect. It is this constrained New York context that drives the reordering of the volumes and surfaces of commercial architecture and has gained such worldwide influence.

The reserve with which New York practitioners work within the grid is not shared by foreign architects when they practise in the city. (As an aside, the essentially pragmatic needs of New York culture have meant that very few have been invited to design here.) For the New York architect, making a facade interesting is little more complex than designing wallpaper. Europeans take a much noisier and more figural view of architecture.

Two recent projects inserted into the grid by European architects were commissioned by European clients. The Parisian practice of Christian de Portzamparc has formed a small infill building for the fashion house of Louis Vuitton. A loft building in a gap-site, its only architecture lies in the fracturing of the facade into complex layers, wasting space in ways that would seem irresponsible to New York developers. It gives a moment from the anxiety of French philosophy to the pragmatic face of the city. A different but equally foreign facade has been given to the Austrian Cultural Center by the Austrian architect Raimund Abraham. Abraham is in truth as American as he's Austrian, having lived and taught in New York for many years, but his strong symmetrical modelling of the street forms a distinct presence and has faint echoes of a younger Abraham whose powerful drawings touched worldwide desire.

The density of the grid continually frustrates the assertion of difference. In all its confusion of textures and chaos and layerings and neglect, any such attempt is simply one moment in a kaleidoscope of enterprising fragments.

the city's commercial architecture emerges from two parallel influences. Among the most status-conscious clients, of which New York has a few, fresh invention enhances reputation. However, developer clients in particular match style with the marketplace and within this process architects are required to produce numerous iterations of a design until form matches client desire. Unlike much of European practice, the architect's personality is suppressed within this process. The context within which architecture is perceived in Manhattan is unique: part of the grid wall at the base, limited freedom above the 12th floor, the only internal articulation in the lobby and perhaps the penthouse. This pattern of constraints frames a very specific set of New York design problems, central among them the character of the facade, which has been an issue in the city since the turn of the century. The architects for Rockefeller Center described the problem as being similar to that of designing a tapestry wall hanging and produced numerous renderings to discover the most satisfying effect. 'Vertical garden' was another metaphor to colour the imagination. This is a highly subjective process and there is no clear objective measure of effectiveness. The use of computers has affected all aspects of practice in the last decade and has been especially effective in supporting tasks that require

PENNSYLVANIA STATION

The destruction of Pennsylvania Station in 1962 has lingered painfully in the memory of the city. This most monumental of the urban works of McKim, Mead and White gave New York a series of heroic public spaces of such permanence and grandeur that it was believed they could last for ever. It was the arrival point for travellers from across the nation and presented immediate evidence of the power and strength of the great city. The noble granite colonnade led to a majestic waiting room and into a central concourse beneath an intricate series of glass and metal vaults. The destruction of this most confident work from the first decade of the century has been kept alive in the photographs of Berenice Abbott. In the early 1960s the Pennsylvania Railroad decided to demolish the building. The railway station would remain below ground while the street level would be developed to produce profits for a major entertainment venue named Madison Square Garden after the most ambitious of the turn-of-the-century entertainment buildings, designed by Stanford White. Despite a highly vocal and well-prepared opposition, strongly supported by public opinion, the vast monument was demolished and below ground the Penn Station remained squashed into an insignificant basement lined with cheap shops and restaurants, with uneasy travellers demeaned by the setting. The loss of the building has preyed on the memory and conscience of the city. The failure to prevent its destruction led to the creation of the Landmarks Preservation Community to ensure that such actions would not succeed so easily in the future. Penn is the busiest station in North America with 600,000 passengers daily being forced through its mean passages.

In 1993 the Farely building immediately west of the station was declared redundant. Conceived on a scale equal to that of Pennsylvania Station, it was the most monumental post office on Manhattan and was also designed by McKim, Mead and White, almost contemporarily with their old Penn Station. Soon after the intentions of the US Post Office became public an idea began to take shape: why not re-establish Pennsylvania Station in the Farely building? All the physical elements were in the right place. The post office sat above the tracks that served Penn Station and that were in exact alignment with the trains from north and west. The idea was made visible in the drawings of the architects Hellmuth, Obata + Kassabaum (HOK), and attracted the attention of the senior senator from New York, David Patrick Moynihan.

As the project advanced HOK lost out as the architects for the project to SOM, whose team, led by David Childs, has produced a splendid fusion of restoration and spectacular renewal. The broad form of the post office is similar to the old Penn Station: the great stone-encased outer band of rooms surrounds an inner glazed court where the mail was once sorted. There are two halves to the building, with the post

office on the east separated from a bulk storage building on the west by a service road. Only the east building will be used, and the service road will become the grand entrance hall to the new station. Although far from being a *fait accompli*, the idea has assumed such compelling rightness that President Clinton chose to lead the unveiling of the proposed new structure personally in May 1999, surrounded by the great and the good of the city with the exception of the mayor – from which it can be deduced that this ambitious project did not have his endorsement. It could just be politics; city issues championed by Democrat Moynihan may steal the thunder from Republican Mayor Giuliani.

Skidmore, Owings & Merrill: computer image of the interior of the proposed relocation of Pennsylvania Station

*Skidmore, Owings & Merrill:
computer image of the new
concourse for the proposed
relocation of Pennsylvania
Station*

The station will serve both Kennedy and Newark airports.

Taken altogether – Columbus Center, the new Penn Station and widely varied commercial projects across the city, including an emerging design for the New York Stock Exchange (exuding appropriate levels of security, and ambition) – SOM New York under David Childs has regained the leadership the practice had in the 1950s and 1960s. The projects from that period – Merchants Hanover Trust, the PepsiCo building and Lever House – have never lost their distinction.

As a curious coda HOK, who gave original form to the concept for the new Penn Station, are currently the architects for the renovation of the old, cramped one. These overlapping plans are because the new station cannot be created before the arrival of high-speed trains.

The shifting pattern of desire that shapes the architecture of New York is the product of many variables. All is made simpler, however, by the overwhelming pragmatism of the process by which it is created. Even the most persuasive theories are marginal in the face of cost-effectiveness. New York is formed first and foremost by investment decisions. Pennsylvania Railroad made money by tearing down the old station. The new station, if and when it emerges, will be created out of necessity not romance. Although high-speed trains and Amtrak will change a lacklustre part of the American economy, rail travel has to anticipate growth well beyond the 600,000 people who pass through the station daily.

The restoration of New York's surviving major station, Grand Central Terminal, has just been completed. Long overdue, and clearly appropriate to a city that depends so much on train travel, it is a thorough and pleasurable work by the architects Beyer Blinder Belle paid for by the Metropolitan Transit Authority, the building's owners. The great pavilion, which presents a triple triumphant arch to Park Avenue South, houses the main concourse 375 feet long by 125 feet wide. The design was won in competition by Whitney Warren of Warren and Wentmore in 1912. The traffic arrangements, both internally and externally, were laid out by the engineers Reem and Sterm. They not only devised systems to separate all different forms of traffic – subway, pedestrian, automobile – but also created the sensational short highway that loops around and through the building, plunging under great arches on to Park Avenue. It is still one of the best metropolitan experiences in the city. (The upper reaches of Riverside Drive offer similar thrills.)

Grand Central was owned by the Penn Central Railroad in the 1960s and, like Penn Station, was also seen as being exploitable. Plans included inserting several floors into the waiting room to accommodate a variety of activities including a bowling alley. Another proposal was to build a 50-storey tower over the waiting room. Grand Central was declared a landmark in the midst of these exploitive plans. The railroad company sued to have the status lifted but failed.

The work of David Childs and his team has never been more confident. The proposal would create the new station around two elements: the roofing of the new concourse and the opening up of the sorting hall. The most spectacular feature will be the new entrance to the concourse. It is formed from a segment of an imagined sphere, created from the centre of the building, which defines the geometry for a sweeping shell of glass and steel that will flow between 32nd and 33rd Streets, enclosing the entrance hall, soaring above the mass of the old building and throwing wings out on to the cross streets to be a visible crown that reframes the old building. The structure that supports it will be a delicate metal lattice. It was suggested that this will be made from nickel and in response Herbert Munschamp, architectural critic for the *New York Times*, wrote, 'This metal takes light like a star. You want to send it a rose.' The screen will become a floating, ethereal veil rising high above the existing buildings to be seen from a distance as being above the classical weight of the post office. The second major element will be the conversion of the sorting hall into the new concourse. Here the old steel trusses will be retained and the floor removed to make the tracks and trains visible. Descending to the tracks travellers will pass through an expansive terrace of shops and restaurants. Special zones will be designed to serve the high-speed trains that will soon begin operation and their interiors will aim to equal and better the ambience of airline travel. Not as ambitious as European railways, the trains will have a maximum speed of 150 mph.

© Peter Aaron/Esto

The BBB restoration lovingly re-creates not only the surfaces but also the sense of grand procession through the halls and passages and over bridges. A new grand stairway and terrace that have been added to the east end of the concourse succeed in making the main concourse feel more powerful and balanced. Viewing the crowds from the terrace bar is to feel that one is at the centre of a great city. The restoration recovered much of the ceiling, which depicts the constellations with the stars picked out in twinkling lights. The recovery of the broad ramps that lead to the lower levels enables one to enjoy a similar but slower pleasure to that of driving along the elevated road that snakes around the outside of the station. With gentle grandeur the great slabs of marble drift easily down to the lower floors passing, only for those in the know, that most New York of institutions – The Oyster Bar. The theatrics of the experience make us once again players on the stage of 19th-century ambition. The 150,000 passengers who daily move through the halls of Grand Central – a much smaller building than the original Pennsylvania Station – are players in every performance in the city. The third B in Beyer Blinder Belle – the Englishman, John Belle – has become one of the doyens of New York architects. In the years leading up to the millennium, his taste and judgement not only renewed Grand Central and 42nd Street, but also shaped the reconstruction of the city's major public space, the Rockefeller Center.

Again Munschamp, writing in the *New York Times*, notes that the renovated terminal was opened on the 20th anniversary of the Supreme Court decision rejecting the Penn Central Railroad's suit to remove its landmark status. He feels that no buildings from the 20 intervening years have merited such status; none has even remotely given the city such grandeur.

Grand Central is a temple to train travel, a climactic building whose scale reflects a rail network that stretched the length and breadth of the nation. The stations of the subway system, by comparison, are little more than raw structures softened by small panels of decoration. Compare the luxury of the experience in Grand Central with travelling the subway system during those years when an explosion of graffiti inside and outside the carriages made one feel the presence of an invisible enemy. But now the stations are being remade and a programme of art will add momentary pleasure to the journey. Architects Lee Harris Pomeroy Associates have completed the extensive renovation of the Union Square station, adding pleasant entrance pavilions around the square and working with the artist Mary Miss to create an *objet d'art* whose effect is enhanced by the movement of the train. Such renovations are planned selectively throughout the system but the physical results, apart from improvements in circulation, are cosmetic. Several new stations are planned where lines are being extended but the architecture is more serviceable than significant. Why is there so little imagination and ambition in the public architecture of the city?

Improving public facilities would surely augment the reputation of any mayor farsighted enough to do so. The stations Norman Foster has designed for Bilbao give as much pleasure as the Guggenheim to the people of the city. The new underground stations of Paris and London have all the elegance of art museums. The objects that enhance the streets and transport systems of Barcelona – from lighting and park benches to stations, bus shelters and new forms of art – present the city as a thrilling public theatre, not as a collection of convenient walls on which to hang advertising. The mediocrity of New York's public facilities stems in part from their formation as competitive commercial ventures and the

Beyer Blinder Belle: Grand Central Station, the Grand Concourse

*Venturi Scott Brown and
Associates: competition entry
for the rebuilding of the Staten
Island Ferry Terminal on
Manhattan, unbuilt*

concourse. But where is there the ambition of such as Cornelius Vanderbilt, who forced the city to accept the massive railway development that forms the great trench that lies along Park Avenue, its multiple tracks on two decks serving Grand Central Station? Or where (God forbid) is the equivalent of the Robert Moses campaign to mechanise and socialise the city? New York is entering the new century with less ambition and shorter horizons than at any time in its history.

Ferries have run between Staten Island and Manhattan since the 18th century and the Staten Island Ferry, run by the New York Port Authority, became a public service when it was taken over by New York in 1905. Though they no longer carry automobiles, the ferries carry 70,000 passengers daily and are popular with tourists and New Yorkers alike for the spectacular views they afford of Manhattan from the water. Following a fire in the Manhattan Terminal in 1991, there has been a series of efforts to design a replacement. Competition produced some memorable, if eccentric, propositions including Helmut Jahn's idea of crowning the terminal building with a lighthouse in the form of a miniature skyscraper. The competition was won by the architect Robert Venturi who proposed that the terminal carry a giant clock facing out to the water, keeping commuters on time. He was among the most inventive and influential architects of the 1970s and his witty and ironic devices – exaggerating scale, applying iconic elements of architecture in a flattened and transparently false form – offered stimulating ideas for a revision of the language of architecture. His influence, however, has almost totally diminished in recent years. Shortly after winning the competition he was asked to replace the clock and the arrival hall with something more modest. This resulted in a lively proposal to face the water with a large screen which would show passengers images of news, events and the thrill of city life. This proposal was also set aside and the terminal will undergo an unremarkable restoration. Reasons for such decisions are never completely open but New York has always been thrifty and cautious.

Every major development site in the city seems to become the subject of intense competition and multiple proposals from developers. Over the last three years Peter Eisenman has used the Staten Island ferry terminal to develop his most ambitious project for New York. The combination of structures around the terminal – two museums and a minor league baseball field – extended his mastery over complex liquid geometries that are able move freely between multiple events and conditions and he produced a proposal that had the force of an act of nature. The final commission to develop the terminal area has gone to the architects HOK, but Eisenman will design one of the museums. Had Eisenman being given the entire complex it would have given New York an artificial destination rivalling Gehry's Guggenheim in the public imagination.

Flight is still the future and airports are a major context for

system is now entrapped in the rival politics of city, state and independent authorities. The crude character of the stations is much less of a problem than the system-wide decline in the structural integrity of tunnels, bridges and elevated railroads. Poorly built from the beginning, in 1904, the infrastructure will shortly need a complete overhaul that will require more money than political will can afford.

The examples of European public facilities emerge from a tradition of state paternalism; New York prefers to maintain such facilities as joyless necessities and demonstrations of fiscal prudence. Improvements in public transport in Europe enhance the pleasure in public life. In contrast, life on the New York subway has much in common with prison: both are environments that support acts of abuse or violence. Treating people badly makes them behave badly. Designing places that ennoble, as Grand Central does, can transform public life. Some signs of change are appearing: the new station planned in the development at Columbus Circle may be allowed to break through the surface of the street to create a grand

© Peter Aaron/Esto

68

architecture. Several major new terminals are being built or are in planning. They are competent buildings by SOM, Boudova and others but they do not assert the importance of New York as Grand Central does. Neither, it must be said, do they compare, either formally or technically, with the works of Norman Foster or Renzo Piano. There are few examples in New York of new structures that compare with the many light and effortless glass and steel enclosures of European cities, or that have the technical exuberance and discipline of Foster's Chek Lap Kok Airport in Hong Kong. There are exceptions; the shell from SOM that will cover the entrance concourse of the new Penn Station takes unusual delight in the elegance of structure, but rarely in New York does one see the poetic pleasure in the aesthetics of technology that characterises the best of European architecture. The French play with the illusion of dematerialisation, the English articulate and refine every structural element to form a language of the structure and the Germans, with lean efficiency, make buildings with the precision of an instrument. Though pragmatic, American architecture rarely elevates or fetishises the materials of production. European architects argue that allowing necessary technology to determine the language of the architecture avoids contrived effects and artifice and gives an unambiguous truth to the objects of reality. In the United States, however, though there is an oppressive use of architecture to support commercial display, the buildings themselves represent a neutral undemonstrative use of technology.

In addition to Grand Central, public buildings are being restored throughout the five boroughs. Many new historic districts have been created and buildings given landmark status. Mapping of the five boroughs showing the major survivors since the 18th century could help to structure community development. This is currently done through the various community boards, including the NYC Landmarks Preservation Commission, but there is a need for more complete public information on historic districts and landmark buildings. The few distinguished surviving buildings from the 17th and 18th centuries are mostly stranded in the midst of disinterested 20th-century developments. Historic districts are expanding and increasing numbers of major structures are being renovated, for example, Ellis Island, Tweed Courthouse just behind City Hall on Manhattan and the Brooklyn borough hall. Distinct from the full restoration of significant monuments

is the renovation of millions of square feet of century-old commercial structures on Lower Manhattan. An area stretching from Ladies Mile, Sixth Avenue south of 20th Street, across Broadway and West Broadway, south of Houston in acres of massive loft buildings and extending through TriBeCa and SoHo and now mostly housing light industry, is entering into a process of ongoing renovation and renewal. This monolithic survivor of 19th-century enterprise will become one vast designated landmark, frozen for ever in the present, removed from the field of speculation. I recall an admiral telling me that he was convinced the decline of the Royal Navy started when the British began to show more interest in sailing ships than in fighting ships. In the same sense, does the city decline when the spirit to conserve becomes stronger than the desire to develop? Imagine huge areas of New York given historic-district designation. Only the grid was meant to be permanent. Limiting the right to speculate would mean the death of the idea.

This conflict between preservation and demolition, between the city made comfortable among the artefacts of the past and a city kept vital by being open to redevelopment, is one that will increasingly complicate the future. Conflict will arise between the architectural value of the historic structure and the land values that appreciate in a process of continual development. Painful as it may seem, New York is a city made for speculation. It would be a high risk to predict that a majority of the structures that now make up the five boroughs will still be standing in 50 years. The city's population is not growing significantly and New York's role as a gateway to immigrants means it is also the gateway to increasing poverty. On a broader scale the northeast of the United States is losing population and there is no evidence that, in the foreseeable future, it will ever again approach the growth rates of the last 100 years. Flat population growth, less and less need for new structures and more need to renew New York's existing infrastructure will lead to increasing support for conservation. A simple listing of the life span of the major elements in the city's infrastructure indicates that the prime activities for architects and engineers in the next century will be the preservation and adaptive reuse of the multiple structures and infrastructures, buildings, bridges, roads, highways, subways, sewers, power plants – on and on – that have grown within the city in the last 200 years.

Beyer Blinder Belle: Grand Central Station, the Grand Concourse

FOLEY SQUARE

Public buildings in the city suffer from the public realm's lack of trust and an evident uncertainty over what form public architecture should take. The new Federal Office building on Foley Square, designed by Hellmuth, Obata + Kassabaum and completed in 1997, illustrates the problem. HOK is the nation's largest architectural practice, with 23 offices worldwide. It is responsive and highly competent, producing well-made acceptable realities for almost any programme or culture. Its architects are masters of intelligent depersonalised realities

commodifying uncomplicated uses. By what process, therefore, does this most responsible of practices create in the name of the federal government such a cumbersome and authoritarian object as the building in Foley Square?

The public face of the building, which houses the Internal Revenue Service, the General Accounting Office and the Environmental Protection Agency in a multistorey stone monolith, is a parody of the insensitive, overbearing power of government. The elevation facing the square is symmetrical.

*Hellmuth, Obata + Kassabaum:
the Federal Office building,
Foley Square*

© Jock Pottle/Esto

The set-back central panel rises to support a strange oval pavilion enclosed by a range of freestanding columns. It is clear from a distance that this seeks to appear as a place of permanence and imperial importance. One presumes that federal projects on this scale are the subject of careful critical positioning and much scrutiny. How can it be that such insensitive forms were shaped for such sensitive bodies as the Environmental Protection Agency? The sources are obvious. Such buildings emerged in the 1920s to reflect ambitions and rivalries in the commercial city, their different functions often signalled by the shaping of their rooflines. Buildings carrying temples at their crown sought to give a metaphysical aura to enterprise. The architects of the Foley building should be embarrassed by their casual distortion of architectural signs and symbols. The entrance halls are heavy with columns and the sculptures on the walls deepen anxiety. An eagle softly carved into limestone claws above a bursting sun. It is an enigmatic work that owes some debt to the symbolism of fascism. High above the city, in the rooms enclosed by curving glass, what business of government is being transacted? The same rooms or faithful reproductions of such, representing the base or seat of demagogues, have appeared in several recent movies. *The Matrix* is an example. Such an image may suit the IRS, but not the EPA.

Architecture is not the most substantial or the most disciplined of languages, but in the misuse of symbols, if misuse it is, it trivialises the process of forming an architecture that represents the public realm with distinction. Democracy is a continuous and fragile experiment which requires from architecture inventive explorations of the way the public dimension of a society can be made visible. The aristocratic culture of Europe has given architecture a well-respected role. The rebuilding of the Reichstag to create the European Courts of Justice, new city halls in Spain and new public buildings in France and Switzerland all display the wide-ranging potential for enhancing democracy and the public realm through architecture. In New York, however, as demonstrated by the city's buildings, public agencies do not seek novelty, and architects rarely offer it. The nearby Foley Square Court House building by Kohn Pedersen Fox conveys the same imperialism, but with more charm.

There are exceptions and two works by Rafael Viñoly in the Bronx and Brooklyn show how architecture can enhance the way in which public institutions are perceived. In the design of the Brooklyn Housing Court he brings a distinctly international sensibility to materials and to the reorganisation of this important but disliked institution. It is the smartest new presence on Grand Concourse in the Bronx, a street which, though stressed by profound shifts in population and culture, has not lost its dignity. It fits simply into the wall of buildings that lines the concourse, dignified and forming an elegant

composition in metal and glass. This is continued into an interior, a model of distinction and refined order, that conveys both the authority of the court and a respect for those it serves. Similarly, his design for the Bronx Supreme Court shows subtle inventiveness in presenting the institution in a new way. At the edge of an area that still shows the devastation of the 1960s, the new court will be organised to be open to the community with visible bridges connecting all the major activities, not only breaking down barriers but also giving excitement to the street. Viñoly had a successful practice in Argentina before being forced out because of his politics. These two projects exemplify a practice unique in New York for its concern not only with technology, but also with the social role of architecture. He maintains practices in both New York and Buenos Aires, and his work in Argentina is strongly community based.

Privately owned hospitals are civil institutions in that they exist to support the community. The power of New York City as a medical centre has created hospital complexes that continue to grow and expand. Hospitals more than any other single building type demonstrate American expertise in creating buildings that function as instruments to deliver complex services and functions. They represent a remarkable convergence of the competencies in which America leads the world, but aesthetic concerns tend to be limited to providing a polite enclosure to the outside and subcontracting the interior to a whole array of specialists who create the laboratories, operating theatres, kitchens, etc. Hospital design is increasingly a specialist practice, however, and architects such as Pei Cobb Freed at the Mount Sinai medical centre and Davis Brody Bond at the Queens hospital have guided the construction of major medical facilities over many years. Davis Brody Bond has a body of work that is strongly community

Kohn Pederson Fox: United States Court House, Foley Square

© Jock Pottle/Esto

based. The practice is not as eccentric as Hardy Holtzman Pfeiffer, yet similar in forming an architecture more from the content of the place and the events it encloses than from fashion. It brings political charm to even the most mundane problem.

In the United States, unlike Europe, housing is not so much designed as packaged for profit, a process that makes no attempt to experiment with life style. Instead it prefers to concentrate on a few – the fewer the better – conventional typologies that appeal to the various contexts and market segments. Housing is a product like any other, and the producer cultivates desire and limits choice. Price is key, but land is the real property. Within the city hundreds of thousands of people are unable to enter the open market and must rely on the work of publicly supported community development programmes. Most rely on the New York Housing Authority. However, there are signs in the public agencies of a changing awareness of the benefits of architecture; the signs are few, but they are clear. Over the last decade the authority has begun to develop sensitive procedures to encourage a variety of incentives to restore and consolidate badly damaged areas. It is developing housing and community centres in some of the more difficult neighbourhoods, and some of the most thoughtful and unaffected architecture is being designed to help restore the large areas of the city that are still recovering from the widespread devastation of the 1970s. Commissions are going to younger more experimental practitioners. Hanrahan and Meyers created a new community centre in converted industrial buildings in Red Hook, and in the Latimer Gardens neighbourhoods of Brooklyn. The Red Hook project is at the entrance to the neighbourhood, near, but not in, the public housing estate. It seems an overly sophisticated object in the midst of the grimy elemental realities of public housing, but kindly nonetheless. A small respectful gesture in a place of dreadful neglect. Within the same programme Agrest & Gandelsonas have produced an engaging and complex community-centre building for the Melrose community in the Bronx. Despite the tales of devastation and the obvious dilapidation, at the Hub on Third Avenue Melrose is one of the liveliest shopping strips in the city. Driven by a sense that fresh and inventive architecture can help rebuild communities, these must be among the housing authority's most ambitious design commissions in many years, and this from a Republican administration.

In the same areas there have been a number of attempts to rebuild the streets and neighbourhoods. Melrose Commons led by the architects Larsen Shein Ginsberg + Magnusson have developed a careful and thoughtful programme of rebuilding. The new architecture seems better integrated than in developments in central Brooklyn, and the planning will renew the texture of the community by integrating churches and stores in the development. The community who have been the clients for the project told the architects, 'Please do not experiment with us'.

The condition of the Melrose community is yet another legacy of Robert Moses' social engineering when poor minorities were forcibly imported into public housing in areas that were already poor. Community projects such as these make more demands than the fashionable reality of commerce on architecture – demands formed in the belief that it has a reformative, and redemptive power. New York is a tough city, expedient and profitable on the one hand, resilient and tolerant of extremes of wealth and poverty on the other. These forces should be the stuff of the theories of architecture.

Like Davis Brody Bond and Hardy, Holtzman and Pfeiffer, Robert AM Stern has a New York imagination. Dean of Yale's architecture school, he has an encyclopedic pleasure in architecture and his early work was every bit as experimental as that of his contemporaries Peter Eisenman and Michael Graves. Slowly, over the years, his work practice has embraced widely ranging architectural styles. The work falls into three broad categories. First, designs for Disney which range from imitations of the great seafront hotels of the 1890s to cartoon-like corporate buildings on the Disney campus. Second, an array of private houses, many on Long Island, thoughtfully and elegantly made in the manner of the English architect Edwin Lutyens and the shingle-style houses of McKim Mead and White. Third, there are the highly conservative commercial, educational and residential works for the city, buildings such as his apartments on the West Side or the dormitory for the New York Law School. This last group is of particular interest in any assessment of the buildings of Manhattan, for they fade wholly into the fabric of the city. They willingly conform to the grid and respect the continuity of form and structure in the island's buildings. The grid sought to constrain enterprise, and limit differences in architecture; Stern's work respects and reinforces continuity. A city needs the imaginations of both Eisenman and Stern, but New York's self view is much closer to the vision of Stern than Eisenman.

The stable institutions and affluent individuals who shape the taste of New York understand the need for risk, and that uniqueness is necessary to create new products and advance new ventures, but where and how they live is defined by convention and conformity and is not a matter for invention. Stern's architecture is willingly in the service of the city

There are few new religious buildings in New York. No architecture has declined more in quality than church building. In absolute contrast to the end of the 19th century, new religious buildings fail to add anything to meet the need for secure and constant values in public life. There are exceptions. Stern's Kol Israel Synagogue is a strong simple brick temple; the congregation could wish for nothing more respectful and

71

conforming. The Islamic Cultural Center on 96th Street and Lexington Avenue stands free within the grid. In the form of a mosque, its geometrically abstracted decoration suggests the fusion of traditional and progressive orders. It has a crystalline quality which unites the form and decoration. A building quite at ease with public place, although there are similarities in character, it has none of the sense of withdrawal that marks the great mosque in Regent's Park in London. Architecture in America is an inadequate medium for conveying sensitive cultural values, yet the centre seems to make a beneficial contribution to public understanding.

Measured by degrees of difficulty, architect Greg Lynn's design for the Korean Protestant church is the most ambitious experimental work in the city. Over many years working with Peter Eisenman, Lynn began a sequence of experiments in the generation of complex geometries, moving to ever-increasing complexity with increases in computing power. The first application of these experiments to architecture is the Korean church which grows out of the old Knickerbocker laundry in Queens. The city has never had much use for personal experiments in architecture, although a small if fragile *avant-garde* has always existed within the modern period. Such experimental practice has enjoyed the influence of science and philosophy and the romantic task of creating forms and spatial conditions that embody the essence of the 'complexity' age. It must be noted that such disciplined conceptual procedures require rich theoretical apparatus and have produced compelling new forms and orders. These are occasionally co-opted by commercial practices to entertain an ambitious client seeking a new image. Lynn's project is one of the few commissions given to an experimental architect in the last decade. For the Korean church he has enclosed a shell in a skin of wave-like forms, dissolving conventional notions of floors and ceilings. This is a restless place seeking new direction which may fuse with the born-again beliefs of Korean Protestantism.

Led by Peter Eisenman, the avant-garde has been effective over many years in making New York a centre of critical writing on architecture, and has given character to two of the United States' stronger schools of architecture: Columbia and Cooper Union. Architecture at Cooper, where Eisenman has taught for many years, has been led by the late John Hedjuk whose only major commission in the city was the renovation of the buildings of Cooper itself. His ability to fashion forms that seem to be the products of complex, often tragic, histories has captured the imagination of a generation of Cooper students. Under the precise administration of Bernard Tschumi Columbia cultivates the most confident students, convinced they are setting the radical agenda. The recent graduates of Columbia are likely to have the most impact on the architecture of the future, less because of theory, which certainly shapes their

Greg Lynn: the Korean Church, Queens

thinking, than because of the school's emphasis on making the most powerful uses of computing.

Contradicting the prevailing mood of conformity among institutions, a few educational buildings represent modest experiments with changing architecture. Public School 217 on Roosevelt Island, designed by Michael Fieldman, achieves spatial freedom and visual excitement in a rich three-dimensional composition with echoes of Mondrian in its colours and geometry. The new building for Baruch College by the architects Kohn Pedersen Fox presents the most original mass of building anywhere in downtown New York in recent years. Here teaching and public spaces are enclosed behind a

*Bernard Tschumi: Lerner Hall,
Columbia University*

soaring, curving wall — more echoes of Mendelsohn. The
impact is of a building mass that takes pleasure in difference
and is physically satisfying, and it gives an immediate
distinction and energy to the college. Pleasure in difference
highlights awareness of the city's conformity. Profiting from
selling space is more significant than difference. Bernard
Tschumi has created an exquisitely different passage within
the fabric of Columbia University. Lerner Hall is a simple
building that provides little opportunity for the conceptual
brilliance that marks many of his works in France but, in its
gymnastic articulation of circulation space and his pleasure in
the materials and connections that carry the extravagant
ramps and form the glass facade, he has brought European
sensibility to the campus. It is in marked contrast to the overall
character of city architecture, which seems more illusions of
reality than reality itself. Tschumi's work illustrates that
differences in architecture derive not only from separate social
histories, but also from distinct differences in sensual and
spatial perception.

Throughout the five boroughs decrepit school buildings are a
major problem. Leaking roofs, weakened structures and run-
down and long-inadequate mechanical systems seriously
damage teaching programmes in the city. In such conditions of
crisis it is perhaps unfair to expect innovation in school design.

However, it is disappointing that several major new school
projects lack distinction. The extensive new Stuyvesant Public
High School at the north end of Battery Park City, designed by
the able architects Cooper Robertson, presents a characterless
and confused set of facades to the waterfront. That a school
with the strongest reputation for quality in education should be
housed in such a conventional work of architecture is a missed
opportunity. Its conventional planning, rambling confusion of
parts and uninspired spaces and places will influence the
thoughts and imaginations of its students. The so-called
prototype public school design led by Ezra Ehrenkrantz
conveys an almost fortress-like presence with its massive
walls and gabled roofs. As with the institutional buildings
discussed earlier, no one is certain what a school should look
like. Compare this state of affairs with the clear civic form that
school building had throughout America for a century.

BATTERY PARK CITY

Battery Park City is the most extensive comprehensive planning district in Manhattan. Covering over 92 acres, a third of which is landfill from the construction of the World Trade Center, it lies to the western tip of the island. The Battery Park City Authority, a state-created public benefit corporation, was founded in 1968. From the beginning it was conceived as a model of public/private enterprise. State bond issues were sold to raise funds to pay for infrastructure and public parks/immunities. Then developers were chosen by the authority to develop a variety of commercial and residential projects. Equity was achieved by investing profits from the private activity in low- and middle-income developments elsewhere in the city. The master plans were prepared by Alexander Cooper and Stanton Eckstut in 1979, and included very precise design guidelines controlling the heights of set-back approaches. The authority allocated 41 per cent of the land to housing, 9 per cent to commercial space and 20 per cent, including the grand esplanade along the river's edge, to open space. The road system made up the rest. The 9 per cent commercial space was developed solely by the Canadian firm Olympia and York, developers of the Docklands in London among much else, resulting in the development of the World Financial Center, designed by Cesar Pelli. The centre has become an extension of Wall Street to which it is connected by bridges, and for which it is a spectacular climax beneath the palm trees across the glass canopy of its Winter Garden, which is one of the most choreographed public/private spaces in the city with a year-round programme of dance and music. The Winter Garden looks out across the busy marina and the staging point for the new ferry service to Jersey City. From here the esplanade runs south past a sequence of neatly arranged housing terraces placed at right angles to the river. They are the work of many architects including Charles Moore, SOM, James Stewart Polshek, Ulrich Franzen, Davis Brody Bond and Gruzen Samton Steinglass among others. The initial phase was completed in 1988. The subsequent development has been less inclined to maintain the uniformity of the first phase. Opinions are divided between those who believe that public order is served by careful adherence to controls on the height and character of buildings, and those who see this overly controlled district, with its rather homogeneous wealthy population, as a withdrawal from the reality of Manhattan as a place of conflict, speculation and promise. The latter feel that such controlled development would inhibit change and overly protect this privileged enclave from the resilient forces that remake the city. The Stuyvesant High School, discussed earlier, adds little to the spirit of neighbourhood. Additional commercial developments and housing are now in planning and will include a luxury hotel with some of the best views in the city. Profits continue to be invested in other less affluent developments elsewhere in the city.

A small park at the southern end of Battery Park City holds a monument to immigration, set on a precise plane of grass. The work of architects Machado and Silvetti, it is a collage of architectural fragments forming a grand arch that frames the Statue of Liberty. The experience is diminished somewhat by the intrusion of clumsy balustrades. The most uncomplicated achievement is the esplanade which provides a truly civilised setting in which to enjoy the Hudson River.

The importance of appreciating the river is slowly spreading in the imagination of the city. Idea competitions to reconceive the whole waterfront as a place of public pleasure have been set, and a number of projects have already been computed. On the Upper West Side Richard Dattner's Riverbank State Park has been developed on top of the North River sewage treatment plant and is used extensively by the inhabitants of the densely populated neighbourhoods it adjoins. The Van Alen Institute is a foundation dedicated to supporting architecture in New York. Under the creative direction of Ray Gastil, the Institute has held several international ideas competitions on the future of the city including several focusing on the vast river front that surrounds Manhattan. In one recent competition the architects Reiser + Umemoto produced, in multiple images, a landscape of structures and landforms that would transform the edge of the East River into a wholly new kind of park. It is by such means that the consciousness of the city will be raised to believe in the potential for a unified park system that could surround Manhattan on a scale and ambition equal to Central Park. A recovery of the belief that sensibility can be gained from landscape could transform the city.

Central Park, however, remains the most powerful assertion of public life in New York. Contrary to rumour, it is relatively safe. And it remains the only place where New York comes together in all its diversity. Since 1980 the park has been in the hands of the Central Park Conservancy, a private agency that has taken on the responsibility for its upkeep and restoration. Maintenance was a rather passive affair in the postwar years and severe budget cuts in 1970 led to a visible decline in the park's landscape and buildings. This neglect led to the formation of the conservancy with the specific mandate of restoring the Olmsted and Vaux Greensward plan. Many structures such as the Belvedere castle and the dairy have been restored and in some cases partially rebuilt. Olmsted's picturesque monuments, such as the sheep meadow, have been restored and new turf has recovered the Great Lawn. Used to capacity by everyone, and sometimes overwhelmed by joggers and skaters, the park continues to impart to every visitor the intentions of its creators.

The further from Manhattan, the less significant the architecture. Apart from the few minor community projects, architectural activity is focused on business development and widely varied projects to restore and conserve 19th- and early

20th-century institutional buildings. The major exception is the Queens Public Library. As mentioned earlier, this is the work of the Polshek office led by Todd Schleimann and the most satisfying demonstration of the ability of architecture to enhance public life.

When the ferry terminal on Staten Island is completed it will be the only significant new architecture on the island. Brooklyn sees similar pockets of activity involving architecture: renewals and additions to the Brooklyn Museum and the Academy of Music, and the concentration of commercial and educational buildings at the Metrotec Center.

The legacy of civic life in the many surviving and knowingly monumental structures from the turn of the century may be encouraging, not only by their renewal but also by the revival of civic conscience. Otherwise where, in the buildings of the present, are such convincing images of permanence and unity? One might expect distinguished architecture from the new schools and colleges, but little of distinction is being produced.

An interesting example of the force of architecture can be seen across the Hudson to the east. New York has Manhattanised the Jersey coast from the extensive condominium developments from George Washington Bridge south. The Colgate Center and all the waterfront of Jersey City opposite Battery Park were planned by Brennan Beer Gorman (BBG), and include the Merrill Lynch tower in New Jersey. Around it is developing a new city which, as it grows, is creating harsh lines between renewal and neglect. New town houses resurrect streets alongside abandoned buildings, new shopping malls stand next to derelict power plants and factories. Nothing softens the division between vigorous healthy city and vast areas of neglect.

In the future Manhattan will emerge from a million divergent transactions. Nowhere – save within the narrow limits of the commercial and public realm – is architecture part of the vision that drives the ambitions and desires of the multicultural communities that will define it.

NOTES

All the material in this section has been drawn and developed from the documentation generously provided by the architect contributors. I must again cite the *New York Times* and its wonderfully eccentric architectural critic, Herbert Munschamp, for being a continual stimulus in developing insights and maintaining a sense of the larger forces at work in the city. Munschamp is one of the very few architectural critics employed by any newspaper in the nation. It is a tribute both to the intelligence of the *Times* and to Munschamp's imagination that he succeeds in maintaining architecture as a vital part of the city and the nation's culture.

The material on the competition to expand MoMA is drawn from *Imagining the Future of the Museum of Modern Art*, 7 in the series of Studies in Modern Art, published by the Museum and distributed by Harry N Abrams, New York 1998.

BUILDINGS 6

Courtesy: Arquitectonica/Tishman Realty & Construction Co., Inc

Commercial High Rise

ARQUITECTONICA
WESTIN NEW YORK AT TIMES SQUARE

The architects for this project researched the history of 42nd Street to create a building that belonged in the context of the Entertainment District. The basic rectangular prism is metaphorically sliced by a curving beam of light. This effect creates 'two buildings' each with its own sculptural profile. The easterly volume is firmly anchored to the ground and is clad in horizontal bands of earth-coloured bronze glass. While bands of black-painted glass in gold and rust emphasise the horizontality of its patterning. The westerly volume rises above the ground, levitating five storeys above the corner of 43rd Street and 8th Avenue in defiance of gravity. An atrium lobby in clear glass ends in an angled ceiling that becomes the underside of this suspended building. In contrast to the easterly building, its thin volume broadens as it reaches towards the sky. It is clad in vertical bands of space-age steel and blue-grey glass. This 52-storey volume rises above the 45-storey side, revealing its lit up curved inner surface to Times Square.

On 42nd Street, the tower appears to rise from a 'rock'. This rock actually houses the suites of the hotel and is shaped like a jagged rocklike form approximately 10 storeys high. It is clad in mosaic and its irregularly shaped collage is punctuated by a checkerboard of glass squares – the windows of the guest rooms.

77

Arquitectonica: studies for the new Westin New York set in the context of a new Times Square

Courtesy: Arquitectonica/Tishman Realty & Construction Co., Inc

Courtesy: Arquitectonica/Tishman Realty & Construction Co., Inc

Courtesy: Arquitectonica/Tishman Realty & Construction Co., Inc

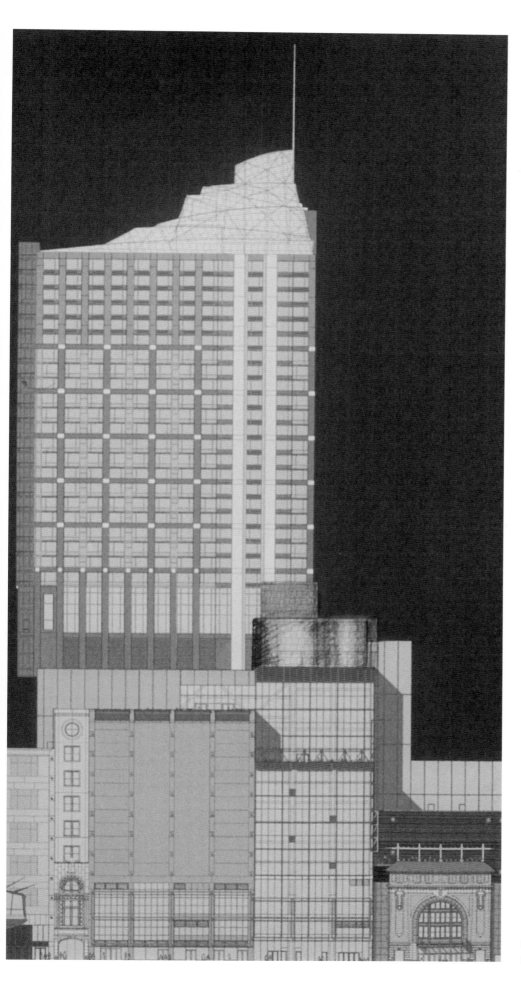

BEYER BLINDER BELLE
42ND STREET

This major revitalisation project for 42nd Street, immediately adjacent to Times Square, will create an exciting mix of specialty and signature retail, restaurants, tourist attractions and entertainment spaces. The new mixed-use building of approximately 850,000 square feet, designed by Beyer Blinder Belle Architects & Planners, is significant for its breadth and complexity of historic preservation issues within a mix of new design and construction.

79

Design phase model of retail/entertainment portion including historic Harris, Liberty and Empire Theater facades.

*Rendering of north-west elevation showing
storefronts, signage and above hotel*

SOUTH ELEVATION

© Jock Pottle/Esto

FOX & FOWLE
REUTERS

At the corner of 43rd Street, a seven-storey drum shaped structure pulls the street wall around the corner towards the north. As its curvilinear facade returns into the building, it forms an exedral space that draws the sidewalk in and forms a three-storey mid-block lobby. On the north east corner, a 20-storey stone-clad mass rises from the street. This exposure has a strong Reuters presence from the street to the building's top. Starting with the lobby behind a 60-foot high all-glass wall, there is a series of 30-foot high video monitors that wrap around the corner of 43rd Street. These monitors broadcast Reuters programming to the 'bow-tie' area of Times Square. On the corner, starting on the ninth floor and rising to the 23rd floor, a wedge-like corner element frames a vertical LED sign that serves as the Reuter's Index, conveying through colour and intensity the importance and character of the day's news.

Above these ground-based masses rises an ensemble of planes and volumes that form the office tower. These elements vary in scale, colour and texture. As a means of further connecting the two urban venues within the space above the low-rise retail elements, the eastern face has a dramatic curvilinear form easing towards the south west. This facade is expressed as a 20-foot thick reflective glass plane with an eccentrically arced top that drives the rising energy towards the corner and creates a definitive protruding edge. The western face is composed of fragments of smaller volumetric components, facade expressions and sign planes designed to complement the historic low-rise buildings towards the centre of the block.

81

Reuters: model viewed from Times Square

Clockwise from left: the corner of 42nd Street;
the first floor plan showing the division between distinct tenants;
multi-media at the Reuters entrance.

© Jock Pottle/Esto

© Jock Pottle/Esto

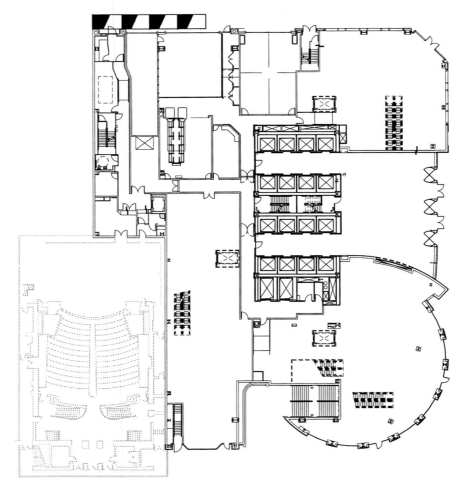

FOX & FOWLE
CONDÉ NAST

Below: view across Bryant Park showing the crowning projection screens;
Below right: the NASDAC sign at 43rd Street.

This 48-storey office tower located at the north east corner of Broadway and 42nd Street occupies a pivotal site, straddling urban spaces with diverse identities. Its design embraces the essence of Times Square while meeting the needs of corporate tenants.

Designed with two distinct orientations, the west and the north sides of the building reflect the dynamic environment of Times Square and are clad primarily in metal and glass, while along 42nd Street and the east facade, a textured and scaled masonry treatment presents a more composed personality, appropriate to the midtown corporate context and the refined style of Bryant Park. A 30 per cent expansion of the original building site has enabled setback massing, allowing the building to evolve from a full streetwall base to a setback tower. A varied composition of interlocking setback forms and facade treatments that respond to the diverse scale and character of the neighbouring buildings has been created. As the main building shaft rises, the collage of volumes and surfaces evolves into a composed structure culminating in a highly energised top. The building top reflects the principal structural support system with its 60-foot square signs and communications tower.

This building is environmentally responsible. All building systems and construction technology have been evaluated for their impact on occupant health, environmental sensitivity and energy reduction, adopting state-of-the-art standards for energy conservation, indoor air quality, recycling systems and sustainable manufacturing processes.

83

© Jock Pottle/Esto

Below: 42nd Street and Broadway;
Bottom right: plan of upper floors showing the projection screens;
Bottom left: the elevation to Times Square.

© Jock Pottle/Esto

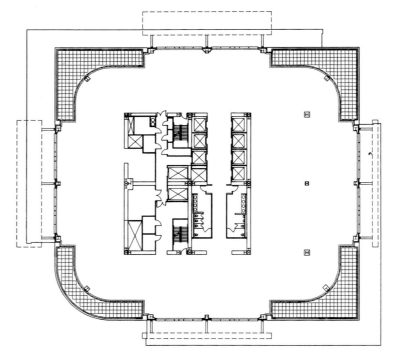

© Jock Pottle/Esto

FOX & FOWLE
EMBASSY SUITES TIMES SQUARE

Located in the heart of Times Square, the 460-suite Embassy Suites Times Square hotel was one of the first projects to be built in accordance with the Times Square signage regulations. Thirty-eight floors of hotel, public and retail spaces were designed to span the existing five-storey, interior landmarked Palace Theatre. The theatre received a new marquee and facade as well as restored and expanded interiors. Illuminated billboards 120 feet high, and characteristic of Times Square, were prominent and mandated features of the new hotel and theatre facade.

Fox & Fowle designed the interior spaces as an integral part of the architecture of the building. They reflect the 'culture' of Times Square as well as Embassy Suites' commitment to quality and hospitality. The six public floors include public lobbies, hotel administration and services, retail shops, a restaurant, piano bar and conference facilities. In addition, Fox & Fowle reviewed the interior design of the 460 suites occupying the upper 36 floors.

85

Left: the view down 45th Street;
Below: sectional projection showing the bridge-like structure over the Palace Theater.

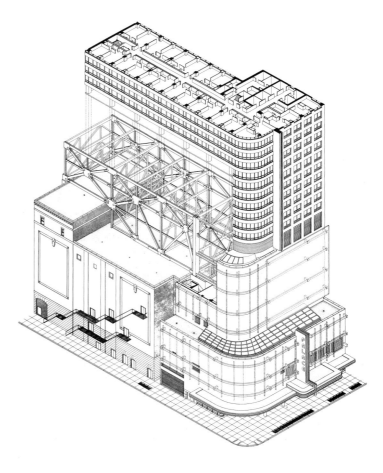

© Andrew Gordon

© Peter Aaron/Esto

GWATHMEY SIEGEL

MORGAN STANLEY

This 52-storey office tower, completed in 1990, houses the world headquarters of an international investment banking firm. Located in midtown Manhattan at 1585 Broadway, the building reflects the aspirations of a traditional skyscraper to present an appropriately scaled public building at the pedestrian base and a strong silhouette on the skyline.

The site's unusual shape and positioning posed a challenge which was resolved by generating forms that address both the diagonal of Broadway and the orthogonal Manhattan street grid. The base responds to the diagonal; the segmented curve of the double-height mechanical floor creates a transition from the rotated base to the orthogonal tower. The changing play of natural light on the building's glass surface produces images of both opacity and reflectivity, of fluidity and permanence.

Its interior design encompasses executive offices, dining and meeting spaces, and boardrooms on the 40th and 41st floors, the main lobby on street level, and dining facilities for 500 people on the lower level.

The two-storey executive floor entry space is rendered in granite, anaigre, mahogany and ebonised cherry woods. Offering a panoramic view south, east and west of Manhattan, the entry acts as the referential interconnected volume for the two executive floors. The selection of materials imbues the entire space with a sense of density, permanence and inevitability. The public lobby is a sweeping expanse broken only by two columns. The walls are finished with grey granite accented by strips of dark green polished marble. Other materials include white, black and dark green marble in a geometric pattern on the floor, and a coffered ceiling of wood.

Top: view from Broadway;
Far left: view from the West;
Left: the lobby.

© Jeff Goldberg/Esto

CESAR PELLI & ASSOCIATES
CARNEGIE HALL TOWER

Built in 1991, Carnegie Hall Tower is the second tallest concrete building in New York City and the eighth tallest in the world. A commercial venture using Carnegie Hall's air rights for development, it is also an expansion of the music hall, designed as a harmonious addition to the landmark. The 60-storey tower, on West 57th Street between Sixth and Seventh Avenues, extends the composition of the Renaissance Revival Music Hall and reinterprets its massing, colouration and system of ornamentation.

The exterior cladding, similar to that of the music hall, is primarily brick over a cast-in-place, concrete structural tube. The colour was selected to complement the music hall; three complementary colours are used to create the pattern in the central fields. Window sills, lintels and accents are pre-cast concrete, coloured to reinforce the terra cotta decoration of the music hall. The frieze at the top of the tower is dark green glazed brick.

The tower recalls the shape of the building's 13-storey additions and is formed of two interlocking slabs of different sizes. The six-storey base relates to and extends the major cornice line of the music hall. The building is set back above this level to allow the Carnegie Hall campanile, with its large overhanging cornice, to stand free.

The facades are organised like those of the music hall. Each side is divided into three parts: two corner 'solids' and a central field. These elements, and the two components of the tower, are bound together by wide coloured bands at six-storey intervals, similar to those of the music hall cornice. The tower top is a dark frieze beneath an open metalwork cornice, analogous to the attic storey of the music hall, but expanded in proportion to the height of the tower. The shorter tower component carries a smaller version of this same top.

87

Above: the tower with Carnegie Hall in the foreground;
Right: the view from Central Park West

© Jeff Goldberg/Esto

CESAR PELLI & ASSOCIATES
WORLD FINANCIAL CENTER

The World Financial Center consists of four office towers ranging in height from 34 to 51 storeys, the public Winter Garden, a glass-roofed courtyard, two nine-storey octagonal gateway buildings and a 3.5-acre landscaped public plaza.

The four glass and granite towers rise from a granite base. The proportion of granite to glass is greater at the base of each tower and gradually lightens into glass skins.

The buildings, which were completed in 1988, surround and define a public plaza that is the heart of the waterfront edge. Adjacent to the plaza, the Winter Garden creates a great public room enclosed in a glass vault. It is the largest public space at the World Financial Center and was designed as a grand glass hall with a huge bay window facing the Hudson River. The space serves as the main connector to all public circulation within the World Financial Center and with the World Trade Center.

The Winter Garden is an integral element to the World Financial Center and Battery Park City. It was designed for the general public as well as for those working in the financial district. Performing arts programmes are regularly scheduled and are extremely popular, especially on weekdays during lunch hours. Visitors descend a large circular staircase from the upper level, which links the garden to the office towers and to the World Trade Center, to a palm grove below. Skyscraper tops are visible through the roof of the garden, and a panoramic view of the Hudson River appears through the grove.

88

World Finance Center in front of the twin towers of the World Trade Center

Jeff Perkell

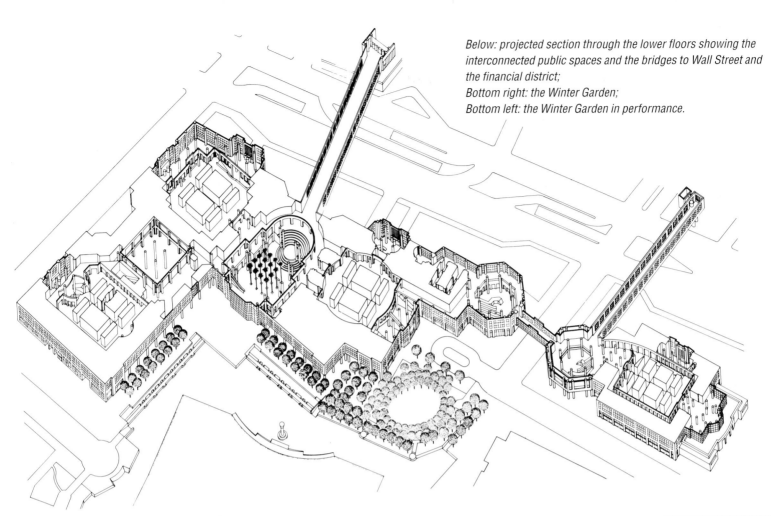

Below: projected section through the lower floors showing the interconnected public spaces and the bridges to Wall Street and the financial district;
Bottom right: the Winter Garden;
Bottom left: the Winter Garden in performance.

Opposite page: the Winter Garden from the marina;
Top right and left: the Winter Garden;
Bottom: plan of the buildings, the landscapes and the river.

Erich Hartmann/Magnum Photos

Timothy Hursley/The Arkansas Office

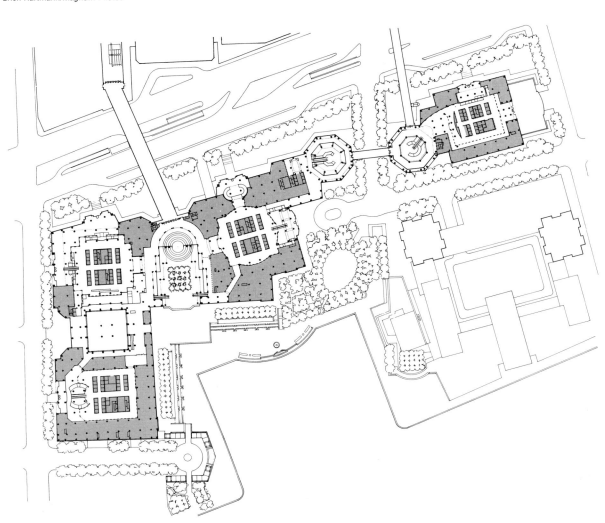

Opposite page: Timothy Hursley/The Arkansas Office

© Nathaniel Lieberman

Above: the grand foyer;
Below: the view from the south.

I M PEI & PARTNERS
JACOB K JAVITS CONVENTION CENTER

The Javits Center is a partially transparent glass structure on the edge of the urban core. Completed in 1986, it was designed to relate to, and regenerate, its environment, and to serve as a vital focus for residents and conventioneers alike. Located at 655 West 34th Street, it contains 720,000 square feet of exhibition space as well as offices, storage and service areas, kitchen and dining facilities and shops. It also houses more than a hundred meeting rooms, most with movable walls for maximum flexibility, making it the largest convention centre in the US.

Among the many challenges confronted, the most exacting focused on structure, integration and circulation. The structure was resolved with a modified space frame and truss system: a lightweight double layer structure in which steel tubes are connected to spherical nodes. The system was selected for flexibility as well as texture and optical effect. The pewter-coloured trellis also assists in integration while the space frame's small rhythmic patterns help to reduce the building's apparent scale. The interior terrazzo pavement, animated by shifting daylight, has the same reductive effect. And so does the building's reflective glass skin, folding precisely around the space frame's corners and bevelled roofline notches. Even more important for integration is the play of solidity and transparency in which the vast interior, flooded with natural light, combines indoor and outdoor views.

Installed along the inner west wall of the concourse (designed for registration, exhibition overflow and flexibility of circulation), is the Javit Center's concrete 'core': a freestanding building within a building over whose low roof natural light filters into the exhibition areas.

© Nathaniel Lieberman

Norman McGraph

PLATT BYARD DOVELL

CHANEL TOWERS

The 17-storey tower completed in 1996 represents Chanel Inc. on the most important retail frontage in the US. On 57th Street in Manhattan between Madison Avenue and Fifth Avenue, the building houses Chanel's flagship boutique as well as a salon and showrooms for fashion shows and other major presentations, and a variety of offices supporting the boutique and other enterprises of Chanel. The design reflects the elegance of Chanel in a building attached to Chanel's European roots but completely at home in New York.

Norman McGrath

Above: the view down 57th Street;
Above right: the elevation, Louis Vuitton now
occupies the gap on the right;
Right: interior.

CHRISTIAN DE PORTZAMPARC & HILLLIER

LVMH TOWER

The Hillier Group was approached by Parisian architect Christian de Portzamparc to make his vision for the LVMH (Louis Vuitton - Moët Hennessy) North American Headquarters a reality. At the crossroads of commerce and fashion, this light-filled building rises like a beacon on 57th Street.

De Portzamparc designed the 100,000 square foot building, located on 57th Street between Madison and 5th Avenues and Hillier served as the co-ordinating architect, providing design development, production documentation and construction administration services, as well as all interior design. The innovative design of the structure incorporates 'smart building' technology, including fully integrated data and telecommunications systems. The interior is comprised of corporate offices, showrooms, a spa and the 'magic room' – a multi-purpose room used for a host of events, including fashion shows, product launches and large meetings.

The LVMH Tower is considered one of the most distinctive buildings constructed in Manhattan in recent years. The concept of the magnificent building is simple. Designers took the layout typically seen on Parisian streets and flipped it vertically. Now, instead of seeing high-end fashion stores side by side on a common street, they are stacked on top of one another with the elevator lobby on every floor serving as the 'common street.'

Each company occupying the tower has a showroom with finishes that relate to its retail stores in Paris to display its line of products. The sister companies of LVMH, which include Christian Dior Couture, Parfums Givenchy, Christian Dior Perfumes, Louis Vuitton, Loewe, Celine and Guerlain occupy the tower.

Opposite: general view.

© Nicolas Borel

LEE HARRIS POMEROY ASSOCIATES

SAKS 5TH AVENUE/SWISS BANK TOWER

This 36-storey, mixed-use office building is sited mid-block immediately behind the landmarked Saks Fifth Avenue flagship department store, directly across from Rockefeller Center. Saks occupies the first nine storeys. The building's contextual design continues the store's classic motifs on the street facades while acknowledging the Rockefeller Center with its own modern front. The chamfered corners recall those of the Saks Fifth Avenue store, and the design is compatible with the materials of the historic landmark.

The rusticated limestone base of the new building carries the theme of composite-order pilasters and the proportions of the punched shed windows of the Renaissance facade of the existing store. Much of the stone detail is machine planed to the precise profiles to match the original facade, but many of the intricate curvilinear and floral pieces were hand carved by stone artisans using essentially the same methods and implements that were employed during the Renaissance.

The tower sets back equally on 49th Street and 50th Street, rising straight up with a cladding of flat limestone panels with a pattern of punched recessed windows. Inside, the 475,000 square foot building includes sophisticated systems: fibre optics, complex security systems; column-free flexible interiors; provision for satellite communications and other high technology installations. A small tower entrance on 50th Street leads to a larger sky lobby and conference centre on the 11th floor. This two-level sky lobby provides a dramatic entrance to the banking offices, overlooking the spires of St Patrick's Cathedral.

Above: the view past St Patrick's Cathedral showing the blending of the tower with the Saks store;
Left: the entrance to the Swiss bank through an extension of the early Saks facade.

ALDO ROSSI, GENSLER & ASSOCIATES
SOHO BUILDING

Above: model study for one bay of the pseudo-industrial building;
Below right: the mixture of facades;
Below: the model showing the ersatz facades on two sides of the block.

Broadway is the main street of SoHo, a New York City district which combines monumental, century-old buildings and a high-energy contemporary scene of culture and commerce. Scholastic, the educational publisher, commissioned Aldo Rossi in conjunction with Gensler and Associates, to design a new building adjacent to its existing headquarters in one of SoHo's most prominent historic structures. Rossi's design is conceived as a connected companion building for its older neighbour, relating to its historic context in a responsive yet completely contemporary way.

97

The building's Broadway facade, in steel, terra cotta and stone, takes its inspiration from the columnar, classically organised facades of its neighbouring commercial buildings. A second facade, equal in scale and dimensions, faces the more utilitarian, industrial environment of Mercer Street. Here, the treatment is a bold response to the powerful, abstract forms and the assembled structural components of historic cast-iron factory buildings. With its unique double presence, Rossi's design reflects SoHo's confluence of people, ideas and creative enterprise, and its diverse context of history and architecture. Here, Rossi reaches toward his ideal of the 'urban artefact': a response to the city as a field of memory and ideas realised in three dimensions; in the architect's words, not just a 'physical thing', but 'history, geography, structure and connection with general life'.

Commercial Low Rise

ARCHITECTURE RESEARCH OFFICE
ARMED FORCES RECRUITMENT STATION

The existing structure is a fixture in the Times Square landscape. It has occupied the spit of land between Broadway and Seventh Avenue since 1946, where it sits above a subway grate.

ARO's new design, executed in 1999, establishes a strong visual presence for the Armed Forces in the constantly changing cityscape. The 500-square foot stainless steel and glass structure has been reproportioned to make the building better fit the scale of the site and is elegantly detailed.

The exterior of the recruiting station takes its cue from the neon vernacular of Times Square itself. Each long facade presents itself to the passerby as an American flag while each glass face fronts 13 bands of fluorescent light. Red, white and blue elements are provided by reflective gels that colour the lights at night and reflect sunlight during the day.

A landscaping programme for the site was also developed. The flags of each of the four services are joined by the American flag in a row at the north end of the island. A series of reflective bollards frame the structure and outline the site's perimeter.

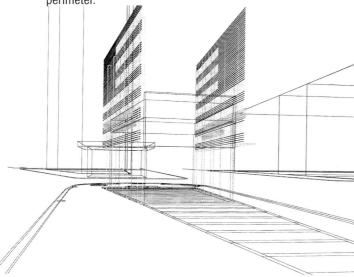

Above: reflections of Times Square;
Left and below: conceptual studies of the abstract
'Stars and Stripes' in lights.

FOREIGN OFFICE ARCHITECTS
BELGO AMERICA

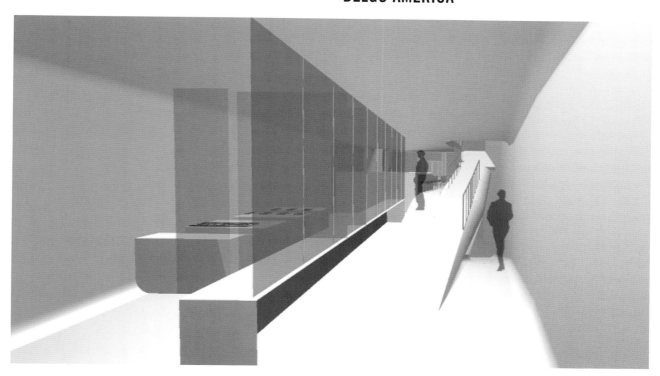

This work develops in an intimate context many of the formal and topological explorations that the London-based Foreign Office Architects have exercised so grandly in their harbour project in Yokohama, which is now under construction. As you enter the restaurant, you approach long, sleek ramps that lead to two levels: the upstairs with its high vaulted ceilings designed to represent the growth rings of a mussel and the downstairs complete with futuristic back-lit posters and multilingual phrases. As you make your way up the ramp you receive your first 'taste' of Belgo as you pass the open kitchen; and as you continue into the restaurant you can catch a glimpse of the recently decorated back wall. It is a brightly coloured mural of 'The Atomium' in Brussels.

Above: computer study for the dividing passages entering the restaurant;
Left: the constructed work.

FRANK O GEHRY & ASSOCIATES
CONDÉ NAST CAFETERIA

The Condé Nast Cafeteria is located on the fourth floor of the new Condé Nast Publishing Headquarters designed by Fox & Fowle Architects at Four Times Square in New York City. The 260-seat cafeteria, intended to provide employees with convenient lunchtime dining and meeting facilities, includes a main dining area, a servery, and four private dining rooms.

The main dining area is organised to provide a variety of seating arrangements in an atmosphere that is both intimate and open. Custom-designed booths that accommodate four to six people each are distributed along the perimeter walls. These walls, which are clad in perforated blue titanium panels that include an acoustic backing to ensure acoustic absorption, undulate in response to the geometry and overall configuration of the booths. Additional booths are located on a raised seating platform which is enclosed within curved glass panels in the centre of the main dining area. Freestanding tables and chairs which will be designed by Frank O Gehry & Associates will be distributed throughout the main dining area. The floor of this area is an ash-veneer plywood, and the ceiling is clad in perforated blue titanium panels that match the perimeter walls.

The servery, which is adjacent to the main dining area, is a fully-equipped facility that provides a selection of different hot and cold entrées. The servery's curvilinear angel hair finished stainless steel countertops, blue titanium walls and canopies, and ash-veneer floor and ceiling complement the sculptural and aesthetic character of the main dining area.

The four private dining rooms are located on the same level as the main dining area and the servery, but they are distinct and separate spaces to be used for special lunch meetings and presentations. The walls, floors and ceilings of the private dining rooms are ash-veneer plywood. Curved glass panels articulate the east wall of each room, providing an even natural light illumination through clerestory windows. The private dining rooms are equipped with state-of-the-art audiovisual capabilities. Three of the four private dining rooms have movable partitions, allowing the three rooms to be transformed into a variety of spatial configurations for special occasions.

100

SHARPLES HOLDEN PASQUARELLI
V-MALL

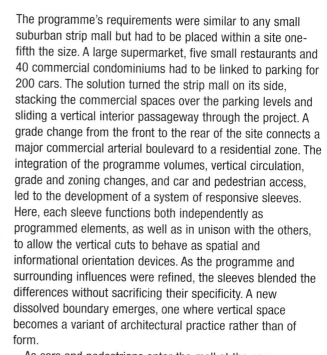

The programme's requirements were similar to any small suburban strip mall but had to be placed within a site one-fifth the size. A large supermarket, five small restaurants and 40 commercial condominiums had to be linked to parking for 200 cars. The solution turned the strip mall on its side, stacking the commercial spaces over the parking levels and sliding a vertical interior passageway through the project. A grade change from the front to the rear of the site connects a major commercial arterial boulevard to a residential zone. The integration of the programme volumes, vertical circulation, grade and zoning changes, and car and pedestrian access, led to the development of a system of responsive sleeves. Here, each sleeve functions both independently as programmed elements, as well as in unison with the others, to allow the vertical cuts to behave as spatial and informational orientation devices. As the programme and surrounding influences were refined, the sleeves blended the differences without sacrificing their specificity. A new dissolved boundary emerges, one where vertical space becomes a variant of architectural practice rather than of form.

As cars and pedestrians enter the mall at the same location, a three-storey media sleeve separates the two circulation zones while advertising images for the shops are projected on to the sleeve. The trees of the park are visible through the retail stores where cuts in the sleeves allow light to penetrate deep into the underground garages.

101

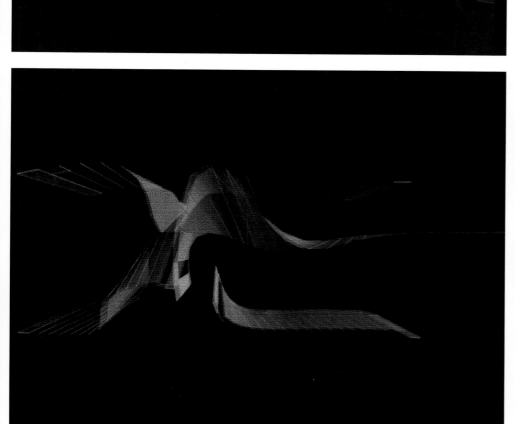

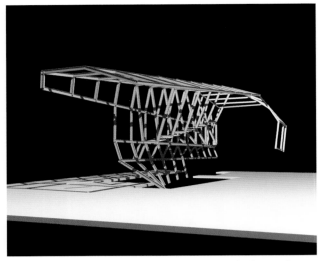

V-Mall: computer studies of the structure of the folding roof

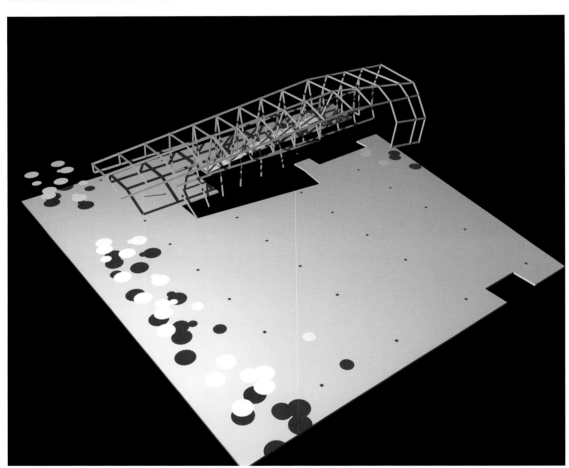

V-Mall: computer studies of roof form and structure

Residential High Rise

GRUZEN SAMTON

TRIBECA POINTE

Gruzen Samton

Above: view from the Battery Park City Esplanade; Right: development model showing the adjoining Stuyvesant High School on the left.

Tribeca Pointe is a 42-storey residential tower on a riverfront site adjacent to Stuyvesant High School at the north tip of Battery Park City. The 79-foot wide tower, soaring over 400 feet, is the tallest new residential structure. The 340 apartments, ranging from studios to three-bedroom units, offer a mix of rental units with views of the Hudson River and the lower Manhattan skyline. While the tower symbolises the entire Battery Park City development, the street facade integrates details recalling the nearby historic TriBeCa area. The exterior treatment of brick and stone with a glass marquee was designed to meet the demanding design guidelines established by the Battery Park City Authority for all the structures in this new community, while elements of floor to ceiling window provide dramatic views.

Tenant amenities include a rooftop solarium and terrace, a laundry and fitness centre with river views, a 1,000-square foot retail space, and direct access into the recently completed Rockefeller Park and on to the Battery Park City Esplanade.

103

Gruzen Samton

FARUK YORGANCIOGLU
353 CENTRAL PARK WEST

Built in 1992, 353 Central Park West is an integrated structure whose interior layouts are an outgrowth of the building's siting and form, and whose facades are a reflection of the functions of the apartments within. The primary rooms of each of the individual apartment units are orientated towards the avenue to take maximum advantage of the panoramic views of Central Park and the city skyline. Service spaces are relegated to the side street, both for better service access at ground level for the goods lift and for reasons of lesser importance of outlook.

Each typical floor affords about 2,400 square feet of functional space for a single apartment. The resulting extremely low density of only 16 units to the entire building gives Number 353 a sense of exclusivity rare in new buildings.

The materials and detailing used on the building's facades are very much within the character of the surrounding streets and reflect an existing general aesthetic which has been consistently applied for over a century. The treatment of the fenestration and the brickwork provides articulation, shadows and a rich three-dimensionality, even within the constraints of the local New York pedestrian protection law which forbids projections greater than 10 inches beyond the building line.

Above: view from across Central Park;
Left: study perspective.

Residential Low Rise

HANRAHAN & MEYERS

HOLLEY LOFT

Completed in 1995, the Holley Loft is an adaptation of an existing 4,000 square foot industrial loft space into a residence for a single person. The space is on the second floor of a loft building in Lower Manhattan.

The space of the project is a loose and relatively open grid of pure formal elements which float within a non-specific and unbounded context. The loft was generated from notions of transparency, light, reflectivity and freedom in the plan, all of which position the work of Hanrahan + Meyers solidly within the auspices of modern architecture, following in the traditions of Mies van der Rohe and Le Corbusier.

The loft contains no solid walls. A single 48 foot long full-height wall of glass and steel marks the major division of master bedroom and bathroom from the rest of the apartment, with sandblasted areas for privacy and a telescoping curtain to control the openness of the space. At any moment, from any position, the full dimensions of the entire loft space can be experienced, with all the elements of the domestic programme distributed freely in the form of low cabinetry and movable panels. This disposition yields a complex space of constantly changing perspectives and points of view. Light from both ends of the apartment penetrates deep into the residence, while the movable panels allow for the creation of smaller, more intimate spaces to accommodate overnight guests.

105

Holley Loft: plan and interior view

© Peter Aaron/Esto

SULAN KOLATAN/ WILLIAM MACDONALD
WITH ERICH SCHOENENBERGER
O/K APARTMENT

This 1997 project involved the remodelling and combining of two separate but contiguous apartments totalling 1,500 square feet. The West Side building was originally built as artists' ateliers and residences. The owners asked for flexibility in the use of the apartment's configurations so that it could function both as a corporate apartment, and serve as a pied-à-terre. Three sleeping areas with variable degrees of privacy respond to this need.

This interior project was conceived in the manner of a 'miniature urbanism' consisting of three phases: the identification of individual 'sites' within the existing space; the generation of these structures through cross-profiling; and the mapping of similarities akin to co-citation mapping.

For the generation of the new structures on each site, section profiles of everyday domestic objects and furnishings were electronically cross-referenced with each other regardless of original scale and category but with an interest in registering formal and operational similarities between them. Based on this information, they were then spatially organised and resurfaced. The resulting structures are chimerical in the sense that the initial profiles as indexes of particular identities (bed, sink, sofa, etc.) are now inextricably embedded within an entirely new entity which they have helped to produce.

106

Above: bathroom;

MAYA LIN STUDIO
NORTON APARTMENT

Commissioned as a surprise gift for a client's wife, this 2,000-square foot apartment was designed as a simple toy box that could transform its shape and functionality. By moving key components (such as a pivoting closet and a shower wall), two bedrooms transform into one, a single bath becomes two and a dining table reduces to a simple bar element.

The apartment is on two levels with an entry mid-way between the floors. As one enters the space, light filters from a rear skylight through the apartment to the kitchen. One has views of the entire downstairs public spaces, while the upstairs private bedrooms and baths are concealed behind frosted glass and sycamore panelling.

The client will use the apartment as a pied-à-terre, but wanted it to work whether he was by himself or accompanied by his family. The artist wanted to design a space that had maximum flexibility and reflected a transmutable way of living, creating an apartment that could work if the client was visiting alone, with his wife or with his two children.

Above: two levels, two moods;
Below: transmutable spaces.

DANIEL ROWEN, FRANK LUPO
NEW YORK APARTMENT

Completed in 1992, this project transforms two traditional apartments at a white-glove Park Avenue address into a 2,500-square foot non-traditional pied-à-terre for a businessman and his art collection. The non-traditional aspects of the design are a result of the client's mandate that all accommodations of normal living be concealed or eliminated so that the visual field is reduced to its essence.

The abstraction of the apartment is further reinforced by the elimination of many windows, the screening of the remaining views, the absence of furniture (the soft stuff is nested behind cabinet doors), and the absence of the intended art collection. The later decision evolved as the client determined that the play of light against the compositional planes of walls, floors and ceilings satisfied his aesthetic agenda.

The apartment's minimalism creates a meditative landscape that radically separates it from the energies and influences of surrounding midtown Manhattan. This reductive separation affords the occupant the possibility of exploring the senses without encumbrance. In short, it is a place to listen to the light, to see the silence and to dream.

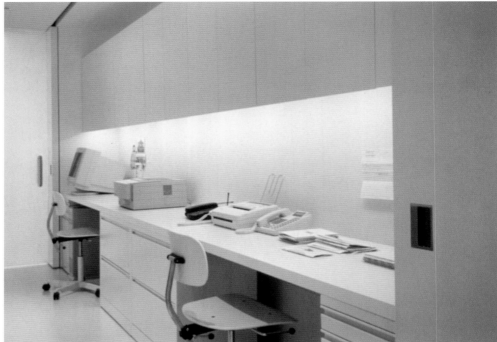

Top: office space;
Above: sleeping space;
Left: the visual field reduced to its essence.

OGAWA/DEPARDON ARCHITECTS
TOWNHOUSE UPPER EAST SIDE

Set in midtown New York, this project was a complete renovation of an existing townhouse. This house is about light. Light reflects on all aspects of the design: the transitions between old and new, interior and exterior, serviced and service space, material solidity and lightness, opacity and translucency.

The house has no interior walls in the traditional sense. They have been replaced by large sheets of translucent and transparent glass to create an illuminated light well through the centre of the house.

All closets, mechanical shafts, dumbwaiter and other service spaces were aligned against the eastern wall and stacked vertically behind built-in cabinetry to maximise the usable spaces such as bedrooms, living room and dining room. This further allowed the infusion of natural light from the stair well and the front and rear elevations throughout the house.

A four-storey extension was added to the rear creating the opportunity for a new glass and steel facade which opens the house to an exterior room and walled garden.

The juxtaposition of new and old is clarified by the use of building materials and their detailing. Stone, steel, glass and wood are assembled with light to animate the interior spaces. A thoroughly modern spatial quality co-existing with a traditional townhouse typology.

Above: rear elevation and walled garden;
Right: central stair and light well;
Below: long section.

TOD WILLIAMS, BILLIE TSIEN AND ASSOCIATES

NEW YORK CITY HOUSE

Compressed into the 30'x100' footprint of two demolished brownstones in a New York City block, this townhouse suggests that it is still possible to build a single family house within the super-dense urban fabric of Manhattan. Sited on East 72nd Street, the immediate context of this building is a five-storey brownstone (a consulate) to the east and an 18-storey apartment building to the west. Other structures on this noisy and wide cross-town street are predominantly 15-storey apartment buildings with the occasional 19th-century brownstone and a 30-storey tower.

In response to the scale of the more intimate buildings and the private nature of the programme, the central element in the quiet composition of the facade is a hammered limestone wall around which are composed translucent and transparent windows. The wall provides a sense of protection and privacy from the street while at the same time connecting it with surrounding built fabric through material and scale. The composition of glass surrounding this stone wall isolates and abstracts it, while bringing filtered light to rooms within. The rear facade, facing a 30'x30' back garden is predominantly glass and is related in its sense of composition to the front of the house.

In order to encourage vertical circulation by foot in this six-floor house and to flood the interior of the house with light, a large skylight illuminates and marks the stairway from the basement level to the top floor. One is able to see from the pool level to the sky. Defining the sense of movement and illuminated by the skylight is a monumental wall, echoing the initial limestone facade. Organisation of spaces is clear and logical, placing elements of the programme in the most effective location with pool in the basement; family, kitchen and dining on the ground floor; and living, study, and library on the second (double-height) floor. The guest room is on a mezzanine level, parents' and child's room on the third level, and staff rooms on the top floor.

Floors in public areas are kirkstone and cherry. Cabinetwork is cherry. All interiors including furniture and carpets are designed by the architects (at the date of this photography, on completion of the house in 1996, the owners' extensive and changing collection had not been installed). While it is clear that this house has been built for a wealthy client, it is also a good neighbour and contributes to the vitality and fabric of the city. It affirms the city as a locus for civilised life and provides an alternative to those who flee the city for bedroom communities.

Above: the rear elevation;
Left: the great room looking out to the walled court below.

© Michael Moran

LARSEN SHEIN GINSBERG + MAGNUSSON / NOS QUEDAMOS COMMITTEE

MELROSE COMMONS

The development of an appropriate density, a minimum of 60 units per acre, is a major concern to the Melrose community. Density means establishing a critical residential mass that encourages commercial and institutional uses to locate here. A mixed use community fosters a pedestrian orientated environment that has access to jobs, recreation and educational opportunities.

The revised plan called for the creation of 1,500-1,700 units of housing woven into the fabric of the existing community. The types of new building are varied, allowing different scales to be developed. The building distribution is as follows: six-eight storey elevator buildings with a commercial base along Third Avenue, East 161st Street and Melrose Avenue; four-storey multiple dwellings along the side streets; and two-three family homes at certain side streets and along mid-block mews. Small play areas are provided on each block accessible from every home. Parking is off-street but not between the homes and the public sidewalks/streets.

In order to create a sustainable community that satisfies the need to house its inhabitants and provides for their upward mobility, a range of occupancy types must be created allowing a mixed income neighbourhood to develop. Additionally, an appropriate apartment mix with the percentage of dwelling units divided between one-, two-, and three-bedroom units must be established. The primary building form in Melrose Commons is residential incorporating both commercial and community facilities.

111

Above: the townhouses scaled to the turn-of-the-century church; Right: dense apartment block housing commercial and institutional activity at street level.

Institutional Arts

RAIMUND ABRAHAM
AUSTRIAN CULTURAL INSTITUTE

The lateral compression
of the site
defines the latency
of its vertical thrust.
Three elementary towers:
The Vertebra / Stair Tower
The Core / Structural Tower
The Mask / Glass Tower.
Signifying the
counterforces of gravity:
The Vertebra – Ascension
The Core – Support
The Mask – Suspension.
The entire tower
rests
on the cavity
of its public spaces.

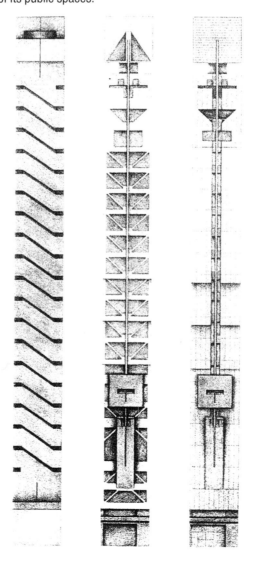

Opposite page left: the model detached from
the compression of the Manhattan grid;
Opposite page right: three elementary towers: stair tower –
vertebra, structural tower – core, glass tower – mask;
Above: structure integrating the three towers;
Right: photomontage in context.

FREDERICK FISHER & PARTNERS

PS1 CONTEMPORARY ART CENTER

Sixteen years ago, the PS1 was on the avant garde of the 'found place' movement in the realm of contemporary art spaces. The movement had several themes, among them: getting art out of the tradition-bound museums, producing art as a response to found space, moving art into the 'streets' and the communities.

Located at 22-25 Jackson Avenue, PS1 is a large, century-old school building in an industrial blue collar neighbourhood of Queens. The vast array of rooms and outdoor space has provided a setting for innovative shows throughout its history. A youth arts education programme and an international artist-in-residence programme have supplemented PS1's exhibit and publications programmes.

After years of ad hoc use and minor remodelling, the building's severe deterioration and functional problems called for a master plan and substantial renovation. As a consequence, the museum has a substantially bigger exhibition area that takes the visitor to every part of the building, to a wide variety of gallery types in addition to the new outdoor 'rooms' of the courtyard.

114

Michael Moran

Michael Moran

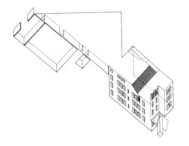
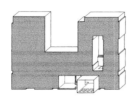

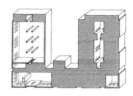
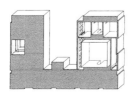

Top: view of the addition with the rear of the old school in the background;
Above: installation in the new gallery;
Left: projected sections showing the new gallery spaces.

Michael Moran

115

Above: raw gallery space carved out of the old building;
Left: external gallery spaces.

Michael Moran

FTL HAPPOLD ARCHITECTS

CARLOS MOSELEY PAVILION

Completely mobile, six custom semi-trailers carry the entire facility to any open performance site. Designed to be set up in six hours with minimal impact on the fragile park locations, this travelling music pavilion has no precedents. The trailers include a self-contained foundation for the pavilion and operable booms required for deployment of the facility. The pavilion's pyramidal open truss structure incorporates a translucent fabric shell, a 40 by 78 foot folding stage, computerised lighting system, video projection screen and a distributed sound system employing 24 wireless remote speakers.

The basic design approach to the project was to allow the engineering of the mechanism to dictate the forms and geometry of the structure. In order not to create arbitrary architectural compositions, it was desirable that the steelwork be permitted to express its essential character. This approach also held true for the fabric membrane in that it took its shape from the reflective acoustic requirements and the need to provide cover for the stage. The architectural poetry was to be found in the proportions and the relations of these elements to each other. Once realised, the design became a mixture of architecture, industrial design and engineering. It was completed in 1991.

Seven semi-trucks carry the entire facility to any open site. The centre trailer contains folding beams which open to provide the 40 by 78 foot structure for the stage. Hydraulic pistons unfold hinged panels which serve as the stage surface. In its final position, the stage rests upon the two front corner trailers and the two rear corner cabs, and the entire assembly is joined together to form one continuous rigid structure.

116

© Jeff Goldberg/Esto

Above: erection;
Top right: in performance;
Right: the structure in plan.

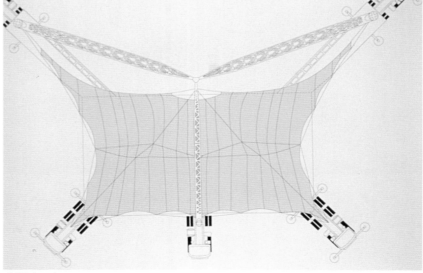

© FTL Associates

RICHARD GLUCKMAN
DIA ART FOUNDATION

This project, carried out in 1987, called for the conversion of a 45,000-square foot, four-storey industrial building into an art exhibition facility for extended installations. It is located at 548 West 22nd Street.

Each installation would last one to two years and changes would often occur within the exhibit during the stipulated presentation period. The challenge inherent in this project was to create an appropriate context for the art on display without compromising the basic, strongly articulated structural language of the building. The electrical grid had to be flexible to accommodate changing installations but also had to demonstrate a more permanent sense of detail.

The skeleton of the structure is deliberately more evident at the second floor, gradually becoming absorbed on the third floor while almost disappearing on the fourth to allow the space and light to become pre-eminent.

The structural order of the space is the primary architectural element. The paring down of details and finishes to a consistent but limited range ensures that the art is not overwhelmed by the space.

117

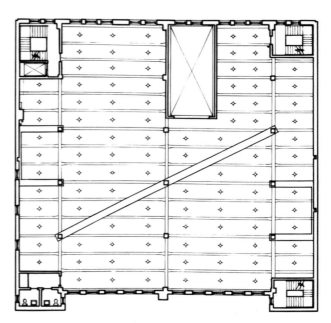

Top left and bottom: installations;
Above: essential floor plan.

RICHARD GLUCKMAN
SECOND STAGE THEATRE

The architectural programme developed by Rem Koolhaas of the Office for Metropolitan Architecture and Richard Gluckman for the renovation and conversion of the existing 17,000-square foot bank building includes a 297-seat performing arts theatre, stage fly, rehearsal space, dressing rooms and offices.

The design preserves the spatial character of the existing building while the insertion of new elements transforms the bank into the theatre. The placement of the new elements – a seating wedge, a control booth and a translucent wall – maintains the integrity of the space. The stage fly creates the ultimate flexibility.

The theatre is entered through the ground floor lobby where the theatre's box office occupies the existing bank vault. The second floor orchestra level remains virtually untouched, except for the insertion of a single wedge that performs the tasks necessary to turn the space into a theatre. It accommodates the seating, defines the lobby and stage, and contains the lavatories. A translucent plastic wall defines the balcony area and allows for the passage of the actors and the concealment of mechanical devices without dividing the space. At the stage, a removed section of the third floor allows for a fly space, increasing the available height of the stage to 43 feet. The third floor contains dressing rooms, wardrobe and column-free rehearsal space created by the removal of existing columns.

New materials set off the existing building. The design of the theatre seating combines simple wood chairs fitted with translucent gel cushions; the curtains, like the windows, allow views of the theatre.

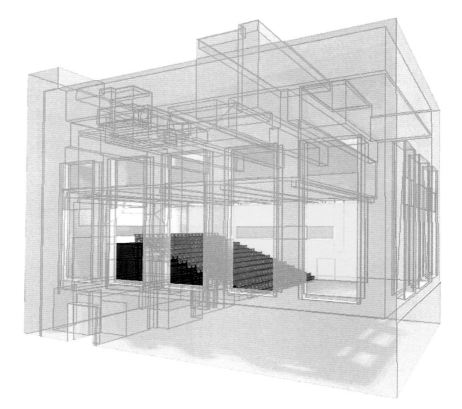

Left: computer rendering of the auditorium;
Top: lobby;
Bottom: computer-rendering showing the auditorium within the volume of the old bank building.

GWATHMEY SIEGEL
GUGGENHEIM

The renovation and addition to the Guggenheim Museum on Fifth Avenue at 89th Street contains 51,000 square feet of renovated gallery space, 15,000 square feet of office space, a restored theatre, a restaurant and retrofitted support and storage spaces. The 1992 addition refers directly to both the original Frank Lloyd Wright proposed annex of 1949-52, and the former William Wesley Peters annex which was originally designed as a 10-storey structure.

The concept for the addition was determined by its two critical intersections with the original building: with the rotunda at the existing circulation core, and with the monitor building along its east wall. At the triangular stair, the addition provides balcony views and access to the rotunda from three new two-storey galleries and one single-storey gallery. The transparent glass wall between the monitor building and the addition reveals the original facades from both the outside in and the inside out.

The pavilions are now integrated both functionally and spatially with the large rotunda as well as with the new addition. Outside, the new fifth-floor roof sculpture terrace, the large rotunda roof terrace, and the renovated public ramp reveal the original building in a new extended and comprehensive perspective. The entire original structure is now devoted to new exhibition space. Existing annex columns on the fifth floor were extended vertically to accommodate the addition.

Within the rotunda, numerous technical refinements have corrected omissions in the original construction and brought the building up to current museum standards, recapturing the quality of light evident in Wright's original design.

119

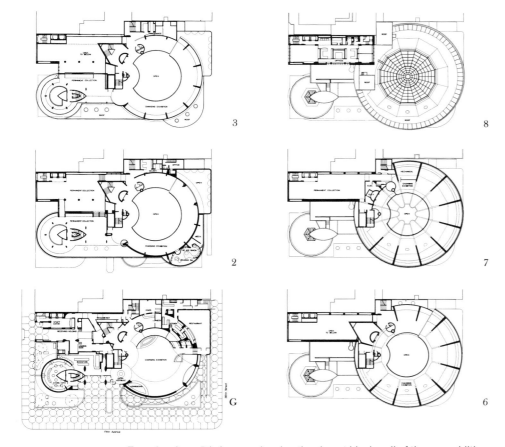

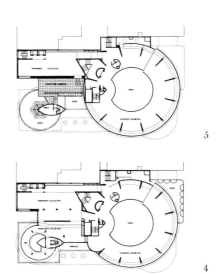

Top: view from 5th Avenue showing the almost blank wall of the new addition; Above: the renovated floor plans. The new addition is to the upper left of the Wright plan.

The climax of Wright's great ramp

© Whitney Cox

HARDY HOLTZMAN PFEIFFER ASSOCIATES
BROOKLYN ACADEMY OF MUSIC

Once a hub of Brooklyn's social and cultural life after it opened in 1861, the Brooklyn Academy of Music, at 30 Lafayette Avenue, has become New York's leading showcase for the *avant-garde*. In 1978 HHPA renovated the building and added a new rooftop rehearsal hall. The first phase of construction converted the Lepercq Space into the new BAMcafé. Once the ballroom and social scene of BAM, this grand open space has been returned to the public. Though located on the second floor, BAMcafé becomes primary lobby space through the addition of a new escalator linked to street level. Furniture and stage platforms within the room can be rearranged (or removed) to accommodate a variety of activities from gala parties, live music performances, lectures and dialogues to video presentations and casual dining. New steel arches inset with corrugated, perforated metal recall the original decorative plaster vaults. Silver-tipped light bulbs set along the red arches accentuate their openwork structure.

121

Then, the Helen Carey Playhouse was converted into a four-screen cinema. This design unites the building's existing ornate plaster proscenium arch and coffered ceiling with contemporary cinema seating and state-of-the-art sound and projection equipment. A harmonious fusion of new and historic elements is also apparent in the concession area, where sleek refreshment stands take their place between intricately patterned arched entry vaults and the elaborate wood detailing of the former inner lobby.

Renewal of the BAM public spaces is achieved in a contemporary vocabulary, by juxtaposing new with old and contrasting technological needs with the ornate details of this historic building.

Top: the Helen Carey Playhouse;
Left: BAMcafé.

© Whitney Cox

HARDY HOLTZMAN PFEIFFER ASSOCIATES

BROOKLYN ACADEMY OF MUSIC, MAJESTIC THEATER

Built in 1903 as a neighbourhood theatre, the 1,700-seat Majestic Theater had an active early life, at one point housing the Broadway try-outs for Gershwin musicals. The story of the building's construction, its use for movies and religious services, and its subsequent abandonment is traceable through its vividly hued layers of finishes.

By the time of HHPA's renovation in 1987, rainwater had reached its interior surfaces, creating a rich tapestry of colour and texture, which became a major element of the auditorium's design. To create a dramatic arena that suggests a Greek amphitheatre, the performance area was raised 5 feet and thrust 21 feet forward of the proscenium. The first balcony was extended towards the stage, and the second balcony was reduced to ensure good sightlines from all areas. The result is an intimate relationship between audience and performer. Both are now actually in the same room.

To ensure public comfort and safety, contemporary electrical and mechanical systems were introduced, and the air-conditioned interior meets every standard of the New York City building code. Erosion of the Majestic's interior now contributes to its performance environment. It taunts the senses with random juxtapositions brought about through the layering of time.

Above: the erosion seen across the auditorium;
Below: the proscenium.

HARDY HOLTZMAN PFEIFFER ASSOCIATES

NEW AMSTERDAM THEATER

Designed by Henry Herts and Hugh Tallant in 1903, the New Amsterdam was the first major Art Nouveau building in the US, celebrated as much for the luxury of its decor as for the size and sophistication of its stage facilities and large public spaces.

The theatre's decaying condition made its restoration a tremendous undertaking. There was extensive water damage to the plaster, wood and painted decoration as well as to the steel structure. Less than 50 per cent of the original decorative scheme was intact. A combination of paint analyses and historical documentation helped determine the theatre's original appearance. Special painting and glazing techniques ensured that elements would not look too new after restoration. Modern technology enabled custom, computer-generated designs of carpeting, seat coverings and stage curtains whose colours and textures were in keeping with the theatre's original decorative spirit.

The theatre's exuberant ornament, including decorative murals, terracotta balustrades, bas reliefs, carved and wood panelling were all recreated. Seating boxes which had been removed to accommodate a movie screen in the 1950s were reconstructed.

At the same time, amenities such as air conditioning, expanded lobby space on the mezzanine and balcony levels, men's and women's lounges and elevator access have been subtly added. Stage lighting, rigging, sound systems and all the technology required for modern performance have also been carefully and unobtrusively inserted. Now used for live performances by Walt Disney Theatrical Productions, the theatre has become an aesthetic pinnacle of 42nd Street's transformation.

123

Above: the restored auditorium;
Far right: the renovated section;
Right: the old New Amsterdam.

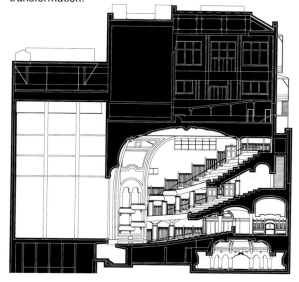

Above: the New Amsterdam, a key element in the renewal of 42nd Street;
Left: before restoration.

HARDY HOLTZMAN PFEIFFER ASSOCIATES
THE DANCE THEATRE OF HARLEM

In 1971 HHPA converted a two-storey parking garage at 466 West 152nd Street, into dance studios and administrative offices. The ballet school, founded only three years earlier had already attracted 400 students to the basement of a Harlem church where classes were held. By 1990, when HHPA was commissioned to design much needed additional space, the Dance Theatre of Harlem had become internationally known for both its accredited school of dance, attended by some 1,300 students, and its professional ballet company.

The project included the renovation of the original 15,000-square foot building and construction of a 13,000-square foot west addition. Consistent brick configurations and window treatments were used throughout visually to connect old and new. The converted garage now appears as one of a collage of elements that invigorate the whole. The addition's juxtaposition of dissimilar architectural forms and materials – red brick, multi-colour shingles set into a diamond pattern, and black and white bands of masonry – reflects the theatre's energy and venturous spirit, setting it apart from nearby tenements and municipal buildings.

Inside, the building comes to life with a palette of earth tones highlighted with intense colours, custom carpeting and terrazzo tile floors that mark circulation pathways. Abundant sunlight filters through skylights and windows placed at the property lines. Fluorescent lights are concealed by a variety of perforated metal enclosures.

The building's vigorous gestures, both inside and out, suggest the choreographic exploration and collaboration which takes place among students and teachers.

125

Above: the rich patterning of the brickwork in the new addition;
Right: rehearsal hall.

HARDY HOLTZMAN PFEIFFER ASSOCIATES

NEW VICTORY THEATER

The New Victory, the city's oldest surviving theatre, resonates with a distinguished and multi-layered history. It was the first theatre on the legendary block between Broadway and Eighth Avenue, when it opened in 1900 as Hammerstein's Theater Republic. Its restoration, the first undertaken by the New 42nd Street, transformed an abandoned landmark into the city's first non-profit performing arts institution dedicated to year-round programming for young audiences.

Hammerstein's Theater Republic awed critics with an elaborately decorated interior featuring a large, guilded dome rimmed with plaster angels. Two years after its opening, the theatre was renovated and renamed as David Belasco took ownership. It reverted to its original name in 1914, when Belasco left and changed again two decades later when Billy Minsky added his name. Each owner both added and eliminated decorative elements.

All existing elements of Hammerstein's facade and Belasco's interior have been restored with a separation of additional new public spaces. On the exterior, the reconstructed grand double stair is adorned with ornate standing globe lamps. Inside, on the main floor, a new public lobby welcomes patrons in space formerly part of the auditorium, which was condensed from 700 to 500 seats. Within the auditorium, detailed plaster and woodwork were meticulously restored, and elaborately stacked boxes, faux plaster draperies and gilded plasterwork were repaired and refinished. Belasco's bumblebee motif, found in the original plasterwork, now patterns wrought iron stanchions and upholstery. Sophisticated theatre equipment, an elevator and new HVAC systems were unobtrusively added to meet contemporary needs.

126

© Whitney Cox

Above: the restored facade;
Left: the New Victory as the first completed element in the rebuilding of 42nd Street.

© Whitney Cox

© Whitney Cox

Above: the restored auditorium;
Right: detail of the renewed metalwork
plaster and painting.

© Whitney Cox

HARDY HOLTZMAN PFEIFFER ASSOCIATES

RADIO CITY MUSIC HALL

Radio City, located on Avenue of the Americas between 50th and 51st Streets, houses some of New York's most awe-inspiring spaces. No other performance hall provides such a combination of history, grandeur and vast capacity.

To re-establish this landmark as one of the world's premier entertainment facilities, a major restoration and renewal of the Hall was undertaken, including the Grand Foyer, the Auditorium and its mezzanines, the Grand Lounge, and six mezzanine lounges for men and women. The glamour of the Hall was re-created using the bold patterns and finishes of the original carpeting, wall coverings and upholstery fabrics. Its murals were restored to their former brilliance and original Deskey furniture and light fixtures were refurbished and restored. Discovered only thorough extensive research of archival materials, much of its historic fabric has not been seen for decades.

Renewal of the Grand Foyer, one of the most elegant spaces in New York, included restoration of the three-storey high mural, *Fountain of Youth*, and re-creation of the decorative carpeting, featuring an abstract design of musical instruments, the original brocatelle wall covering, and dramatic gold-coloured ceiling. The Auditorium features new seating for nearly 6,000 people, replicating the original, a new silk house curtain recalling the original in colour and texture, and re-creation of the linen wall fabric to include its full pattern of singers, musical instruments and other images symbolic to Radio City.

Back-of-house areas and theatre technologies have also been improved. Some of the original stage machinery and technical systems remain in use, supplemented by new production lighting, sound systems and rigging.

128

© Whitney Cox

© Whitney Cox

Above: the entrance from 6th Avenue;
Left: the restored auditorium;
Opposite page: the Grand Foyer, with all surfaces renewed, carpets rewoven and the Ezra Winter mural restored.

MAYA LIN STUDIO
WITH DAVID HOTSON
MUSEUM FOR AFRICAN ART

The design of the museum as a path – an educational passage – is a journey in light and dark, and night and day, incorporating intuited, hand drawn shapes in the staircases that lead one through the museum. The museum, at 593 Broadway, is on two levels, the lower level accessible via a dark stairway, the upper level via a brightly painted staircase. The project was completed in 1993.

The cultural implications of removing a work from its original context and placing it in another culture's – perceiving some works as art and others as artefact, led to the design of the shop. In the shop's display of everyday African objects the artist wanted to show a deference to these objects. The shop is a series of discreet limited display niches which exhibit the crafts. Its display opens up completely only in the bookstore where books exclusively on Africa and African art and culture are sold as a way of further emphasising the educational purpose of the museum. Also a straight path through to the museum allows the visitor to avoid the shop if desired, emphasising once again the primary purpose of the museum.

130

Above: the shop with display niches;
Left: the brightly painted stair.

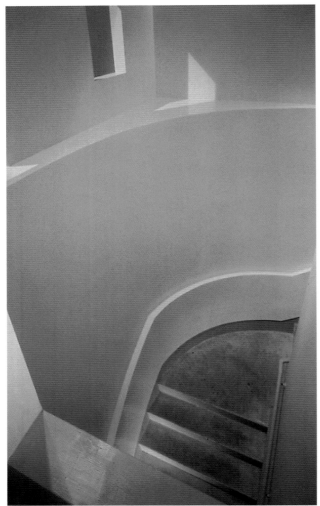

Paul Warchol

Dan Cornish

PLATT BYARD DOVELL ARCHITECTS
THE NEW 42ND STREET STUDIOS

This 10-storey, state-of-the-art rehearsal studio/theatre/and office complex rises on the site of the former Selwyn Office Building and an adjoining one-storey parcel.

The New 42nd Street Studios' intrinsic mission is to provide rehearsal space, a small flexible theatre and office space predominantly for non-profit arts organisations. The ground level incorporates a lobby entrance for the adjacent Selwyn Theater, a retail store and an entrance to the studios, offices and theatre. The 199-seat black-box theatre is located on the second floor and second floor mezzanine.

A total of 14 studios occupy five floors of the building. Each studio is column-free, with sprung floors and high ceilings. The studios offer audio-visual systems and are supplemented by dressing rooms and lounge facilities. The two studios located on the building's third floor provide areas for special events. Pragmatically designed office space occupies the building's remaining three floors.

While much of 42nd Street's redevelopment reflects the block's glorious past, the exterior design projects the excitement and promise of the future. The entire facade of The New 42nd Street Studios functions as a fluid, luminescent sculpture. Conceived as an innovative 'structure of light', the building's shimmering, ever-changing exterior reflects the artistic experimentation and vibrancy within its walls. A state-of-the-art system of multi-coloured lights floods the building at night. The final element of the design is the 175-feet spire of light rising from the west end of the building. Through its mission and architecture, The New 42nd Street Studios symbolises the principles guiding 42nd Street's revitalisation: to bring a dynamic mix of activities and people back to the street.

131

The 42nd Street facade as fluid luminescent sculpture

POLSHEK PARTNERSHIP ARCHITECTS

ROSE CENTER FOR EARTH AND SPACE AND HAYDEN PLANETARIUM AT THE AMERICAN MUSEUM OF NATURAL HISTORY

The primary design challenge in the completion of the north side of this historic complex on Central Park West was to redefine the image of a 128-year old institution for the 21st century while still respecting its architectural integrity. A logical sequence of exhibits unifies the new building with the museum and heightens the public's understanding of the importance of astronomy and its connection to the natural sciences. The central element of the plan is an illuminated sphere, nearly 90 feet in diameter, surrounded by a transparent cube of glass and steel, which evokes images of the rich local architectural tradition of the 1939 World's Fair. The iconic sphere contains a state-of-the-art planetarium and 'Big Bang' theatre, whose programme describes the origins of the universe. Other project elements are a new entrance to the museum, the Cullman Hall of the Universe, expanded restaurant and retail facilities, a new educational resource centre and parking facilities beneath the landscaped Ross Terrace.

132

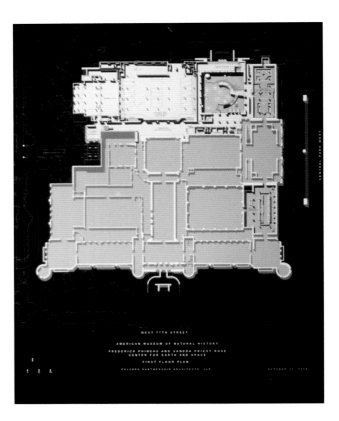

Above: computer rendering of the ramp to the planetarium;
Left: the plan showing both the historic museum and the new addition across the north end;
Opposite page: metal sphere and glass cube.

© Jeff Goldberg/Esto

134

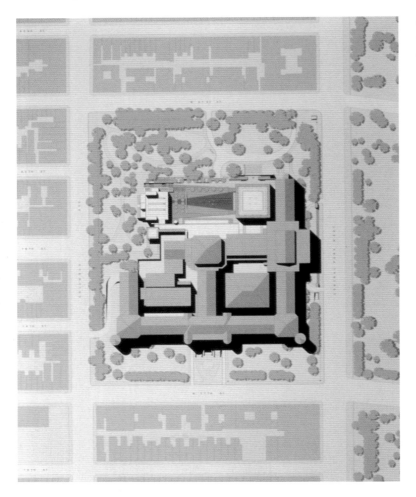

*Above and opposite page: the sphere in the cube against
Central Park and the New York skyline;
Left: the massing of the building old and new.*

© Jock Pottle/Esto

POLSHEK PARTNERSHIP ARCHITECTS
WITH ARATA ISOZAKI AND ASSOCIATES
BROOKLYN MUSEUM OF ART

The master plan for the addition of 320,000 square feet to the Brooklyn Museum of Art, on Eastern Parkway and Washington Avenue, and the renovation of the existing building was selected in an international competition in 1986. A new plaza, around which the new galleries, auditorium, education wing and restaurant facilities are arranged, contains outdoor performance spaces and exhibit areas overlooking the Brooklyn Botanic Garden. A basic principle of the scheme is the rationalisation of circulation, which separates services, scholars, individual visitors and educational groups. Further, the design solution re-establishes pedestrian connections to the adjacent, but presently inaccessible, Brooklyn Botanic Garden. A modern architectural vocabulary, defined by a flush limestone grid with sand-blasted stainless steel infill panels, unifies the unfinished rear facade of the existing building. Parking for 1,000 cars and all loading and art storage facilities are located under the new addition. The Brooklyn Museum of Art expansion and renovation balance the need for new technology – including ultra-sensitive temperature, humidity and filtration climate control systems, as well as extraordinary lighting and security requirements – with the equally demanding concerns for the preservation of this 100 year old McKim, Mead and White landmark.

136

Above: master plan showing the new plaza and galleries between the old museum and the Brooklyn Botanic Garden;
Left: model study for new galleries.

KEVIN ROCHE JOHN DINKELOO AND ASSOCIATES

THE METROPOLITAN MUSEUM OF ART

Master planning for the museum, which began in 1967, involved extensive review of existing considerations and the development of a comprehensive plan for its completion – galleries, curatorial and administrative spaces, work rooms and storage, together with circulation systems that would permit ready access to the many different collections. All this had to be done while respecting a magnificent existing structure and keeping the unaffected sections open for normal use.

The first phase was the redesign of the space in front of the museum's facade on Fifth Avenue, to create an urban plaza with appropriately scaled and terraced steps up to the entry into the restored Great Hall. This entry axis is reinforced by the addition of the Lehman Pavilion on the west side, with its skylighted court as a terminus.

The master plan responds to the need for large galleries by adding the Sackler Wing for the Temple of Dendur to the north and the Michael C Rockefeller Wing, with the Andre Meyer Galleries above, to the south. The adjacent corners are completed by the respective additions of the new American Wing and the Wallace Galleries for 20th century art. The areas between these wings and the existing museum are left as skylighted courts, or relief spaces. These afford the visitor a chance to rest from the intensity of gallery viewing. The new additions, completed in 1990, maintain the high ceilings characteristic of the Metropolitan, while the proportions of the galleries vary according to the works displayed, often with natural light from extensive skylights.

Above: the grand entrance on 5th Avenue. The staircase has become one of the great gathering places in the city; Below: the museum from the air showing the accumulation of additions within Central Park.

137

Above: the new American wing; Right: the Lila Acheson Wallace wing.

*Right: the department of Asian art;
Below: the Sackler wing and the
Temple of Dendur.*

Above: sky-lighted court or relief space on the south side; Right: the Lehman Pavilion.

The view looking north from the tip of Manhattan

KEVIN ROCHE JOHN DINKELOO AND ASSOCIATES
MUSEUM OF JEWISH HERITAGE

Located on a narrow, triangular site at the lower tip of Manhattan, this memorial commemorates the victims of the Holocaust and tells the story of the Jews before, during and after the Nazi persecution.

The Museum of Jewish Heritage is a simple, austere and dignified building that houses a powerful message. This hexagonal museum serves as a structural reminder of the six million Jews who perished during the Holocaust. In addition, its six sides embody the six pointed star of David that celebrates the Jewish people and culture that survived this terrible event.

Its facade of openings and recesses alerts the approaching visitor to the seriousness of the events that occurred. This effect is echoed over and over again in the roof. The roof elements reflect the daylight and at night will be illuminated so that all day and all night this reminder will be with us.

The structure of the museum is a physical symbol devoted to a deeper appreciation of Jewish heritage, an awareness of the Holocaust, and a heightened sense of the sanctity of human life.

141

Institutional Public

BEYER BLINDER BELLE ARCHITECTS

ELLIS ISLAND MUSEUM OF IMMIGRATION

One of the most significant symbols of American history, the Main Building at Ellis Island was restored and renovated in 1990 for use as the National Museum of Immigration. Considerable archival and on-site photographic, historic and archaeological research was undertaken by the design team. Uses of individual rooms over time were studied, documented and compared with analyses of the architectural significance of the spaces. The most important areas, both historically and architecturally, were faithfully restored. Other spaces were converted for modern needs, such as exhibition galleries, theatres, a genealogy library, a cafeteria and a gift shop.

Because some of the Main Building's most important architectural elements had been removed during earlier remodellings, replacements needed to be designed that would fit into the restored spaces but would not be perceived by visitors as pieces of the building's original fabric. An example of this is the famous stairway immigrants had to climb to reach the Registry Room. At the top of this entry stood medical examiners eyeing the recent arrivals for any signs of physical or mental impairment. The rigorous climb often betrayed infirmities and immigrants failing this '60-second medical exam' were marked for further inspections.

Unfortunately, the staircase was removed many years ago and no record remained of its design. To help visitors understand the immigrants' experience, it was imperative to create a new staircase. The architects' design for this stairway uses contemporary materials (stainless steel, reinforced concrete and granite) to capture the essence of the original, while clearly stating its modern construction.

142

© Peter Aaron/Esto

© Peter Aaron/Esto

© Norman McGraph/MetaForm

Top: the Registry Room;
Above: the main building with a new entrance arcade;
Left: exhibition in the National Museum of Immigration;
Opposite page (top): looking across Ellis Island to Manhattan and the Hudson;
Opposite page (bottom): the point of entry.

COOPER, ROBERTSON & PARTNERS
STUYVESANT HIGH SCHOOL

Completed in 1992, the Stuyvesant High School warranted the creation of a special identity appropriate to its status as one of the country's top public high schools. Located in Manhattan at the northern end of Battery Park City, at 345 Chambers Street, the new school replaces the structure built in 1904 on the Lower East Side. The small, 1.5-acre site required a vertical configuration of the 400,000 square feet necessary to fulfil the complex programmes which include a robotics lab, advanced science and computer facilities, a swimming pool and two gymnasia. A distinct urban solution to the more extended, campus-like model that is normally expected for large high schools, Stuyvesant is a 10-storey building connected by a sophisticated express escalator system. The priorities in terms of the users were to make the facility understandable, to create a proper sense of orientation, to allow efficient movement between classrooms, and to provide distinctive views and establish a sense of identity for each of the departments and all of the major spaces.

The design strategy was the alternate use of warm colours on odd numbered floors and cool colours on even floors. Each floor of the school is marked by a set of 'front doors' which helps identify the department or facilities located there and serves as an introduction to the stairway leading to the corridors and classrooms. Each entry has its own distinctive floor pattern which acts as the major clue to the perception of a particular floor or hallway.

Above: the school with the World Trade and World Financial Centers in the background; Right: view from West Street Riverside Drive showing bridge to the city on the left; Below: isometric projection from the north.

144

© Jeff Goldberg/Esto

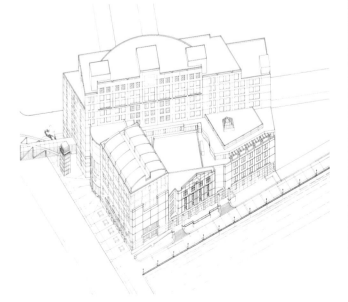

© Peter Mauss/Esto

CHARLES CORREA
WITH BOND RYDER AND ASSOCIATES
THE PERMANENT MISSION OF INDIA TO THE UNITED NATIONS

This building houses the Chancery of the Indian government, as well as living quarters for mission employees. It was designed by Charles Correa, a leading architect in India, and Bond Ryder and Associates served as the architect of record, coordinating the work of a full architectural and engineering team located in India and New York City. Bond Ryder assumed leadership of the project after the completion of schematic design, while continuing to work with the design team in India until the completion of construction in 1993.

The lower four floors of administrative offices form the base of the 21-storey residential tower, which also includes a recreational floor for tenants and employees. The 66,000-square foot building is set on a narrow through-block lot that is 42 feet wide on the 43rd Street side, and only 24 feet wide on the 44th Street side.

The base of the tower is clad in red granite with large cut-outs forming terraces for the workers on those floors. The canyon-red aluminium curtain wall on a reinforced concrete structure was selected to blend with the red granite base, as well as to echo the red sandstone architecture of northern India.

145

The entrance with an aura of Northern India

146

Hidden view from behind the street showing an unusually elegant orchestration of the building volume

DAVIS BRODY BOND
NEW YORK PUBLIC LIBRARY

In 1982, the New York Public Library realised it had reached a critical point at its landmarked main research library on 42nd Street. Its librarians needed solutions for a multitude of facility problems. The 1911 building was showing signs of age and the library was short of space; offices and support spaces had taken over once public rooms, while other grand spaces were used for storage; mechanical systems were inadequate; information technologies were unavailable in the existing space; and major segments of its collections had been shipped off-site to an annex where access was restricted.

These problems were approached by proposing a multi-phased master plan which would return the grand spaces of the building to the public, while creating state-of-the-art environmental and information retrieval systems for the collections.

With the relocation of its science, industry and business collections to a new site in 1996, the library was renamed as the Center for the Humanities. As part of its new identity, the library wanted to introduce new facilities and upgrade existing ones.

Among the projects underway are the restoration of the five-storey main reading room, the creation of the Cullman Center for Scholars and Writers, and the relocation of the Wallach Division Art and Architecture Collection. This project made possible the preservation of one of New York City's most beloved spaces, restoring it to its original glory, while at the same time optimising access to the collections it serves and introducing the infrastructure to provide the latest in electronic, online services.

147

Above: the Deborah, FP Samuel Priest and Raphael Rose main reading room;
Right: looking into the reading room at night;
Opposite page: the carved wooden gate the Reading Room.

EHRENKRANTZ ECKSTUT & KUHN ARCHITECTS
ALEXANDER HAMILTON US CUSTOM HOUSE

EE&K Architects was responsible for the complete restoration and adaptive reuse of the nationally landmarked Alexander Hamilton US Custom House, designed in 1900 by Cass Gilbert. This major undertaking involved the upgrade and repair of all mechanical and electrical systems, fire safety alterations, interior lighting design, space planning, and office layout and design as well as the conservation of interior artwork and the restoration of exterior stonework and sculptures.

The fine arts restoration of the Custom House included the treatment and restoration of interior marbles, decorative metals and paintings, and Reginald Marsh's rotunda murals. The result is a beautifully reconditioned interior which does not appear new or over-restored.

The Smithsonian Institution's National Museum of the American Indian within the Custom House includes approximately 19,000 square feet of exhibition space, a state-of-the-art 345-seat auditorium, a museum shop, staff and support offices, a resource centre and exhibit support space. The exhibition space required a special air quality control system to monitor the temperature and humidity in the air to preserve organic materials contained in the exhibit artefacts. Natural wool carpeting, waxed ash wood panelling and Winona Travertine stone from Minnesota were used to create an environment sensitive to the cultural objects displayed.

The US Federal Bankruptcy Court, also within the Custom House, is an elegant installation of a modern courthouse into a significant historic building. The courtrooms are finished in the stone and hardwoods appropriate for a federal court. In addition, it boasts a state-of-the-art security system built into the courts with no adverse impact on the historic character of the building.

149

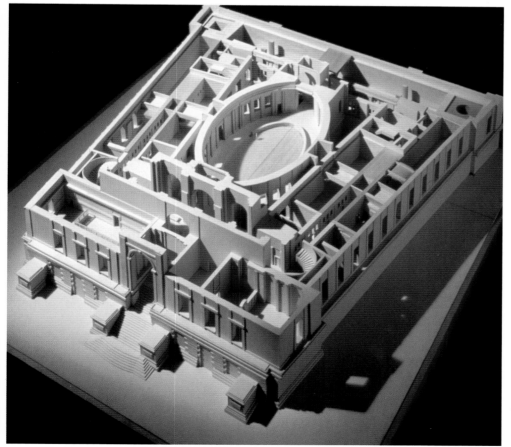

Top: the Rotunda;
Bottom: study of the complex reorganisation of the internal spaces.

ELLERBE BECKET ARCHITECTS
NEW YORK PSYCHIATRIC INSTITUTE

Gil Amiaga

*Above: aerial view form the west showing
the bridges to the main hospital;
Below: view past the ramp to the George Washington Bridge.*

This project replaces the New York State Psychiatric Institute's outdated facilities on Manhattan's Upper West Side (1051 Riverside Drive). The site's shape, location and topography contributed to the internal planning of the building. Slated to contain a mix of in-patient and out-patient treatment and research facilities, laboratories, administrative and teaching spaces, the building plan had to undergo extensive review by the state and the surrounding community. A number of concerns had to be addressed in the design of the building: strict limitations on building height (limited to six storeys), and restrictions on the size and configuration of the proposed bridges.

The east face of the building is more solid, with precast concrete and metal panels enclosing its orthogonal mass. The west face stands in dramatic contrast. The views from this side are spectacular with unobstructed panoramas on to the Hudson River.

Patient care areas were placed nearest the Milstein Pavilion on the north side to facilitate patient movement, while laboratory spaces were placed nearest the Kolb Annex, also on the north. At the juncture of these two areas, a dramatic six-storey tall atrium was created at the intersection of the building's geometries. One of the greatest difficulties of the project was posed by the patient room windows which had to meet the required safety standards. The building is also confronted with dynamic wind and environmental conditions. These elements, as well as the presence of two major highways, had a significant impact on the design and influenced the location of air intakes, fume hood and generator exhausts and curtainwall design. Intakes were positioned high on the west face while exhaust locations were carefully studied to ensure that no cross-contamination would occur.

© Peter Aaron/Esto

Clockwise from left: the atrium from the outside and the bridge; Milstein Pavilion views from within the atrium.

MICHAEL FIELDMAN ARCHITECTS

ROOSEVELT ISLAND SCHOOL, PS/IS 217

Completed in 1993, this school centres on the formation of social and abstract values where the physical environment contributes directly to that process. Its numerous parts continually open on to each other, linking the younger with the older students and linking both groups to the adult world outside.

By infusing the spaces and building forms with meaning, the interaction of the users with these forms can establish significant identity and affection in the children for their school. A subtle though real objective is to enrich the design so that the children take possession of their surroundings. Each part has validity and relates in a meaningful way to all other parts. A generous circulation system filled with natural light brings vitality to the whole; it is interesting, lively and fun. The building's structure is exposed so it can be easily understood. Materials are left in their natural state to further an appreciation of their intrinsic value.

The school entrance is a generous intersection for parents, children and teachers where welcomings and farewells take place. In the kindergarten area, the space is scaled both in building plan and section for very young children. Small windows are deliberately kept low to the floor, miniature bay windows with 4 foot 9 inch ceilings creating 'cosy nooks' off limits to adults. The articulation of the colourful house-like forms along the corridor's curving length creates a child's townscape. The concrete columns become decorated street trees, the enormous central bay window becomes the village square. Similarly throughout the school, the building's architecture has the opportunity actually to expand a child's education.

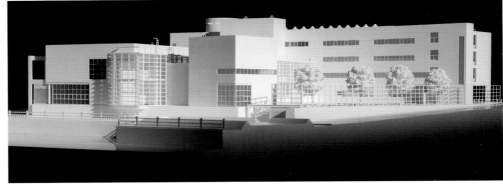

Top: the view from the East River;
Above: study model;
Below: view towards Manhattan from the central hall.

ELLERBE BECKET & MICHAEL FIELDMAN

NEW YORK CITY POLICE TRAINING ACADEMY

Dan Cornish

With a total programme area of 969,000 square feet and the orderly organisation of a compact footprint that rises above its plinth, the 8-storey academic and training facility is a state-of-the-art structure. It was completed in 1998, and is situated in the Bronx.

To establish clear and concise definition to the various elements within the programme, the building's form and architecture are expressed as volumetric distinctions between programme components. In their sequences and compositional definitions, the components are: entry/lobby/atrium; academic block; administrative block; physical education block; Muster Deck assembly unit; and outdoor track and par course. The six components are arranged and stratified in a way which strengthens functional and operational adjacencies to minimise extensive walking. On a more intimate level, spaces are clustered as cohesive units tied directly to the differentiation between academic and fitness programme requirements.

The building contributes to the revitalisation of the training programmes through an innovative design that is dignified, enduring and an inspiring symbol. It is intended to heighten the seriousness of law enforcement with a facility that supports greater involvement with the city, public life and safety.

153

Above: study model;
Below: computer model;
Right: computer rendering of the central atrium.

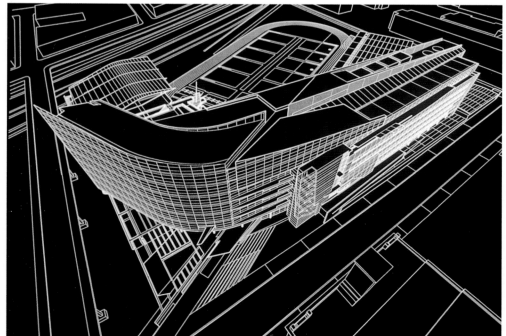

HANRAHAN + MEYERS

LATIMER GARDENS COMMUNITY CENTER

© Jock Pottle/Esto

154

Latimer Gardens Community Center is located on 137th Street in Flushing, Queens and is part of a complex of four high-rise housing blocks owned and managed by the New York City Housing Authority. The Community Center is very active and hosts programmes that serve all age groups in the community. Hanrahan + Meyers were hired to design a 5,000 square foot multi-purpose gymnasium/theatre adjacent to the existing 8,000 square foot centre, which they are also renovating. The project is due for completion in 2001.

The new multi-purpose structure places an additional building south and west of the existing Community Center. Within the restricted zoning envelope of 85 feet by 49 feet, the architects designed a structure which is as large as possible to accommodate sports, as well as future theatrical productions. In order to accommodate theatre further, a removable stage has been designed to fit one end of the new addition. There is also theatrical lighting located above a removable stage area at the western edge of the space, and lights in the main space are on a dimmer system.

The roof, the principal design feature of the new building, is a reflective bent plane running east-west and resting on columns at either end of the space. It will be visible to the ten-storey housing blocks surrounding it and was designed as a sculptural shape with standing seam stainless-steel cladding. The reflecting pool adjacent to the building, which passes under the entrance sidewalk and appears as a depression in the ground on the side of the entrance across from the building, is an extension of this surface. The roof folds down to create the building's west elevation.

The new multi-purpose space is entered from the existing Community Center. A new entrance on the existing Center's south elevation leads to a new lobby, adjacent to the addition.

© Jock Pottle/Esto

HANRAHAN + MEYERS
RED HOOK COMMUNITY CENTER

This project, completed in September 2000, is a redesign and reprogramming of an existing community centre in Brooklyn which includes two additions to the existing building: a new entrance pavilion on the street side of the building and a new outdoor theatre at the rear. The lower lever of the Community Center is home to an alternative high school programme, and the redesign of the building also includes the incorporation of new windows into this lower level.

The project has been sub-titled 'Open Corner: Lines of Light' by the architects. 'Open Corner' refers to a strategy for creating a new entrance building which literally 'opens' Red Hook Community Center to the rest of Brooklyn. 'Lines of Light' articulates the sense in which the new Center was designed as a series of prosceniums through the site, with an outdoor theatre at its southern edge.

The street facade of the new pavilion is aluminium frame with glass in-fill. A large rectangular punch acts as a window within the glass curtain wall through which the Community Center communicates with the larger community of Brooklyn to the north. This window is a 'proscenium' for the infiltration of light and communication. A second proscenium crosses through the pavilion at the threshold between the new and existing building. This second 'line of light' brings reflected daylight into a new neighbourhood gallery. At the edge of the gallery a plane floats between the upper and lower floors. This is a cast glass mural wall designed as a plane of transparency and reflection for the new and future residents of Red Hook. The next proscenium marks the edge between the stage and the outdoor seating area. This creates a new facade that opens the building to Red Hook Houses, where most of the patrons of the new Community Center live.

'Lines of Light' is a means of establishing a new order of social interaction in Red Hook. This is accomplished through programming, space, and the inscription of lines of light into the Community Center site. A language of light permeates a darkened 19th-century housing complex, and through light and enlightenment a new sense of hope, desire and optimism about the future brings the 21st century to Red Hook today.

HELLMUTH, OBATA + KASSABAUM

FEDERAL OFFICE BUILDING AT FOLEY SQUARE

Located directly north of City Hall, Foley Square has long served as the civic heart of the city. The expansion of this government complex in 1995 constituted the first major change in the area since the early 1970s. The design integrates the classic, dignified tradition of American federal architecture with contemporary aesthetics for high-rise architecture in a dense, urban area. The tower, buff-coloured granite with decorative banding, is capped by an illuminated, barrel-vaulted roof. The tower base was sculpted to introduce streetwalls and setbacks compatible with, and respectful of, the adjacent Sun building. Pedestrian, subway and vehicular linkages in and around the site were incorporated into the design.

The original design included a 25,000-square foot pavilion connected to the main building which was to house day care facilities and an auditorium, extend the public arcade and accommodate 55,000 square feet of parking below. The design, however, had to be modified upon discovery of an African-American burial ground.

The Internal Revenue Service offices, located on five floors, provide 135,000 square feet of office space, IRS training floors, conference facilities, a criminal investigation division and support areas. The US Attorney Office encompasses 165,000 square feet of space on seven floors and houses executive office suites, private and open office space, a library and conference facilities serving both the civil and criminal divisions.

Sophisticated security requirements, including a secured lobby with state-of-the-art detection devices, and an interconnecting staircase are among the project's special features.

© Jeff Goldberg/Esto

Above: the crown in the form of a temple;
Below: the view from Foley Square showing the building up to the crown;

© Jeff Goldberg/Esto

RM KLIMENT & FRANCES HALSBAND ARCHITECTS
RENOVATION OF THE US POST OFFICE & COURTHOUSE, BROOKLYN

The building provides renovated and new space for the US Bankruptcy Courts, the US Attorney and the US Postal Service. The original building was completed in 1892 to house federal courts and a general post office. An extension in matching style was built in 1933, and the renovation was carried out in 1998.

A monumental flight of steps, scaled to the existing building, connects the entrances to the street. A new 45,000-square foot mezzanine is constructed over the first floor of the 1933 extension. Added on each of the upper four floors are 10,000 square feet to provide efficient office space and to form a courtyard that opens south to the 1892 building and to the Brooklyn Borough Hall beyond. A new skylight and a new laylight in the atrium of the 1892 building replace the originals which have been destroyed.

The US Bankruptcy Courts occupy the entire 1892 building. Four new courtrooms are added on the second and third floors of the 1933 building. The US Attorney offices occupy floors two through eight in the 1933 building, including the area of the addition. The US Postal Service occupies the existing loading platform at ground level, as well as the first floor of the 1933 building and the new mezzanine.

The exterior of the 1892 and 1933 buildings is cleaned and restored. In the interior of the older building, the original wood and marble are cleaned and restored, and the paint colours and decorative patterns replicated. The renovation and additions are designed to reinstate the building as a significant formal and functional presence in the civic life of Brooklyn.

157

Top: presentation drawing of the proposed renovation. Note the rationally ordered office court inserted to the left; Above: computer rendering of the renewed atrium to the 1892 building.

KOHN PEDERSEN FOX

BARUCH COLLEGE NEW ACADEMIC COMPLEX

The heart of this building is a great central room which twists and steps vertically to the roof. This room connects three dominant pieces of the building: the business school, the school of science, literature and arts, and the shared social amenities. Symbolic of the Baruch community, it is a vertical interpretation of the traditional college quadrangle.

The building occupies almost a full block between 24th Street and 25th Street along Lexington Avenue. The New York City zoning code for this district established the parameters for the building's form.

158

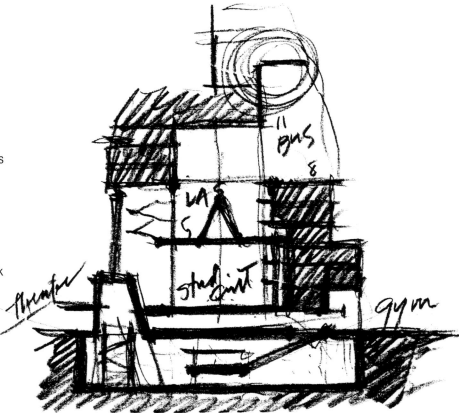

Right: architects conceptual drawing;
Below: model of the project in context.

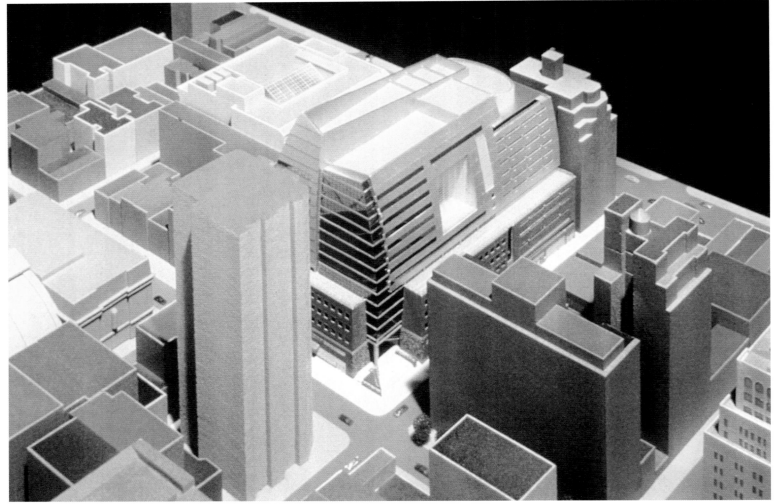

© Jock Pottle/Esto

*Left: computer study of the view
from Lexington Avenue;
Below left: the first floor plan;
Below: the lateral section; compare
with the architects' sketch.*

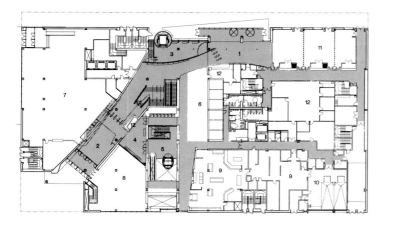

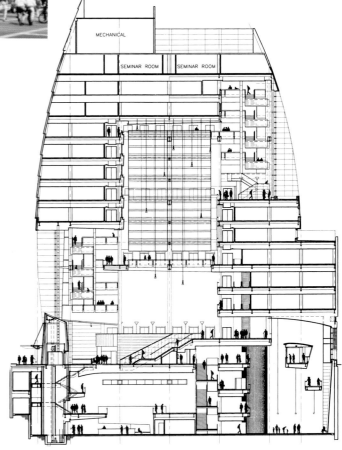

KOHN PEDERSEN FOX

FOLEY SQUARE COURTHOUSE

The highly sensitive site is sandwiched between the residential communities of Chinatown and Little Italy and the Foley Square civic precinct. The solution's basic geometry is dictated by its internal biology. The four clustered courtrooms prescribed a particular shape and required access to three separate systems of circulation. The T-shaped site allowed two basic massings to emerge: the 27-storey tower housing the courtrooms and chambers faces the Foley Square precinct, while the 9-storey wing, housing the support agencies, faces the residential community.

In the company of buildings by Cass Gilbert, Guy Lowell, and McKim Mead and White, this project borrows their colour palette and the spirit of their details. In spite of its large size, a very intimate pedestrian-scale public plaza was created adjacent to the 1903 Guy Lowell Courthouse. Since its completion in 1995, the plaza has been recognised as one of the most successful new urban spaces in New York City and incorporates the Maya Lin sculpture, *Sounding Stones*.

160

Above: the new yet unchanging theatre of the law.

MAYA LIN STUDIO
WITH DAVID HOTSON
ASIA PACIFIC NYU CENTER

Maya Lin Studio

This design plays with daylight, shifting or sharing the light throughout the public and private spaces. Light is sifted through book shelves in the outer offices which are backed with frosted glass. The resulting patterns of shadow and light can be seen from inside the central main gallery. The design also allows for maximum flexibility of space through the use of sliding panel doors hidden in the walls. The doors can open up or close off spaces, thus accentuating a feeling of continuous movement.

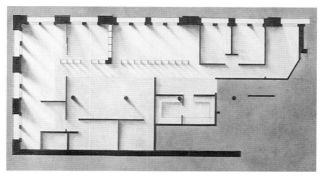

*Top and left: translucent wall;
Above: plan.*

OHLHAUSEN DUBOIS ARCHITECTS
RESTORATION OF THE NEW SCHOOL FOR SOCIAL RESEARCH

Built in 1929-30, the New School for Social Research was designed by Viennese architect, scenic designer and decorative artist Joseph Urban. The building was a herald of the emerging influence of vanguard European Modernism on American architecture of the late 1920s, and is widely recognised as an important precursor of the International Style in New York. Urban's pioneering work in theatre design and his notable contribution as an architect were brought together in this commission. The auditorium, in particular, is both an architectural masterpiece and a skilful example of innovative theatre planning, and was restored by Ohlhausen Dubois Architects in 1995.

In its abstraction of form and all-enveloping design, the auditorium of the New School has been compared to the Expressionist work of Hans Poelzig. The 550-seat, egg-shaped New School auditorium was conceived to minimise the separation between audience and stage by linking the sides of the room into one curving form, by providing a low, rounded stage platform, and by adding stage extensions with open niches. Urban resolved technical challenges in the scheme by designing a suspended, perforated plaster ceiling that produces acoustical conditions similar to those of an open-air theatre. The dramatic space is illuminated by lights concealed in the concentric rings of the vault. At the rear of the space are two upper-level balconies wedged into the curving form, and the Cubist openings of the projection booth.

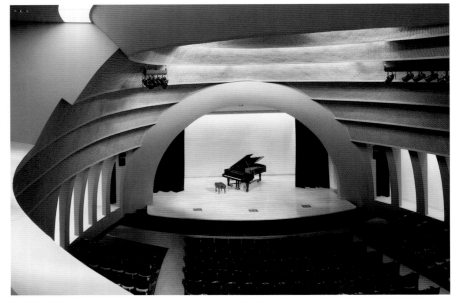

Above: perforated plaster ceiling;
Left: the auditorium.

© Paul Warchol

PEI COBB FREED & PARTNERS

GUGGENHEIM PAVILION MOUNT SINAI MEDICAL CENTER

The new Guggenheim Pavilion was undertaken as the first step in a massive reconstruction and renovation programme to meet Mount Sinai's goal of becoming one of the top academic medical centres in the US. In 1992, a major new building at the northern edge of the campus (Fifth to Madison Avenues and East 98th to 102nd Streets) was erected, in which related departments could be grouped together and the hospital as a whole be made more flexible to accommodate current and future needs. The Guggenheim Pavilion gathers together 625 medical/surgical and intensive care unit beds and incorporates the emergency room, nuclear and rehabilitation medicine, administrative offices and the hospital kitchen and cafeteria, all transferred from remote and outmoded facilities. In addition, it houses new programme elements such as state-of-the-art operating rooms, a conference centre, a chapel, a synagogue and, for the first time, a main hospital lobby.

163

The 11-storey pavilion rises from a rectangular base that locates public spaces and services for easy access from the street, while accommodating major medical areas on large floor plates for maximum flexibility. Patient areas, by contrast, are housed in three linked towers raised atop the base away from the city bustle and angled to maximise perimeter surface.

Of all the challenges confronted, the greatest was circulation. The new building separates incompatible traffic both horizontally and vertically. Public corridors in the patient towers allow staff and visitors to move freely without encountering carts and stretchers, as service traffic is supported by an independent network of dedicated elevators and passages. Circulation is further enhanced by bridges, stairs and elevators that separate medical and materials traffic from the general public.

Above: main hospital lobby;
Right: new complex, centre right.

© Jeff Goldberg/Esto

POLSHEK PARTNERSHIP ARCHITECTS
QUEENS BOROUGH PUBLIC LIBRARY

Located in a vibrant multilingual, multicultural neighbourhood, this 76,000-square foot, four-storey public library is the largest branch of the Queens Borough Public Library, which has the largest circulation of any system in the country. Its design emphasises the asymmetrical qualities of its triangular site, which results from the intersection of two main thoroughfares. Unlike the vault-like and often impenetrable character of some public libraries, transparency is employed as a metaphor for accessibility: the architecture is intended to demystify the library experience by making the facility's collections and functional organisation visually accessible from the street. The public facade on Main Street is a glass membrane. The Kissena Boulevard facade is rendered with articulated stone, its design alluding to the book stacks within and its opacity allowing perimeter shelving to be maximised and affording privacy to both staff and neighbours.

As part of the New York 'Percent for Art' programme, public art is integral to the architecture and is intended to enhance the building's accessibility to its many and varied users. From inside the entry at the apex of the building, the anatomy of the centralised free-plan layout is repeated floor by floor, and connected by a stair and elevator core just inside the exterior glass wall. Reading areas are arranged along the south side, while stack areas occupy the north and east walls. At the lower level is the 227-seat auditorium, a multi-purpose room for 150, conference rooms, exhibition areas and the Adult Learning Center. The International Resource Center, which occupies the top floor, houses the extensive foreign language collections and provides flexible exhibition space.

164

© Jeff Goldberg/Esto

Above: the junction of Main Street and Kissena Boulevard;
Left: integration of public art;
Opposite page: reading areas.

At the junction of Main Street and Kissena Boulevard

© Jeff Goldberg/Esto

The view from Main Street

BERNARD TSCHUMI ARCHITECTS

LERNER HALL STUDENT CENTER

The student centre at Columbia University contains lounges, meeting rooms, a bookstore, a 1,500-seat assembly hall, dining and kitchen facilities, a radio station, student club and games rooms, a night club, administrative spaces, a theatre and 6,000 mailboxes as well as expanded computer facilities for student use.

The two principal wings, which face Broadway and the campus, remain faithful to the massing of the master plan by McKim, Mead and White and the materials of the existing campus, which are primarily brick and granite. The student centre translates the exterior public courtyard which the McKim, Mead and White plan had intended to place between these wings into a linked series of enclosed spaces for the public elements of programmes. These spaces include the main multi-functional student lounge and the theatre. To tie all of these programmes into the activity of the central campus, they are separated from campus only by a glass wall that stretches between the two wings.

The building interior accommodates the needs of student life at a contemporary university. Located directly behind the glass curtainwall, the Hub is the student centre's main space of social and circulatory exchange. It is comprised of a dual system of opposed ramps that link the split-level wings into a continuous circuit, thereby joining traditionally disassociated floors and activities into a space of fluid communication. During the day the light filters through the suspended glass ramps. At night, as light glows from the inside, figures in movement along this route appear as if in a silent shadow theatre.

© Peter Aaron/Esto

Below: the Hub and its dual system of opposed ramps;
Opposite page (top): the view from Broadway is consistent with the
mass and character of the McKim, Mead and White master plan;
Opposite page (bottom): night view of the Hub from the campus.

© Peter Aaron/Esto

Opposite page: the Hub;
Below and lower left: Tschumi's conceptual drawings of the
social and circulatory exchange;
Below right: the view out to the campus from the Hub.

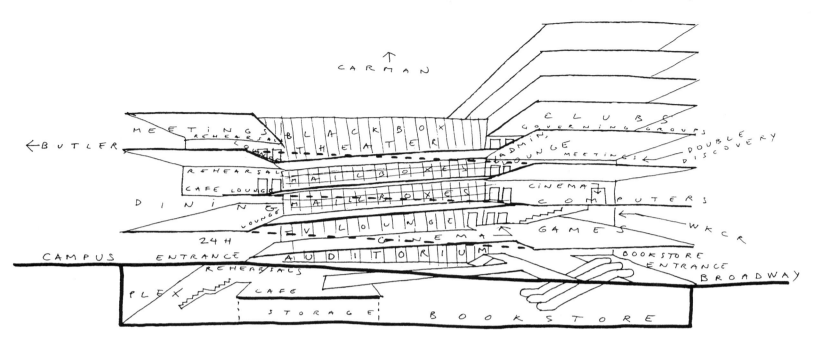

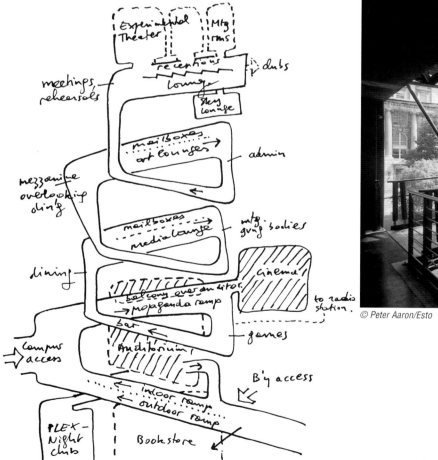

© Peter Aaron/Esto

8/94

TOD WILLIAMS BILLIE TSIEN & ASSOCIATES

MUSEUM OF AMERICAN FOLK ART

Located on 53rd Street, this new eight-level building devotes the four upper floors to gallery space for permanent and temporary exhibitions. The museum is capped by a skylight above a grand interior stair with openings at each floor allowing natural light to filter into the galleries and through to the lower levels. Art will be integrated into public spaces, utilising a series of niches throughout the building that offer informal interaction with a changing series of folk art objects. The experience of the museum visitor will be an architectural journey, encouraging novel encounters with both new and familiar objects by using multiple and sometimes redundant paths of circulation. The museum's collections and exhibitions are presented through both straightforward and non-traditional display spaces, creating a comfortable environment for adults and children, frequent and first-time visitors alike. The building also incorporates a number of additional facilities. The mezzanine level, with a view out to 53rd Street, houses a small coffee bar and looks back over the main hallway with a dramatic view of a two-storey atrium. The building extends two levels underground: one floor holds the new auditorium and classroom facilities, while the lowest level houses museum offices, a library and archive. At the entrance level there is a museum store, with access during non-museum hours via a separate exit to the street. The facade of this building is designed to make a strong but quiet statement of independence. It is sculptural in form, recalling an abstracted open hand.

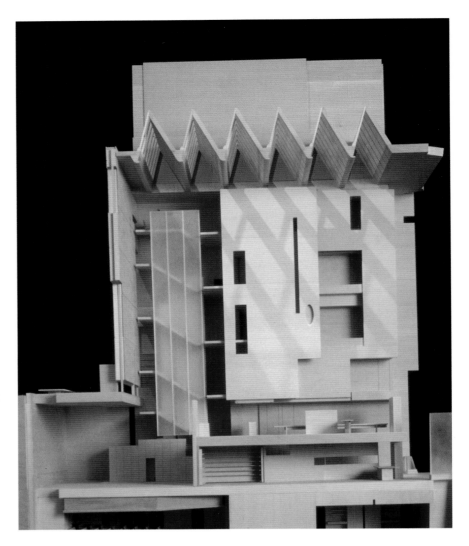

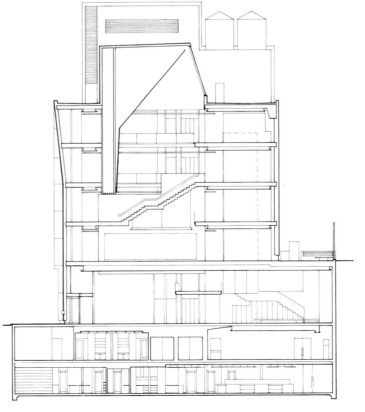

Above: the view from 53rd Street;
Above right: development model and section.

Atmospheric photomontage of the work in context

© Jeff Goldberg/Esto

RAFAEL VIÑOLY ARCHITECTS
THE BRONX HOUSING COURTHOUSE

The Bronx Housing Courthouse is located on a narrow, mid-block lot in the newly designated Special Grand Concourse Preservation District. The programme includes 13 courtrooms, offices for the clerk and the court, ancillary agencies and judges' chambers. The Courthouse exemplifies the integration of a modern structure with a large and complex programme into an urban context with a very prominent and distinctive character.

Along the Grand Concourse, there are several buildings of civic importance. The new Courthouse, completed in 1997, participates in a dialogue with these, as well as responding to the geometry and volumetric configurations of the immediately adjacent buildings. The Courthouse also respectfully adapts to the street wall height of its residential neighbour to the south. The building is clad in sandstone and roman brick on concrete masonry unit backup. Aluminium and glass curtainwall is used to create monumental openings into the public areas or to clad special functional elements.

The first five storeys vertically organise the courtrooms and public areas of the Courthouse. The tower portion of the building, containing the private functions of the court and the judges' chambers, is set back from the construction line to align with its freestanding institutional neighbour to the north. The volume containing the judges' library is canted so as to be visible when crossing the Harlem River from Manhattan into the Bronx.

© Jeff Goldberg/Esto

© Jeff Goldberg/Esto

GREG LYNN, DOUGLAS GAROFALO & MICHAEL MCINTURF

KOREAN PRESBYTERIAN CHURCH OF NEW YORK

The existing building, originally the Knickerbocker Laundry Factory, was built in 1932 in Sunnyside, Queens. The architectural approach to the re-use of the factory as a church was to retain the industrial vocabulary of the existing site and transform its interior spaces and exterior massing into a new kind of religious building. The conversion and additions were completed in 1998.

In the Korean Presbyterian Church, the traditional programme has mutated to provide a whole constellation of cultural programmes in addition to religious services. The church becomes a much larger and more complex, self-contained urban entity which simultaneously opens itself to the city seven days a week as a public institution. The new church seats 2,500 people in the main sanctuary addition to the roof of the existing building. Space is provided for 80 classrooms for school and various social groups, a wedding chapel, four multi-purpose assembly spaces, a choir rehearsal space, a cafeteria with kitchen, the reverend's apartment, parking for 350 cars and an on-site guardhouse.

The construction materials employed for the new additions are relatively unconventional with respect to church typology. The approach, given the extremely tight budget constraints, was to choose the materials and building systems that would provide the most flexibility for each of the four main building morphologies. The main sanctuary is a continuation of the louvered shell system that surrounds the exterior fire stair. Each exterior shell splits into two shells on the interior and these are made up of light-gage metal framing and clad in painted drywall, all of which is suspended from the long-span trusses above. The main altar area is finished with aniline-dyed veneer plywood wall panels and flooring.

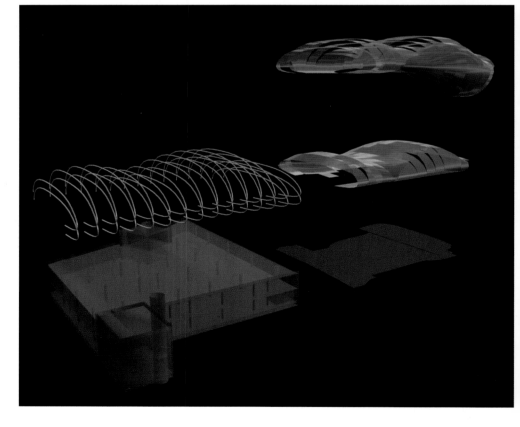

Above: louvered shells system around the exterior fire stair;
Right: early computer studies of forms of enclosure to go over the existing industrial building.

Left and below: computer models of the exterior and interior of the Presbyterian Church.

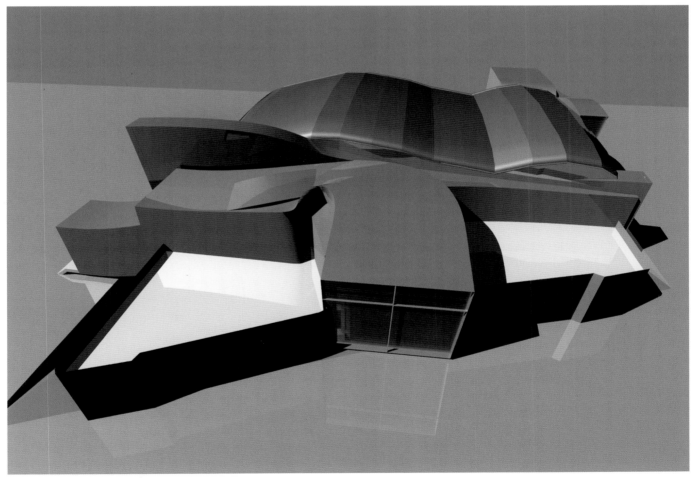

The main sanctuary

Top: long section showing the wave-like ceiling of the sanctuary;
Above and left: views looking out and within the louvered shells.

SKIDMORE, OWINGS & MERRILL

THE ISLAMIC CULTURAL CENTER

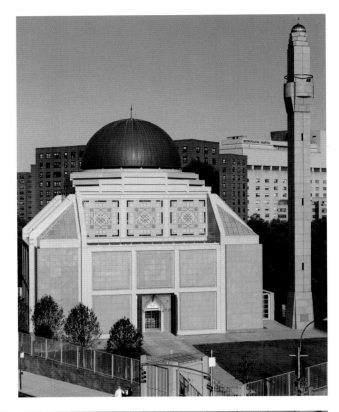

Located on a dense urban site (1711 Third Avenue), the 21,000-square foot mosque is the first liturgical centre built for New York's Muslim community. Completed in 1991, the centre comprises a mosque, an assembly room and a minaret. The design of the mosque encompasses both the traditions of Islamic architecture and contemporary building materials in keeping with the design of a classical mosque.

A structural system of four large steel trusses forming a nine-square grid supports the dome and creates a column-free interior space. The expression of the structure and the non-load bearing qualities of wall surfaces form the basis for the external articulation of the mosque. The exterior is organised in three sections. The lower tier, which follows the basic square outline of the plan, has a masonry expression. The middle section, set back from the square outline to the plane of the intersecting trusses, is developed as a metal and glass composition. Finally, a copper clad dome completes the envelope.

At the lower tier, solid granite L-shaped elements form the four corners of the mosque. Between the corners, six large square granite panels are set within secondary steel frames. In the middle section, large glazed panels patterned with fired ceramic surface decorations fill between the members of the primary structural trusses that span the prayer hall which is entered through a monumental portal fronting the court. The upper portion of the portal is formed by a composition of squares and cubic inscriptions in carved relief. In the lower portion, 15-foot bronze doors open to reveal an abstract arch motif of layers of glass cut in rectilinear patterns.

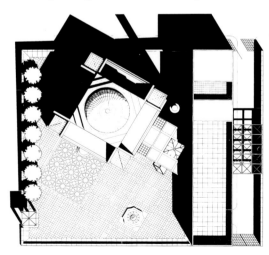

Top right: view of the exterior, masonry base, metal and glass enclosing the intersecting trusses carrying the copper dome;
Right: the prayer hall;
Left: the site plan showing the intersection of the Manhattan street grid with the path to Mecca.

180

ROBERT AM STERN
KOL ISRAEL SYNAGOGUE

This synagogue situated on Avenue K in Brooklyn and designed in 1989 for a growing congregation, occupies a corner site in an established residential neighbourhood. To complement the Mediterranean quality of the surrounding houses, a vocabulary of red brick and stone walls sheltered by a red tile roof was adopted.

Stringent setback and height limitations led to an unusual arrangement whereby the entire site was excavated to 19 feet 6 inch below grade. This created the largest possible area for the light-filled main sanctuary, which rises up past the entry level and balconies to achieve a height of 34 feet.

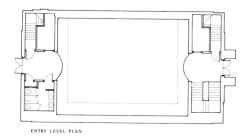

ENTRY LEVEL PLAN

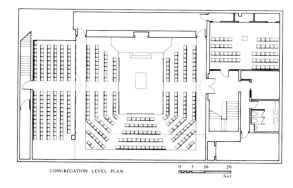

CONGREGATION LEVEL PLAN

Above: the sanctuary. The dado running across the centre marks the area below ground;
Top right: plans showing the visible building (top) and the extent of the excavation (bottom);
Right: the visible building.

BEYER BLINDER BELLE ARCHITECTS

GRAND CENTRAL RESTORATION

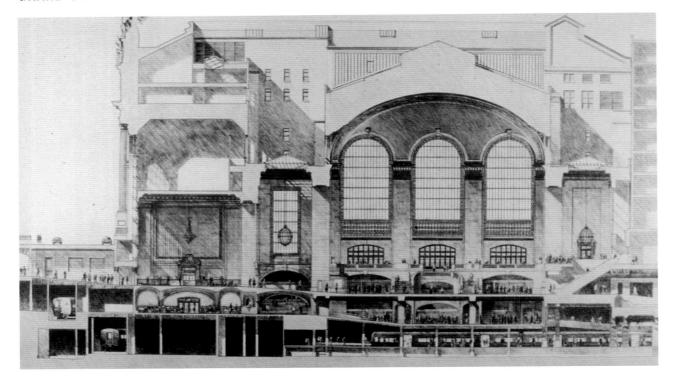

Above: lateral section through the grand concourse;
Left: the Vanderbilt entrance.

Completed in 1913, this was the world's first all-electrified, subterranean railroad station. Half a million people per day pass through the ageing structure which now requires wholesale revitalisation. The six-volume 1990 restoration master plan is designed to improve railroad services, update the building's infrastructure, restore its architectural splendour and improve its civic and retail uses. The first construction phases include restoration of the magnificent waiting room, relocation of the stationmaster's office, reconstruction of the Guastavino-vaulted Vanderbilt entrance and portions of facades and monumental sculptures.

© Peter Aaron/Esto

© Peter Aaron/Esto

Left: view from 42nd Street;
Below: the restored ticket booths.

© Peter Aaron/Esto

© Peter Aaron/Esto

© Peter Aaron/Esto

© Peter Aaron/Esto

© Peter Aaron/Esto

Opposite page (top): the grand concourse; Opposite page (bottom): the view from the elevated roadway on Park Avenue South; Top: the stellar constellations traced in lights on the ceiling of the grand concourse.

© Peter Aaron/Esto

FOX & FOWLE ARCHITECTS

MAIN ENTRANCE TO THE TIMES SQUARE SUBWAY STATION

Times Square subway station is located at 42nd Street and Seventh Avenue and is the city's largest, serving nearly 500,000 users daily. The exuberance of Times Square has been captured by means of a vibrant, undulating canopy, topped with brightly lit animated signs that announce the subway's presence on the street and orients passers-by to the 11 subway lines that the station serves. The 'waved' canopy form continues into the station, becoming the ceiling over the token booth and turnstiles inside, and evoking an appropriate sense of motion. Smoothly undulating sculpted forms and cove lighting serve as the ceiling for the progression from street level to the tracks below, floating over the escalators and stairs. On the track level, a curved lighting and sign element, suggesting an old Broadway theatre marquee, brings the flavour of Times Square street life into the heart of the station. This marquee becomes the focal point of the station and helps to orient the subway rider within the station complex.

In an effort to integrate the new entrance into the traditional aesthetic of the station, a well-preserved mosaic has been relocated from the original station into the new street level space, providing a touch of the old subway within the contemporary entrance setting.

186

View from 42nd Street

© Andrew Gordon

RM KLIMENT & FRANCES HALSBAND ARCHITECTS
LONG ISLAND RAIL ROAD ENTRANCE PAVILION AT PENNSYLVANIA STATION

The entrance building of the Long Island Rail Road at Pennsylvania Station serves 90,000 commuters each day. It is the only component of the Long Island Rail Road station visible above ground. The site is a small lot in a block of single storey commercial buildings surrounded by office buildings, hotels, Madison Square Garden and Macy's department store.

187

The 1995 building shelters pedestrian access to the station, and accommodates climate control equipment for the entire Long Island Rail Road concourse below. It is comprised of three elements: a brick outer shell, a steel and glass tower, and a marquee suspended by cables from a mast. The outer shell supports the cooling tower and other components of the mechanical system.

The structure of the tower is composed of painted steel laced columns and struts, similar to those of early train sheds, bridges, and the glazed concourse of the old Penn Station itself. The glass of the walls and roof is transparent, colourless and supported by a mullionless stainless steel flush-bolt system. A clock, salvaged from the old Penn Station, is suspended in the tower. A folded metal ceiling with integrated lighting is suspended over the escalators connecting the street with the concourse level below. The floor is grey granite and the walls are beige marble, both extended from the concourse below. The walls are coursed marble and brick.

The stainless steel mast and cables support the painted steel and glass marquee, which reaches over the sidewalk of 34th Street. The mast is capped by a radiating light beacon.

Above: view from 34th Street;
Right: inside the steel tower.

© Jeff Goldberg/Esto

LEE HARRIS POMEROY ASSOCIATES

UNION SQUARE SUBWAY STATION REHABILITATION

The 14th Street/Union Square Station complex is the third most heavily used in the New York City transit system. Three different subway lines converge below Union Square Park. The 1999 design included the rehabilitation of all station access points above and below grade as well as its co-ordination with the existing historic Union Square Park: all station finishes and signage, waterproofing and structural alterations as required, and replacing all lighting, plumbing, mechanical and public address systems. Two of the lines are made accessible to the disabled with new elevators and the elimination of barriers. Mechanical ventilation is added to the platform levels of all three lines. The architects collaborated with Mary Miss, the Arts for Transit artist whose work focuses on historical and inner workings of the station. This work will be a common thread throughout the entire complex.

188

Top: Union Square from the air. Below ground, the network of tunnels connecting three different subway lines covers the whole area; Above: a renovated station, the steel and vaulted structure dates from early last century.

© Peter Mauss/Esto

WILLIAM BOUDOVA
TERMINAL ONE, JFK INTERNATIONAL AIRPORT

The facility consists of 675,000 square feet on four levels, arrivals level, sterile corridor level, departures level and the mezzanine level. Terminal One is a visual gateway to the JFK terminal complex. The concept of the unique geometry of the ticketing hall was developed by creating a structural torus for the roof that is intersected by the north glass curtain wall. The result is a striking parabolic facade that serves as an introduction to the radial long span structure within.

Upon entering the ticketing hall the structure is immediately perceived as both the dramatic and the unifying element of the volume. The tripartite arrangement of the roof plane was planned through the use of transparent and solid materials visually to organise the volume into its essential elements of vestibule, airline services and retail.

The use of tinted, insulated and fritted glass throughout Terminal One ensures abundant daylight throughout, modelling the space with the changing light conditions. During the evening hours the terminal is a geometric composition of light as seen by arriving passengers both airborne and driving the roadway networks.

189

Above: the baggage hall;
Below: aerial view showing the parabolic facade of the ticketing hall.

SMITH-MILLER + HAWKINSON

PIER 11

As part of a long-term project to improve the city's alternative transportation infrastructure, together with the desire to improve waterfront public access in Lower Manhattan, the New York City Economic Development Corporation and the New York City Department of Transportation are rebuilding Pier 11 and the Wall Street Esplanade. Smith-Miller + Hawkinson were commissioned to design the Wall Street Ferry Terminal Building. The building is intended to provide a seamless transition between interior and exterior, land and sea.

The main waiting area is a transparent space which can be transformed from a fully interior environment to an open porch, indistinct from the rest of the Pier. The walls swing out of the way to extend the interior space to the exterior. Canopies extending east and west of the building, constructed of steel and translucent fibreglass, elongate the space of the waiting area to the ferries, and back to land.

The terminal provides both shelter and shade, a place not only for the traveller, but for the local community as well. An indoor/outdoor café will also serve both commuter and visitor.

The building materials include galvanised corrugated metal, corrugated fibreglass, large areas of glass, and exposed structural steel – all materials which are functionally sympathetic to waterfront construction, and are evocative of the working, industrial history of New York's waterfront.

190

© Jeff Goldberg/Esto

Above and below: day time and night time view of the plant.

THE HILLIER GROUP
COGENERATION PLANT

Situated in the centre of JFK International Airport, this facility will provide electrical power and hot and chilled water to meet the needs of the airport. The project consists of three primary elements: a 30,000-square foot renovation of the existing Central Heating and Refrigeration Plant (CHRP), a 12,000-square foot chiller addition and a new 45,000-square foot cogeneration facility. The unusual nature of the programme and unique site required a singular design solution. Highly visible from every point in the central terminal area, the buildings respond with a series of curved, streamlined forms providing a bold sculptural presence in tune with the geometries of the surrounding terminals. Rather than obscure the equipment within, glass walls enclose the chillers, turbines, and CHRP. The machinery inside has been made prominent with bright paint colours and lighting. The twin heat recovery units and stacks are accented with space frame screen walls. The choice of materials – glass, metal panels and screen walls – complements the mechanistic image of the facility.

191

© Jeff Goldberg/Esto

Industrial

POLSHEK PARTNERSHIP ARCHITECTS

THE NEW YORK TIMES PRINTING PLANT

This 475,000-square foot facility significantly expands the production capacity of the *New York Times* and provides for the introduction of colour into the paper's daily edition. Located in a bleak industrial area adjacent a major six-lane expressway, the new building is highly visible to a million passing motorists each week. The design recomposes the typical industrial shed into a series of dynamic building forms whose volumes are distilled from the separate components of the printing process and serve to dramatise and articulate its various stages.

Distinct volumes express the paper storage, printing, sorting and distribution elements of the programme. Defined by the machinery within, these volumes are arranged to best order the site and to optimise views from the outside to the printing presses within, perhaps the most important and emblematic of the parts. Large expanses of glass offer dramatic views of the machines and of paper threading through the building. Bold colours and graphics enliven the long highway facade, and the skin of the plant provides a striking wall along the adjacent highway by employing simple and inexpensive materials appropriate to the building type in unexpected ways.

© Jeff Goldberg/Esto

© Jeff Goldberg/Esto

© Jeff Goldberg/Esto

Above: the elevation to the expressway;
Top left: aerial view showing the expressway in the foreground, Manhattan in the distance;
Bottom left: the presses.

Landscape
BEYER BLINDER BELLE ARCHITECTS
ENID A HAUPT CONSERVATORY, NEW YORK BOTANICAL GARDEN

© Frederick Charles

The view at dusk

Constructed in 1898 by Lord and Burnham Co, this conservatory previously underwent a series of alterations that compromised architectural elements but failed to solve recurring environmental and maintenance issues. Beyer Blinder Belle developed a rehabilitation programme including a glazing system replacement, structural work, modern life safety, ADA, and new state-of-the-art environmental systems. A preservation maintenance plan assures the future of America's greatest steel and glass conservatory which is a designated New York City landmark.

RICHARD DATTNER
RIVERBANK STATE PARK

In 1965, a federal court issued an order requiring New York City to treat all its remaining raw sewage before discharging it, and a search began for a suitable site along Manhattan's Hudson river front. Several sites were studied and rejected because of intense community opposition and political pressure.

In 1993, a park was finally built on top of the sewage plant. The 28-acre plant roof, almost a half-mile long, was constructed, consisting of 14 separate sections moving independently as the roof expands and contracts due to changes in temperature. Each roof plate can support a different load, depending on the column spacing below, up to a maximum of 400 pounds per square foot. The entire park buildings, landscaping and site features are strictly controlled because of the limited load bearing capacity of the plant's caissons, columns and roof spans. The park had to be constructed without affecting either the remaining construction of the plant or its operation.

The selected conceptual design organised the four largest park buildings around a south-facing courtyard sheltered from winter winds. A skating rink, multi-purpose cultural building and a gymnasium are linked by enclosed passageways. An enclosed 50-metre swimming pool is reached by a covered walkway to facilitate circulation in bad weather. In warm weather, an outdoor 25-yard pool, wading pool and large surrounding terraces supplement the indoor facility. The park's restaurant is sited to take advantage of views north to the George Washington Bridge and the New Jersey Palisades. In warm weather a large terrace is opened for outdoor dining.

194

© Julio Olivas

© Norman McGrath

Above: aerial view showing Riverside Drive and the extent to which the filled land extends into the Hudson River;
Left: from the terrace with the George Washington Bridge in the distance.

JOHN DI DOMENICO
QUEENS WEST PARK

The Queens West Park system wraps around 1.25 miles of diverse East River waterfront. Located directly across from the United Nations in the Hunters Point area of Long Island City, the parks encompass one of the most visible and easily accessible waterfronts in New York City.

Hunter's Point Community Park was designed to serve the active recreational needs of the adjacent community. Court games such as basketball and handball are accommodated in the fluidly divided spaces of the park. A children's play area at the western end enables the community park effectively to address a cross-section of ages and activities.

Gantry Plaza is the centrepiece of the Queens West Park system. This waterfront park informs visitors about its industrial heritage and provides unequalled opportunities for viewing the Manhattan skyline, recreation, and public events. Historic remnants of New York City's industrial legacy define this park area: preserved gantry cranes, which once transferred railcars from barges to land, stand framed by unparalleled views of the Manhattan skyline. Five rebuilt piers extend into the East River providing public pedestrian access.

The 1-acre peninsula's layout is flexible to accommodate a variety of activities. A terraced lawn and concentric seawalls facilitate viewing of performances on the stage area at the water's edge.

The North Gantry Plaza provides for major public events such as performances, festivals and exhibitions whereas the marsh grasses of the South Gantry Interpretive Park provide a contemplative zone encouraging outdoor classroom environmental and historical education.

195

Top: site plan, East River at the bottom, the north and south gantries are shown as horizontal bars;
Above: rebuilt pier with Manhattan in the background;
Right: North Gantry Plaza.

JOHN DI DOMENICO
WITH LEE WEINTRAUB
OCTAGON PARK, ROOSEVELT ISLAND

Octagon Park is the realisation of the original Roosevelt Island plan that envisioned a large ecological landscape. Changes in the way open space is programmed and used, from more pastoral pursuits to a more demanding constituent-orientated series of spaces, necessitated a broad-based participatory planning process to determine these uses. This empowering process has facilitated a unique design consensus, which has helped to enable timely implementation.

The product of this planning process is a park that functions as a series of specific rooms that respond to an evolution of the current culture of recreation. That culture is activity orientated. Lawn spaces allow for a range of athletic endeavours. Octagon Park is not only a series of sportsfields, it is a place where one can participate in sports activities and at the same time enjoy the rich tapestry of a traditionally landscaped park, all with the Manhattan skyline as the backdrop. The landscape serves as a foil and as a common thread, seamlessly weaving these discrete elements together and softening their presence, along over a mile of the East River.

196

Above: the terrace looking towards Manhattan;
Left: the site showing the park extending to the tip of Roosevelt Island.

EHRENKRANTZ ECKSTUT & KUHN ARCHITECTS
SOUTH COVE PARK, BATTERY PARK CITY

Below: bridge, viewing tower and floating island;
Bottom: the bridge with Battery Park City and the World Trade Center in the background.

The Battery Park City master plan has created an entirely new neighbourhood on a 92-acre waterfront landfill on New York's southern edge. The plan established a Commercial District, a South Residential District and a North Residential District, all organised around a series of parks and other focal points. A stringent set of design guidelines was developed to ensure quality among the various parcels of development. Each parcel is orientated around a park or other public space with the intention of capitalising on river views and public interaction.

The South Cove Park and Waterfront were designed to continue the New York City park theme established in the Battery Park Esplanade, while introducing new materials, furnishings and plant materials. A lower wood-lined walkway system provides a means of bringing people on land in closer contact with the water. Other design features include a bridge, a viewing tower, a floating island and a jetty that extends over the water.

Liberty View Apartments is a 28-storey tower in Battery Park City. It is the first high-rise residential property to be developed on West Street in the south cove area. Although it utilises standard building components, its sensitive use of colour and accented materials creates a highly distinctive residence.

Finally, the Esplanade is the area's central feature, providing access to the waterfront and serving as a prototype for public spaces throughout Battery Park City.

197

FTL HAPPOLD
DEJUR AVIARY AT THE BRONX ZOO

The Dejur Aviary at the Bronx Zoo had been in existence for more than a hundred years when, in the early spring of 1995, the old building dramatically collapsed as its steel-pipe structure (which had rusted from the inside) failed under the weight of an unusually heavy snow fall. The new aviary was to be based on the existing site but would be 30 per cent bigger, more interesting to visitors and more tailored to the requirements of the birds.

In order to maintain historic continuity and make the most of existing features, much of the old false rock work was incorporated into the new design as were the mature dense trees that surrounded the site. The 3,000 square metre building is situated within a sinuous, concrete perimeter wall that in parts is submerged below ground, though it emerges at each end to accommodate cave-like entrances. These are important design features that maintain the illusion, despite the enclosing mesh, of a completely uninhibited external environment.

Though the new building is both visually and environmentally transparent, it must be able to resist snow loads, which can still gather on the mesh, and wind loads, though this is significantly less than for a comparable sized membrane structure. Though the building is symmetrical in section, its structure transfers visually from one side of the site to the other, creating an organic continuity that cannot immediately be understood, but which is still clearly resolved.

198

Above: cave like entrance;
Left: the illusion of an uninhibited external environment.

DAVIS, BRODY AND ASSOCIATES
WITH HARDY HOLTZMAN PFEIFFER ASSOCIATES
BRYANT PARK RESTORATION, BRYANT PARK GRILL AND BP CAFÉ

The restoration of the derelict, 5-acre park was reclaimed for public use through the introduction of pedestrian amenities, open access and seating. To encourage easy visitation new entrances and ramps to the north and south were added and existing access points were altered. Perimeter hedges were removed, creating openings in the central lawn's balustrade. Landscape architects and garden designers restored the bluestone and granite terraces, which are planted with bosks of sycamore trees. A 300-foot long flower border defines an entire cross-town block.

The park's overall redevelopment, carried out in 1992-5, is anchored by food kiosks at its edges and the Bryant Park Grill and BP Café which flank the William Cullen Bryant monument on the West Terrace of the New York Public Library. These structures make the relationship between architecture and landscape ambiguous, softening their differences so that seasonal changes visit both the pavilions and the park. The composition of the restaurant is made of an inner layer of glass and steel and an outer layer of woven aluminium and weathered-wood trelliswork, supporting ivy behind large flower boxes. The roof offers uninterrupted views of the outdoors. Careful interventions in the landscape, new public amenities and proper maintenance have made the park a safe, year-round urban oasis.

199

Left: the view in winter;
Below: site plan of the café terrace with the library in black.

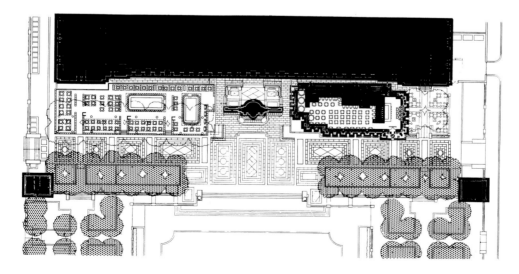

Left and bottom: the café terrace in summer;
Below: food kiosks.

MACHADO AND SILVETTI ASSOCIATES

ROBERT F WAGNER, JR PARK

This park occupies a unique site, characterised by its relatively small area located at the centre of colossal surroundings such as the immense scale of The World Trade Center and the Hudson River. The main function of this public space is the privileged viewing of the Statue of Liberty and New York Harbor.

The design of the park comprises three main components: a pair of alleys that brings pedestrians towards the main park entrance, extending the sidewalks of Battery Place coming from the north and of Battery Park from the south; a pair of pavilions connected by a bridge constituting the main building; and a lawn terrace framed by continuous paths and benches. This 'Y' shaped architectural ensemble is the backbone of the park, resting in gardens and fields of grass that connect to the Battery Park City Esplanade and to Battery Park.

The upper level, 18 feet above the ground, is the truly significant public situation on the park, since the ground level houses restrooms, a café and maintenance spaces. The pair of balconies – furnished with tall-backed wooden benches and portable tables and chairs – is the ideal place for contemplation, lunching and general relaxation. Each balcony is quite different in character from the other: the northern balcony offers a view of the river framed by a large arch, while on the south, the experience of the view is more open and unprotected. From the centre of the bridge connecting these two, the viewer's direct relation to the Statue of Liberty is 'face to face'.

201

Above: detail of the brick work;
Right: the two pavilions and the bridge against the backdrop of the World Trade and Financial Centers.

PERKINS EASTMAN ARCHITECTS

THE BUTTERFLY VIVARIUM, AMERICAN MUSEUM OF NATIONAL HISTORY

202

Computer models and studies

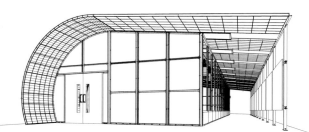

The butterfly vivarium is a custom fabricated, temporary shell structure that sits within one of the museum's existing galleries. It has been designed to be a 'kit of parts', which can be broken down, stored, then reinstalled in future years. It is a completely sealed, self-contained environment and is maintained by its own HVAC system. Butterflies are contained within the adult flight area which is enclosed by a shell consisting of a series of arched panels springing from the existing terrazzo floor along the west side of the exhibit, and supported on the opposite side by a row of columns. The north and south enclosing walls are made of aluminium panels. Running the length of the vivarium to the east is a transparent wall made of acrylic panels.

Before entering the vivarium, visitors line up along a covered passageway. Once inside the vivarium, visitors will walk along a serpentine path with landscaping on both sides. Throughout the exhibit, there are information panels about butterflies, as well as nectar feeding stations. In the centre of the flight area is a self-contained pupa display case where guests can observe the pupas emerging. Visitors exit through the south vestibule.

PERSPECTIVES 7

The Remaking of 42nd Street

Rebecca Robertson

Introduction

'Naughty, bawdy, gaudy 42nd Street.' A single legendary block in New York City on the southern edge of Times Square that over the 20th century represented the best and the worst of Gotham's sybaritic tastes. It was the 'New Rialto' and 'the Deuce', the centre of culture and entertainment for the moneyed classes and the home to drug dealers, prostitutes and 10-year-old runaways. 42nd Street has offered operettas, musicals by Porter and the Gershwins, revues, plays by Shakespeare and Ferber, and vaudeville as well as burlesque, grind movies, flea circuses, freak shows, slasher and porn films, and peepshows. In the first decade of the century, Theodore Dreiser called it 'lush, gossamer and magical'. In 1981, no less an authority than *Rolling Stone* magazine called 42nd Street between Broadway and Eighth Avenue the 'sleaziest block in America'.

Then the civic leaders and planners stepped in.

The story of the redevelopment of 42nd Street is about how one mythic location was recreated in the last part of the 20th century. The richness of the big-city experience depends on places that are steeped in layers of meaning, inspire dreams and hyperbole and convey a sense of being somewhere special. These places have usually evolved over time. 42nd Street was such a place. Its presence, in good times and bad, gave richness and texture to the city of New York. But for many citizens, when the bad began to outweigh the good, it was time to 'clean up' 42nd Street.

How that 'clean up' proceeded touches on a number of real-world issues about the planning and renewal of famous places.

Urban planners and complexity: Marshall McLuhan is reported to have commented that 42nd Street was a relic of a bygone era and should be preserved as the urban counterpoint to colonial Williamsburg.[1] His remark underscores the problem of using urban renewal to propagate the complexity of the elements of a place that has evolved. It can be argued that preserving a place by freezing it in time is just as false as wiping it out. The remark speaks to the fundamental differences between forced and natural evolution. Urban renewal is too often limited in its aspiration and dimension, focusing on physical change and a single politically saleable idea. What creates a famous place is multidimensional, dynamic and the result of many minds and players over time. Conventional urban renewal may be too blunt an instrument for the fragile web that is woven around places of meaning, unless planners are willing – and able – to set a high value on the intangibles that have made the place what it is.

Politicians and complexity: There would seem to be a natural tension between the needs and objectives of politicians and civic leaders and the fine grain of place and culture. Most American civic leaders are interested in crime reduction, business growth and retention and a strong tax base. The concept of re-creating the forces that make a place special is too esoteric to attract political support, despite the fact that famous places are proven generators of economic growth. Politicians also like to focus on a product that is achievable during their term in office. Short-term political demands may obviate subtle and complex solutions.

The role of shifting civic values: Places that evolve naturally reflect cultural shifts, rejecting some and incorporating others as the marketplace dictates. But urban renewal often demands that the values of a particular time are thrust upon the place. It is a common characteristic of large projects that they are a product of their time. But in rebuilding a place with history and character, is this the right outcome? What if the values of the day run contrary to its history?

A necessary planning goal – generating mythology: Planning for a mythic place is like making an 'art' movie. In the long run, its success in becoming part of the collective consciousness is more important than how much the film cost at the time, or who gets the credit for it. Both great films and great plans should result in a story that speaks to the public with resonance and generates its own myths. Planners and civic leaders may not see their role as myth-spinning.

The planning of 42nd Street

There were many initiatives to clean up 'the Deuce', the sleazy version of 42nd Street. We will focus on the three plans, beginning in the late 1970s, that ultimately led to the present rebuilding. Each plan might have been implemented if the economic times had been different. Each would have resulted in a very different 42nd Street.

The First Plan: the city at 42nd Street: 1980

The first efforts to clean up 42nd Street began in the 1930s. New zoning was proposed and enacted then and in the 1940s and 1950s, and every mayor from La Guardia onwards implemented law-enforcement strategies. But the culture of 42nd Street remained entrenched.

By the mid-1970s, 42nd Street and Times Square had become symbols of the urban decay that plagued the city. It was on the verge of collapse: businesses were leaving, crime rates were high, the subway and park systems were in complete disrepair and New York just barely averted bankruptcy.

In response, in 1978, a group of business and civic leaders

raised $1.5 million for the planning of an ambitious remake of the Deuce to serve as a catalyst for the renewal of midtown Manhattan. The plan contemplated a $600 million, 6.6 million-square-foot project that included four large office buildings, a massive merchandise mart and a $100 million cultural, entertainment and educational complex with exhibitions by major corporations, state-of-the-art film presentations and indoor rides. The proposed complex was described as 'a city in a capsule' and would contain sound stages and studios; a multimedia history of the lively arts; a continuous parade of fashion (just to the south of 42nd Street was New York's garment district); reborn theatres with catwalk views into the home of the Ziegfield Follies; a simulated vertical experience through a 'slice of the Apple' from the underground maze of tunnels and pipes to the tips of the famous skyscrapers; and the world's largest movie screen (employing a new technique called Imax).

The design by Richard Weinstein and Jaquelin Robertson was more abstract than real, but was presented in magnificent minimalist graphics and models that communicated a lively vision of futuristic change. A much-circulated rendering of the entertainment complex with theatres with glass walls and sky bridges was more florid, and I believe pointed out the major flaw in the plan – that the entertainment complex as proposed was a complete fantasy.

The implementation structure was as innovative as the plan itself. It was a multimillion-dollar project, the financial burden of which would be borne in the first instance by the private sector (a brilliant stroke as New York was still in dire financial straits). The city would use the private funds to expropriate 13 acres of midtown Manhattan and would turn this over to the private participants. (It was assumed that the block could not be redeveloped incrementally because of the seriousness of the street conditions – a much-argued point but probably, in retrospect, correct.) The private sector would also fund restoration of the historic theatres and renovation of the subway and would be compensated through deep tax breaks. It was a bold strike – urban renewal with flare, financed by the private sector.

The plan bore little obvious relation to the 42nd Street of legend. And yet, the spirit of fantasy and hucksterism on the street was very present in the plans and the graphic materials. The new 42nd Street experience sought by the planners was offbeat and vivid (at least in the literature), and the entertainment complex was the centrepiece. Oscar Hammerstein I, one of the most flamboyant speculators on the early 42nd Street, would not have been ashamed of these plans.

Mayor Koch recognised that there was the kernel of a powerful idea here. However, in May 1980 he rejected the plan as 'Disneyland at 42nd Street', insisting that he wanted 'Seltzer, not orange juice'. Within one month, he had invited the state to join him in formulating a new plan for the rescue of the street.

The city-state plan: 1981–2

The stated goals for the new plan were, first, to eliminate blight and physical decay on the street and, second, to create an entertainment mecca for all New Yorkers. A large team of consultants was hired to provide advice on land values, commercial feasibility of the theatres, environmental issues and urban design. When released, the new plan was in many respects like the one that had been rejected. It had four large office towers and a merchandise mart. It relied on private capital to fund the condemnation, and looked to the developers to fund the restoration of the theatres and the renovation of the Times Square subway.

Cooper-Eckstut, who would so brilliantly develop the design guidelines for Battery Park City a few years later, prepared the design package, but were greatly limited in what they could do. The city and state, urged on by interested developers and financial interests, did not give the planners an opportunity to consider the issues of use, activity patterns or density. These important elements had been predetermined by the developers' strong interest in building 4 million square feet of office space and a 2.5 million-square-foot wholesale mart in the heart of midtown Manhattan. The guidelines were about physical design only, and were directed towards breaking up the bulk of the larger buildings, encouraging reflective materials, changing expression at the base, encouraging retail continuity and variation and mandating high transparency requirements at grade. They were surprisingly silent on the issues of large signage and lighting. Signage was permitted, but not required.

The vision for the new 42nd Street was left to the politicians, who never came up with one. It is telling that there was never a single image that captured the essence of the city–state plan. Even the beautiful watercolour elevations prepared by Cooper-Eckstut were not well circulated. This absence of visual materials, on a street where visual chaos was a hallmark, was an indicator of (1) the gulf between the real 42nd Street and the plan; and (2) the lack of any overall idea from any of the main players. What the new plan mainly said about 42nd Street was that its history was irrelevant and that it would be treated as raw land in a prime location, dotted with historic theatres that would be restored as a 'public amenity'. This was a plan about 'clean up' and starting construction.

The city–state plan was put out to bid in 1982, and 26 responses were received. After various negotiations a line-up of developers was selected. The most dominant of them was George Klein who won the right to build the four office towers. His vision for 42nd Street dominated the project until the early

205

1990s. It was exemplified by the image that became most associated with the redevelopment of the street: the four Postmodern granite-clad office buildings designed by Philip Johnson. Pristine and sleek, the towers did not satisfy the Cooper-Eckstut guidelines for architectural variety, reflective materials and articulated facades, nor were they designed for any kind of signage. Klein proudly touted the project as the new Rockefeller Center.

The project was extremely controversial, in part in reaction to the sterile vision of 42nd Street. Forty-eight lawsuits followed the public approvals in 1984. Philip Johnson redesigned the buildings twice, each time with more variation and finally with large supersigns. In 1988, ground leases were signed with George Klein and his new financial partner, Prudential Insurance Company of America. By that time, developer proposals for the merchandise mart and the hotel were floundering at the western end of the block, and in the midblock the theatres were without a viable plan. All attention was focused on the four office towers, which were seen as the only catalyst in the project.

The final plan: 1991 to the present

On 18 April 1990, Prudential posted a letter of credit for $241 million that allowed the state to move forward with the condemnation (expropriation) of two-thirds of the project area. Under the agreement with the state, Klein and Prudential had to commence construction of the first office building within a year of the clearance of the first two sites by the state. However, by the end of 1991, when the sites had been vacated, the office market had evaporated. It was not possible to move forward with the plan that had been approved in 1984. The developers asked for a standstill until the office market came back. The planners had other ideas.

Relieved of the responsibility of delivering a new world-class financial complex, the state planners were able to turn their attention to the street. The first notable fact about the area was that, even with the worst economic recession in years and a block nearly emptied by the condemnation, 42nd Street and Times Square were staggering in terms of sheer volume of people: 17 million tourists annually; 12,650 hotel rooms with the highest occupancy rates in the city; highest grossing sales at Gap and McDonald's; and a count of 45,000 people a day or 16 million a year on Seventh Avenue between 42nd and 43rd Streets. Despite its seedy reputation 42nd Street was still famous, and visitors wanted to see it. There was life in this entertainment strip. It just needed resuscitation.

Armed with these notions, in August 1992 the state announced a new four-pronged strategy to put life back into 42nd Street:
   – reorient the plan towards entertainment;
   – develop and implement an aesthetic vision for the block

that shouted chaos and dazzle and would make the street as recognisable as the Statue of Liberty;
   – use public funds to complete the condemnation of the last sites so that the government, not the developers, could control the vision;
   – jump-start the new plan by immediately installing new entertainment venues and tourist- and entertainment-related retail plus fabulous supersignage into the sites where the office buildings would eventually go.

Robert AM Stern was hired to develop the plan together with Tibor Kalman and a host of other talented designers, financial consultants, entertainment and retail experts and market consultants. The fundamental goal of the planning process was to develop a framework that would re-energise those forces that had made 42nd Street work. The thesis was that the desired product would result 'naturally' if the forces were right. The conundrum was that the chaotic, unpredictable qualities of the street seemed antithetical to a planning process.

Information was collected from a variety of sources: books and newspaper clippings; focus groups of people who had come to 42nd Street as children or worked there now; surveys of entertainment, retail and restaurant operators; and discussions with the area's old-timers. Tourists were also surveyed; they complained that there was nothing to see and nothing to do, but said they would come back anyway (such is the draw of a famous place). The changing patterns of ownership, usage, signage, marketing, visitations and reputation were analysed, as was the current market demand for entertainment and related uses. The planners also walked the street daily and absorbed its energy and craziness. The magnificent ruins of the theatres, the bright and gaudy lights of the peepshows and porn shops, the street life of drug dealers, commuters, pimps, evangelists and tourists – these created a vivid experience, and raised the bar on what the new experience had to feel like. The new 42nd Street needed to be safe, but it also had to be imperfect, unpredictable and special.

Seven principles were developed that governed the new plan and its implementing infrastructure of use, design and operating regulations, land control and financial incentives:

1 Layering: This embodied the notion of exposing the layers of 42nd Street – layers of time, layers of ideas, layers of signs. Like an archaelogical dig, the strata reveal generations of commercialism and entrepreneurial efforts, made more flamboyant by the nature of the entertainment business. The new 42nd Street would show its age lines, reminding us of its history. The restored buildings would mix with new ones, good architecture with bad. Traces of the old signage would remain and new layers of signs and facades would be added.

2 Unplanning: The analogy was with the English garden which (unlike the French formal garden) is planted and then cultivated as it grows, producing wild and random vistas. It is prodded, not forced. The concept was that the selection of uses would set the tone, and the design guidelines would prohibit coordination or theming of any kind. Within this framework each tenant, each user, would be permitted to grow at will. Similarly, the mandated requirement for abundant and brilliant signage would define the outlines of the garden above the street level. Competition for attention would define the specific character of the complex over time. By setting the parameters of the key elements – in this case visual chaos, abundant lighting and signage, and entertainment – the rest of the garden would fall in line. The spectre of a canyon of sober, restrained corporate-headquarter buildings would be banished.

3 Contradiction and surprise: This had been a street driven by commerce of a particular nature: entertainment. It was a commerce of illusion, hucksterism, flamboyance and risk-taking. By defining a concentrated multiplicity of usage (entertainment, retail, offices, live theatre, hotels), of architecture old, new, high and mid-scaled, and forcing brilliant signage and late-night hours, it was hoped that the concept would result in the random fairground-like chaos that had defined 42nd Street for decades. The surprises would come as individual entrepreneurs worked with and against each other to attract attention and audiences in their own way. Chaos was also encouraged in the signage, where developers were prohibited from any kind of coordinated design and were required to provide at least five kinds using at least three different techniques or signage types.

4 Street life: Creating a rich and safe pedestrian experience was of paramount importance, particularly given the reputation of 42nd Street. The sidewalks would glitter, all ground-floor stores would be mandated to have a high percentage of transparency (a problem in some well-known superstores which use every square foot for selling space) and abundant and varied signage would be required at street level – in the store windows, on the sills, over the doors, etc. Stores on key corners would be required to stay open until the early morning to continue the tradition of 42nd Street in 1910, when it was known as 'the block that never sleeps'.

5 Visual anchors: The street needed visual anchors at the block's east and west ends – icons that would act as exclamation points to identify the area. At the eastern end, a sign was mandated (a replica of a British Airways Concorde flanked by two enormous video screens), and at the western end the icon was a building (a brilliant multicoloured glass structure, designed by Arquitectonica, with a comet that

explodes at its base and in the tower a map of Times Square that can be seen for miles).

6 Aesthetics as attractions: The goal was to make the street a visual icon, an internationally recognisable streetscape that would attract the world to its doorstep. 42nd Street has always been about attracting crowds. In its new incarnation, as in its old, it would use every available trick to do so.

7 An achievable plan: The viability of retail or office buildings on the new safe 42nd Street was not an issue. However, in 1993 the entertainment component was not so assured. Thus, the financial incentives offered by the city and state as part of the new plan were directed at attracting new entertainment uses to the street. The Disney Company received a $26 million low-interest loan to be the first entertainment tenant on the block; Madame Tussaud's was given a low rent and a deep tax subsidy; the first movieplex on the block also received tax subsidies. In addition, an independent corporation was formed to ensure that there were not-for-profit performing arts on the street. The city and state subsidised it for the first nine years, and gave it the lease on six theatres to provide a rent-stream into the future to fund its non-profitmaking activities.

The plan was released in 1993. Today, the 42nd Street project is almost completely built out. It includes: two restored musical theatres (the New Amsterdam and the Ford Center); two restored non-profitmaking theatres (the New Victory – New York's first theatre for children, and the Roundabout Theater at the Selwyn); a 60,000-square-foot not-for-profit rehearsal centre with a small 'black box' theatre; two movieplexes with 39 screens; Madame Tussaud's; three virtual-reality arcades including an ESPN zone and a home-grown New York penny arcade; two hotels; a blues club; several restaurants; and the headquarters of two major media companies. The signage is abundant and dazzling, and the street throngs with crowds although many of the major attractions are not yet open.

It is not clear whether the new 42nd Street will be as vibrant or chaotic as the old one. Only its evolution over time will provide the answer. But it is without a doubt New York's oldest and newest entertainment destination. The competition between the tenants is loud and lively, and there has already been one big bankruptcy and scandal. It is a real, live street.

Notes

1 Stanley Buder, 'Forty-Second Street at the Crossroads: A History of Broadway to Eighth Avenue' in *The Bright Light Zone*, Graduate School and University Center of the City University of New York (New York), 1978, p71.

207

New York City, Planning for a Bright Future

Joseph B Rose

New York City holds a dominant place in America's urban consciousness. For much of the past half century that role, often as not, was as a symbol of urban troubles. Yet, while New York's imminent demise has been often reported, the past six years have shown these assumptions to be wrong. New York is undergoing a dramatic renaissance that is returning architectural, commercial and cultural innovation into the heart of the city, reshaping its national and international image. Private employment in the city is growing faster than at any time since data collection began in 1950. In 1999, employment grew faster in New York than in the booming national economy and the city is now on the verge of surpassing its previous employment peak of 3.8 million. The next census may even show that New York has surpassed its population peak of 7.95 million in 1970. Manhattan's per capita income is now substantially higher than that of any other county in the United States, and its concentration of educated and talented workers has become unparalleled in the world. In addition, the Giuliani Administration has transformed the city from the perceived capital of crime to the model for crime control. New York City is now by far the largest of a small number of dense, diverse, pedestrian- and transit-oriented American cities that have not just retained, but improved their vitality. Why has this happened? More importantly, what is happening to ensure it will continue?

First, New York's historic acceptance of immigrants has helped attract millions of new residents to the city, stabilising its population numbers while adding phenomenal energy and vitality to the city's neighbourhoods and economy. Immigrant entrepreneurs have opened so many small businesses on the city's 400 neighbourhood main streets that while in 1960 New York contained an excess of commercially zoned land, today there is shortage of commercially zoned land. Immigrants and other new households have also poured billions of dollars, and millions of hours, into the renovation of neighbourhoods throughout the city that had been in decline for decades.

Second, New York has made far-sighted decisions throughout its history to nurture its greatness. The consolidation of the pre-1898 City of New York, comprised of Manhattan Island and a portion of what is now the Bronx, with the City of Brooklyn, Staten Island and portions of suburban Westchester and Nassau Counties (which became the larger part of the Bronx and the borough of Queens) gave the city's population room to expand. The city's system of great bridges, tunnels and highways has knit the New York archipelago together. The creation of a vast subway system and commuter rail network has allowed for the transportation of a dispersed labour force into Manhattan's Central Business District. This district now holds more than three times the employment of its nearest rival, Chicago, and nearly as much as the combined employment of the next five largest American central business districts (Chicago, Washington, San Francisco, Boston and Los Angeles).

Third, New York has a famously solid and adaptable collection of buildings. As the city's economy has evolved from one dominated by factories to knowledge-based industries, adaptive reuse has blossomed in New York as thousands of buildings are used today in ways very different from those intended by their original builders – industrial lofts as residences or offices, office buildings as residences and department stores as libraries. Places such as the Midtown South area of Manhattan, famous for its Flatiron Building, contain a building stock originally constructed for commercial use, then reused for light industry as commerce moved on, then left substantially vacant as industry moved on. Now this area is the dynamic centre of Silicon Alley, New York's concentration of 'new media' businesses providing content and services for the Internet. Recognising that adaptive reuse is not only important to the city's economy but provides the essential economic underpinning to support a flourishing preservation movement, New York City policy has evolved accordingly to embrace reuse.

Beyond these three factors, all of which were in place prior to the current renaissance, there have been years of thoughtful involvement on the part of the public and private sectors in initiating redevelopment. Areas that had become blighted and depressed have regained their prior importance through a combination of tax breaks, environmental and security improvements, coordinated marketing, and zoning liberalisations. The fruits of this work can now be found all over the city and are the finest examples that New York City's rebirth is still a work in progress.

The best known of these areas is Times Square. Although it is the place with the finest mass transit connections in the United States, 15 years ago Times Square was a seedy district of poorly maintained buildings with its famous theatres in financial distress. In the 1980s, the city and state sought to redevelop the area by acquiring several blocks for massive new office buildings, together with extensive tax breaks for new construction and new zoning that temporarily increased permitted density. However, as the economy went into recession these buildings failed to attract enough tenants and the major development for the centre of Times Square failed to move forward. One part of the plan that was a success, however, was a change in the zoning to require large, brightly lit, animated signs. Though the new buildings were initially empty, the signs proved to be hugely profitable and allowed Times Square to maintain a character very different from that of standard, staid, corporate office buildings. Today these signs are a multicolour extravaganza that attract corporations looking for office space, millions of tourists and even New Yorkers themselves.

Another critical component of restoring Times Square to its original splendour was overcoming the concentration of anti-social behaviour that made the area menacing and uncomfortable for most people. In 1995, adult entertainment zoning restrictions were put in place to break up the concentration of sex businesses in Times Square and prevent another concentration from developing elsewhere. In addition, the city cracked down on gambling, ticket scalping, pickpockets, littering and illegal peddling in the area, while a business improvement district (funded by dedicated real estate taxes) removed litter, cleaned graffiti and maintained street furniture. As a result, serious crime fell, pedestrian traffic soared, and Broadway attendance increased by over 50 per cent. Four major office/studio buildings, three major retail and entertainment developments, three new hotels and two large apartment buildings have been built or are under construction. Several other buildings, including old theatres, have been renovated. To continue to allow expansion in Times Square while preserving landmark theatres, the city adopted an extended transfer of development rights programme in 1999. This programme will allow theatre owners the right to transfer additional floor area to a wide range of properties in this part of Manhattan.

Lower Manhattan, New York's historic financial district, was in great distress in the early 1990s. As the financial industry automated, consolidated and retrenched older buildings became virtually unmarketable. The city sought to promote adaptive reuse through residential conversions and upgrading for small technology-oriented businesses. New property tax reductions were made available to older office buildings in Lower Manhattan for conversion to residential use, for the installation of new wiring and communications infrastructure and for the signing of long-term leases with commercial tenants. The city also changed the zoning rules to merge a large number of complicated special zoning districts covering the area, make it easier for architects to adapt the irregular floor layouts to new residential uses and allow additional neighbourhood commercial uses. Almost 5,000 apartments have already been built or are under development.

Under the joint federal-state-local 'Empowerment Zone' programme enacted in 1994, redevelopment projects on 125th Street, the historic 'Main Street' of Harlem and in nearby areas of Manhattan and the Bronx became eligible for up to $340 million in federal, state and local tax credits. Tax benefits, a marketing programme, and a reduction in crime have spurred development in the area. The first projects, which have been recently completed or are nearing completion, primarily serve area residents – a supermarket, a chain drug store, and Harlem USA, a large new complex with a motion picture theatre, a health club and several other stores. Recently approved projects are expected soon to re-establish 125th Street as a major destination for residents of the entire city. These include a large shopping centre, hotel and office building complex – Harlem Center – and another large shopping center – East River Plaza – on nearby 116th Street. The historic Apollo Theater is also being renovated.

In Downtown Flushing, a 1920s regional business centre in Queens which has become the focal point of one of the city's major concentrations of Asian immigrants, two obstacles to redevelopment have been removed. The city constructed underground tanks to hold excess stormwater runoff which had been fouling the adjoining Flushing River. Obsolete zoning, which had prevented the historic commercial core from expanding, was changed in 1998 to allow for a more urban oriented zone, lower parking requirements and small office expansion. The adjacent area near the improving river was also re-zoned to permit large scale commercial redevelopment and require new developments to build public walkways along the waterfront. A new hotel has already been built in the re-zoned area, and major private waterfront developments are in the planning stage.

At the southeastern corner of Central Park, on Columbus Circle, another large redevelopment project is taking place at the site of the Colosseum, the city's former convention centre. Though it is traversed daily by more than 40,000 commuters using its subway station and 60,000 vehicles, Columbus Circle for years was more of an obstacle course than an urban destination. With the opening of the I. M. Pei-designed Javits Convention Center on the far West Side, attention was focused on the long-neglected circle and the major site adjoining it.

When the Metropolitan Transportation Authority (MTA), the site's owner, recently offered it for sale, the MTA worked closely with the city, its consultants and civic and community groups to craft a set of design guidelines attached to the Request for Proposals. At the same time, the city redesigned the circle itself. Traffic crisscrossing the circle has been rerouted into a circular pattern freeing up a large vehicle-free public space in the centre for pedestrians.

The city insisted on making architectural design and sensitivity to community context, rather than simply purchase price, the most important considerations in selecting a development team. The design guidelines included using less than the maximum floor area permitted by the zoning, a height restriction to limit shadows on Central Park, a view corridor through the site, a curved streetwall to respect the geometry of the circle, publicly accessible space within the development and materials consistent with neighbouring buildings. The city also required that the developer include 100,000 square feet for a permanent home for Jazz@Lincoln Center, the first theatre built expressly for jazz. The MTA, with the consent of the city, selected a team comprised of related companies with the architectural firm of Skidmore, Owings and Merrill. The winning scheme incorporated all the key features of the design guidelines and represents a major architectural statement and promises to be an icon for this critical site.

The most recent of the current plans to improve New York involves not a specific area or site, but the zoning code that affects the entire city. The 900 pages of the current Zoning Resolution have become full of both impediments for business people and homeowners as well as loopholes that allow unpredictable and out-of-context development. In addition, the Resolution has its origins in a 1950s vision of rebuilding the city as Le Corbusier-inspired towers-in-parks. The public, as well as architectural and urban design professionals, long ago came to believe that this prototype does not produce the attractive and vibrant urban streetscapes that New York benefits from. As a solution, the Department of City Planning has proposed the Unified Bulk Program, a comprehensive reform of the regulations governing the bulk of new and enlarged buildings. The new zoning would contain the simplest regulations compatible with the city's planning objectives. More importantly, it would uphold values of urban form, streetscape and neighbourhood character and scale while assuring that New York city is able to grow and develop the housing, commercial space and community facilities that its economy and populace require.

Recognising New York's architectural heritage, the Unified Bulk Program is also designed to use the market's preference for taller buildings as an incentive for developers to give exterior design more consideration. The programme would include a City Planning Commission special permit for significant exceptions from zoning rules, including height limits and tower coverage requirements, for developments found to have, among other considerations, high quality designs. A panel of architects and others concerned with design issues would be established to advise the City Planning Commission on the design merits of these special permit applications.

With its embrace of new cultures and ideas, valuable public transit system and roadways, and seemingly endless supply of great buildings, New York city has an innate capacity to regenerate itself. With the hard work of the city, businesses and citizens themselves, New York is turning its potential into reality.

Taniguchi's MoMA: Preview

Kenneth Frampton

The last half of the 20th century was not kind to Manhattan, this mythical citadel of modernity that for much of the century served as the quintessential symbol of the new. One thinks at the outset of an image drawn from the *Deutsche Werkbund Jahrbuch* of 1913, when what was the latest German transatlantic liner of the Nord Deutsche Lloyd company, the *Kronprinzessin Cecile* was captured by a camera in its passage along the Hudson against a backdrop of skyscrapers that then made up the skyline of Wall Street including McKim, Mead and White's City Hall, Cass Gilbert's Woolworth building, both still standing, and Ernst Flagg's Singer Tower of sewing machine fame, demolished in the mid 1960s. There followed in the roaring 1920s and the New Deal 1930s, the inimitable Chrysler building (1930), the Empire State (1931) and above all, Rockefeller Center (1933), this last being much more than a one-off scraper with a distinctive Art-Deco profile. Rockefeller Center was virtually a city in miniature as opposed to a free-standing tower and indeed this stepped concatenation, faced in limestone, and grouped around the central pinnacle of the RCA (now GE) slab remains to this day an exemplary civic set-piece, soaring to some 110 floors at its apex, while at the same time discreetly aligning its low-rise, outriding wings with the Fifth Avenue frontage. Hence the subtle integration of the Saks Fifth Avenue building and St Patrick's Cathedral with the microcosmic continuity of the Rockefeller complex.

The next heroic moment in the evolution of modern architecture in mid-town Manhattan came with the Pax Americana of the 1950s and early 1960s, with the fertile decade and a half that produced, in short order from the hands of Walter Gropius, Mies van der Rohe, Wright, Skidmore, Owings & Merrill and Kevin Roche, a series of remarkable works that assured the city its continuing global reputation as a modern *civitas*. I have in mind such works as the Pan Am Tower (1957), the Seagram building (1958), the Guggenheim Museum (1959), Gordon Bunshaft's Lever House (1952) and Pepsi-Cola buildings (1960) both designed for SOM and, last but not least in this illustrious company, Kevin Roche's Ford Foundation building (1967), 'the house of Ivy League values'. This, along with Lincoln Center by Johnson, Harrison and Abramowitz (1962-66) and other Skidmore megaliths of the period in midtown and downtown Manhattan is what the city as an architectural set-piece had to show for itself in the mid-1950s. All these works, if not always in the most sublime manner, were, on balance, impressive achievements from both a technical and tectonic standpoint.

There followed an inexplicable regression in both architectural and civic terms, that despite the best efforts of the Lindsay administration, produced little of consequence and moreover initiated a continuous wave of developer speculation in high- to medium-rise construction that further transformed the skyline of the city, without adding a single building of merit to its urban matrix. This decline in civic patronage that lasted for almost 30 years without break, began to lift towards the end of the century, first with Raimund Abraham's winning entry for the Austrian Cultural Institute Competition of 1994 now under construction on 52nd Street between Madison and Lexington and then with Yoshio Taniguchi's winning design for the overall expansion and rearrangement of the Museum of Modern Art. It is surely significant that both of these promising late modern pieces should have come to the point of realisation in the centre of Manhattan as the result of the competition system, even if the former was an open competition restricted to Austrian architects, and the latter was the result of a judicious two-stage selection process from a limited list of ten pre-selected architects comprising Wiel Arets, Herzog and de Meuron, Steven Holl, Rem Koolhaas, Williams and Tsien, Rafael Viñoly, Bernard Tschumi, Dominique Perrault, Toyo Ito and, finally, Yoshio Taniguchi.

In terms of the *vox populi* prevailing at the time, it could be said that the selection of the Taniguchi design was an unexpected outcome given that the other two entries on the final short list of three were by the Swiss team of Herzog and de Meuron and Bernard Tschumi Associates of New York. The fact that Taniguchi finally carried the day is perhaps best accounted for in urbanistic terms, since his entry attained a level of civic resolution that was absent in the projects of the other finalists.

First and foremost, like Rockefeller Center, only at reduced scale, the Taniguchi scheme displays exceptional skill in relating the prevailing average cornice height of the 53rd and 54th Street frontages to a single existing high-rise structure in the centre of the block, in effect the 54-storey Museum Tower, completed to the designs of Cesar Pelli in 1978. In addition to achieving a balance in terms of the overall mass between this curtain walled residential high-rise and the adjacent brownstone-scale to either side, Taniguchi will also reveal for the first time the full height of the 54-storey tower at its eastern corner as the former impinges upon the Abby Aldrich Rockefeller garden.

Of equal import on both the 53rd and 54th Street elevations are the 80 foot high blank facades composed of slate and darkened glass fronting the expanded museum facilities, aligning on the 53rd Street front with the cornice of both the original Phillip Goodwin building (1939) and the Philip Johnson addition, dating from 1966. While on 53rd Street, the single blank facade will enclose a bookstore on the first floor with virtually windowless galleries above, on 54th Street, one of the blank facades will house the new education wing comprising offices, study centres, libraries and archives. This block will receive unfiltered daylight from its glazed northwest return facade facing the garden. A similar side lighting strategy will be adopted in the case of the second blank face on 54th Street housing the temporary and permanent collections on the site of the former Dorset Hotel. These opaque facades, faced in slate, will convey a feeling of impassive calm to the main street elevations of the new museum and thus help to sustain the horizontal impetus of the 600 foot and 460 foot long elevations running along 54th and 53rd Streets, respectively. This horizontally balances the vertical thrust of the tower and the stepped mass of the galleries and new offices stacked high in a setback formation at the western end of the complex. This was an enormous amount of accommodation to pack on to a very limited site and Taniguchi seems to have been able to achieve this without a sense of overcrowding. In part, this has been achieved through the horizontal profile and in part through integrating this linearity into the scale and rhythm of the surrounding urban fabric.

Among the more sensitive aspects of Taniguchi's design is surely the way in which the history of the institution has been physically and culturally incorporated into the matrix of premises. Thus the organic entrance to the Goodwin Foundation building of 1939 is reinstated in its original form – particularly with regard to the former semicircular recessed entry on the 53rd Street front together with its equally organic canopy projecting over the sidewalk. This typical organic curve of the late 1930s is echoed by an equally curvaceous ticket counter, both gestures entailing a faithful restoration of Goodwin's original design. It is fitting that this somewhat theatrical approach will be used to provide access to the existing museum auditoria, mainly for the purposes of attending lectures or film screenings in the late afternoon or evening.

Taniguchi has gone out of his way to maintain the original stair shaft of the Goodwin building in which there still hangs Oscar Schlemmer's famous painting of the main stair in the Dessau Bauhaus. This time-honoured, symbolic juxtaposition will be maintained in the new museum while the stair itself will be restored to its original form so as to descend to the basement auditoria or alternatively rise up to serve the photography and architectural/design galleries, the two departments of fact that, aside from painting, played prominent roles in Alfred Barr's polemical Modernism of the 1930s.

Taniguchi has not been so attentive to the Phillip Johnson east wing and north wing additions, the former being in any event little more that a multi-storey flexible space, clad back and front by monumental neo-Meisian facades, a feature which he will maintain on the 53rd Street front of the east wing

while demolishing its counterpart facing the garden in order to increase the overall footprint of the building and link its stacked staff offices to the education wing. This reworked six-storey building will be furnished with a staff restaurant at the first floor facing the garden, while the offices above will be capped by a new founder's room, together with an equally ample roof terrace for summer reception, overlooking the garden.

The theme of the city-in-miniature which I ascribed to Rockefeller Center will be returned to a diminutive scale in Taniguchi's new MoMA, where the idea of a labyrinthic micro-urban space, inserted into the larger labyrinth of Manhattan, will first be touched on in the main lobby which will assume the form of galleria linking the 54th and 53rd Street entrances in a straight shot. This relatively low, deep space opens up to the member's counter, coat check and bookstore on one flank and to the museum proper on the other, bringing the visitor to confront a long view of the garden before accessing the galleries above either by a typical Taniguchi scala regia or by free-standing, high-speed elevators. These elevators will be augmented by an escalator hall affording continuous pedestrian movement between the second and fifth floors. This is the core of the Taniguchi scheme, featuring relaxing visitor sitting areas overlooking the garden and a subtle link between a void over the 54th Street entrance lobby and the five-storey atrium above poised in the centre of the stacked galleries housing the main collection. This in typological terms is the galleria as city-in-miniature, first introduced as modern trope in Frank Lloyd Wright's Larkin building of 1904.

The idea of a city-in-miniature is returned to in the distribution of the restaurants in the first and second floors, the bulk of them facing the garden on the first floor, but similar 'density' is also pursued in the placement of the auxiliary cafés so as to induce more diverse itineraries throughout the interstices of the building.

Much of this compact and ingenious scheme still surely waits to be studied and refined as its working drawings are developed, and one feels that it is at this stage that Taniguchi will finally come into his expressive own. There are those who are of the opinion that this design is far too corporate and understated to serve as an appropriate home for the Museum of Modern Art at the beginning of the 21st century. These critics seem to underestimate the difficulty of accommodating such a dense and highly complex brief on an extremely compact and, in some senses, compromised site with all sorts of service shafts and entryways which cannot easily be changed or even modified. But aside form these pragmatic and programmatic constraints, that out of sheer necessity have imposed a normative, orthogonal geometry on the work, it may be just as readily argued that the minimalist character of Taniguchi's architecture is appropriately neutral for a complex

212

whose primary purpose is to preserve and exhibit art, that is to say, it will serve as a suitably dematerialised background for art rather than compete with it. But beyond this there lies the promise of the specific poetic of Taniguchi's architecture that resides as much in the details as in the work of other modern minimalists such as Mies van der Rohe or, for that matter, his Japanese colleague, Fumihiko Maki.

Anyone who pays even the most cursory attention to Taniguchi's career over the past two decades, that is to the 17 public buildings that he has realised between 1978 and 1998, six of which happen to be museums, can hardly fail to be impressed by the technical precision of the work and by the way in which quite minimal elements have been used to achieve tonal effects of remarkable subtlety and power. I am thinking in particular of his consummate capacity in handling metal and masonry revetment of various kinds, from corrugated sheet to stack-bonded tiles and of his ability to induce a warm and varied aura of ambient light from the materials themselves. Aside from these skills, one must also note his capacity to discriminate tectonically between earthwork and roofwork, not to mention his particular penchant for the design of light fittings and furnishings with which he habitually highlights his spatial effects (see in particular his Sakata Kotutai Kinen Gymnasium of 1991).

If there is one Taniguchi building that comes close to the tectonic and material syntax that one might expect from him at the Museum of Modern Art in New York, then it is surely the Marugame Genichiro-Inokuma Museum of Contemporary Art also of 1991, located opposite Marugame Station in the Kagaw Prefecture. Here, one finds virtually the entire repertoire of the MoMA *avant la lettre*; from blank stone walls to pleated metal revetment, form luminous spot-lit interiors with accented fields of colour and translucent partitions, to high clerestory lighting in double-height gallery space and precision curtainwalling, from lean metal handrails to classic furniture, be it either bespoke or off the peg. It is all there in Marugame City, as well as elsewhere in the Taniguchi dossier and one only hopes that the Museum of Modern Art will allow him to operate at the same level in New York. As his client in Marugame apparently told him, 'Make it a large rich space. How you do it I leave up to you!' Should a similar level of patronage finally materialise behind the Taniguchi design then there is no doubt that by 2005 MoMA and Manhattan will once again be an undisputed mecca of modern architectural culture. Until then, we shall have to make do with what we were left with as a legacy some 35 years ago.

213

Demanding Audiences: The Future of New York's Public Realm

Raymond Gastil

214

In this world, the future of the 'public realm' is at risk. The 'realm' of public life has always been a balance of abstract and concrete, concept and space, but the decline of physical places thought to embody the public realm, a decline started by the highway in the 1950s and thrust into its endgame by the Internet at the century's end, threatens that balance. While they may have described the 'public sphere' of, say, the town square, as a liberal bourgeois conceit that never met its own ideals of access, interaction and discussion, many critics confronting today's conditions would welcome back such aspirational squares, streets and parks. However imperfect their access and activity, these spaces had at least the apparent complexity of public life as opposed to the simplicity of the monocultural, consumerist enclaves that pass for public spaces today, spaces which may even pass away themselves in the frenzied clicks of online shopping. Without a city square, as form or metaphor, is there still a public life?

In the next few years this question may well be erased by the energies of e-life, but for the moment it is still vital, and especially so for the future of New York. Throughout the 20th century, the city has successfully promoted itself as the most important public space in the world, the one where anything and everyone goes. While its tenure may not be indefinite, New York's public space will remain a potent image for at least the next generation, if only because of the enormous film, video and literary library of 'content' the city has already produced about itself.

Yet if the city is to continue to produce such 'content', its value will depend on actual experience, physical conditions that designers and policy-setters will determine even as they decide whether consciously to design public space primarily for 'export' (film, video, etc) or for local use. The first question for these designers is: can they identify a persistent, valuable character to New York's public space, a character that both serves its residents and may also have meaning for the rest of the world as a symbol of public life? And if so, can it be designed? Can it be implemented by policy, facilitated by benign neglect or simply left to indifferent accident?

To address this question this essay focuses on a specific site, a churning artery at the city's heart: the East River. Running between the Bronx and Manhattan on one side, and Queens and Brooklyn on the other, it has been called a river since the Dutch arrived, though the solemn and informed cannot breathe

the name without intoning that it is not a river at all, but rather a tidal strait between Long Island Sound and New York harbour. Not even a river, it is rarely offered up as a paradigm of anything, even though it has been at the centre of things in the putative capital of the 20th century since 1898, when New York's century began with the consolidation of Manhattan, Brooklyn and Queens, together with the Bronx and Staten Island.

Why the East River? In addition to its central location, of all the spaces in New York it is one of the easiest to grasp, despite its scale. Looking at the 8-mile stretch from the Brooklyn Bridge to the Triborough, before it angles west into the Harlem River and east to Long Island Sound, it can be interpreted as a thoroughly contemporary space of flows (transport, tides, cultures), yet in the end it is a figure, as identifiable as Central Park or Times Square, a broad gap in the grid. The 4-mile 'reach' from the Williamsburg to the Queensboro Bridge is perhaps the paradigmatic figure, almost a negative to Central Park's positive. While it may be mostly known as a barrier to get over or go under by bridge or tunnel, whose one great shared function is as the site for the Independence Day fireworks, it is nonetheless a negotiable, comprehensible public space 365 days a year.

Furthermore, it is in flux. In its final phase of de-industrialisation, it has vast tracts of undetermined, undeveloped land on the Brooklyn and Queens side, and more room for change on the Manhattan shore than most acknowledge. For all the efforts to give it a postindustrial identity, which it may finally surge towards if it becomes the transit corridor for the 2012 Olympics, for now it is still an unfinished, half-wrecked relic of the industrial age.

Finally, not unlike Times Square, the East River is haunted by a memory of 'publicness' as dangerous as it was exciting. Like any port it combined opportunity and risk and, more specifically, for more than a century, the river was the city's backyard and bad conscience, a place to dump toxic waste and toxic people – the criminal, the mad and the infected. Bordered for decades by the city's roughest tenements and grittiest industries, the East River is still where the struggle between Manhattan and the other boroughs, white collar and blue collar, commerce and industry, real and virtual, local and international, honest and criminal, industry and leisure, nature and synthesis and *laissez-faire* and command economy will be fully played out – a proving ground for the future of the city's public life.

There are formative examples of public space in New York besides the East River, of course. The image and reality of the labour protests in Union Square before the Second World War, and the homeless-anarchist protests of Tompkins Square in 1988, were gritty enough, but had a purposeful political dimension absent from the everyday encounters of the waterfront. Olmsted's ideal was the absence of grit, a sentiment he expressed in the sound appreciation of his own work in Central Park, where he observed that people of all different incomes and ethnic backgrounds peacefully coexisted, relieved from the jumble and business of the streets. In the moment after the Second World War and before the explosion of crime in the late 1960s, New York held up its public spaces as fitting the political ideal of Hannah Arendt's public realm, wherein an individual could negotiate a multitude of perspectives, thoughtfully, not overcome by the irrational momentum of prejudice or mob, and could in so doing become a fully realised citizen. Jane Jacobs's evocation of life in Greenwich Village was as ambitious as Olmsted's or Arendt's in its aims, explaining that the 'sidewalk ballet' of the street, in which the 'dancers' nodded hello and watched out for each other's children was the performance of small pieces that built up into the great exchange of public life.[1]

But the waterfront presents a darker ballet, part of a cultural tradition and reality of seeing New York's public space as dangerously alive. Fred Siegel, a social historian who was one of the key champions of bringing 'civility' back to New York's streets in the 1990s, nonetheless acknowledged the special power of New York's not always civil public realm. In 1993, he wrote how: 'New York's dynamic diversity – its mix of touts and tribes, characters and con men – gave total strangers a shared satisfaction in watching the drama of daily life unfold in our parks and plazas. For many, the public character of their private selves was revealed in the pleasure they took in being described as streetwise. This 'streetwise' attitude of 'shared satisfaction' might not equal an Arendtian participation in the public sphere, but it was part of a negotiation, part of a 'balance between pride in being part of the action and prudence in interacting with strangers'.[2]

Looking at New York before the controversial quality-of-life initiatives of the Giuliani administration, Siegel wrote that even the most hard-bitten, proudly 'streetwise' New Yorkers were being overwhelmed by a sense of 'menace', whether from drug dealers, squeegee men, aggressive panhandlers or fed-up residents ready to devolve. The city's leaders demanded a new type of 'shared satisfaction', one less like an episode of a crime drama and 'more urban'. For the founders of the Central Park Conservancy and the Grand Central Business Improvement Districts, civility could be constructed not only by programming and security and cleaning personnel, but also by a commitment to architectural language and form that reincarnated an ethic of visible civic patronage. For many, this was urbanity built on a bourgeois Parisian example, out of date and out of place in New York, yet whatever the class connotations and conflicts, not to mention the enlightened self-interest of these patrons, the campaigns effectively asserted that public space could be controlled – that the 'menace' could and should be removed.

At the same time, New York made its greatest commitment to public space, in policy if not in investments, to the waterfront. The comprehensive waterfront plan first issued in 1992 staked its claim for virtually unlimited public access to the waterfront. Whether from the mayor's office, the borough president's or the city council's (often conflicting powers in the municipal government), the message was the same: the waterfront is the next great public space of the city.

Not surprisingly, these documents didn't announce the goal of promoting the 'streetwise' encounters Siegel described. They did declare their intent to preserve at least some maritime industry districts on the Brooklyn waterfront, but didn't romanticise the social conditions in these areas. Not that their 'seedy' character was entirely out of the planning discussion. In the 1970s, during one battle in the 40-year war to 'clean up' Times Square, Mayor Koch suggested that Manhattan's West Side waterfront be turned over wholesale to pornography shops, a suggestion made when there was more than a little crime, menace and unpoliced behaviour (and a floating prison barge) on that part of the Manhattan waterfront. But city governments, and the planners and designers who work for them, rarely endorse uncontrolled activity, and in the 1990s put that vision behind them. Except, of course, in Times Square, where they passed zoning text that required, in a regulated way, the traditionally exuberant, uncontrolled signage that had typified the district, even as it worked to eliminate the uncontrolled behaviour that had accompanied the uncontrolled designs of the past.

Yet what will be a sustainable future for the East River? Given that few would endorse a zoned district for 'victimless' crimes, is there some prospect of a more varied environment than a waterfront serving as a front garden for a homogeneous population? Can a city sustain or endorse 'incivility', or an 'otherwise civil' city? Symbolically, at least, the preserved 'float bridges' of the Gantry Park at Queens West in Hunters Point speak of a rich, not always clean, history for the site, but what steps can or should be taken to a more complex present? A brief sketch of the East River's 20th-century history may illuminate its potential.

At the time of the city's consolidation (1898) there was only one bridge across the tidal strait, the Brooklyn Bridge (1883). Yet the infrastructural links soon matched the political ones, both above the water with the Williamsburg (1903), Manhattan (1909) and Queensboro (1909) bridges, and below with the first IRT line running between Manhattan and downtown Brooklyn (1904). The ferries that had crossed the river back and forth disappeared, while the swiftest up- and downriver traffic continued to be by water.

What was the urban form of the East River shore before the First World War ? On the Manhattan side the port was still active, but the era of the great packet boats was finished and

215

most international shipping had moved to the Hudson River piers. Just beyond the waterfront, hundreds of thousands of tenements and tenement-dwellers lived in what may have been the greatest residential density in history. The infamous 'Red Scare' map, adapted by John B Trevor for the Lusk Committee of 1920, was colour-coded to show the 'subversive' nationalities living in this 'tenement belt' along the East River from the Brooklyn Bridge to Yorktown. And while the majority of the tenement-dwellers worked inland, the waterfront was thick with shipping, industry and the services of the vast city: coalyards for fuel, cattleyards for food and hospitals for the sick (Bellevue at around 30th Street, which had been on the East River since 1811). In the midst of it, the river still served for recreation, whether in unorganised swimming off the piers or in the public bathhouses.

In the strait's centre, today's Roosevelt Island was known as Blackwell's Island, and had a panoply of buildings for the city's outcasts – prisons, smallpox hospitals, almshouses – scarcely reached by the forces of reform. On the opposite bank Newtown Creek, between Queens and Brooklyn, had been home to oil refineries since the 1860s and was a thriving industrial and shipping centre. The creek was famously foul, yet intensely busy as the second most active (in terms of tonnage) commercial waterway in the country. Brooklyn's Greenpoint waterfront was lined with huge terminals and industrial operations while to the south, in Williamsburg, there were both major private industrial plants and the Brooklyn Navy Yard, the national centre for building warships from the Spanish-American War through the Second World War.

By the 1920s shipping activity along the Manhattan side of the East River was in decline, and while the city continued to stitch itself together by tunnels and bridges east to west, the master builder Robert Moses also drew the north–south Manhattan shore into his highway system. For Moses, the East River Drive (fully completed in 1941 and later renamed the FDR Drive) was inevitably more than a serviceable road: not only did it link to the Triborough Bridge (1936) at the north, but it was also part of a transformation of an industrial waterfront and tenement district into a very different vision of urban life. The road did not erase all that came before – it had to be elevated for long spans to accommodate still-active industry and shipping – but it did dissolve the jagged, industrial edge, turning it into a smooth bulkheaded line. It proposed a new type of city, with the green fields of East River Park on one side and, among others, the Vladeck public housing project (1940) on the other, with the long-muscled road in between. In *Vers une architecture* (1926), Le Corbusier had offered the prospect of 'architecture or revolution'. Along the East River, looking back at the Lusk 'Reds' map of 1920 and the built reality of 1940, it seems that some of the intent behind this building campaign was, as Le Corbusier recommended, to prevent revolution.

Before its reform the East River shore was a site of startling social contrasts, both in fact and fiction. Starting in 1920, the wealthy began to occupy waterfront districts formerly reserved for tenements, from Sutton Place at 57th Street to 42nd where Tudor City rose above the cattleyards from 1925 to 1928. Rich and poor lived cheek by jowl, as portrayed in Sidney Kingsley's *Dead End* (1935). The play, and William Wyler's film with Humphrey Bogart two years later, underscored the East River's character as a place of terrible lights and darks, between great wealth and poverty, colossal infrastructures like the Queensboro Bridge and puny tenements, the freedom of the river and the captivity of the neighbourhood. The Dead End Kids could look across to the centre of the river, where the renamed Welfare Island was still a site for the unwanted, although its early 20th-century reforms had included building modern hospitals in the 1920s and removing the notorious prison to Rikers Island in 1935.

The United Nations might have been expected to transform the East River once and for all. The most powerful players in New York participated in a fast-paced deal to ensure that the city became the UN's headquarters. In 1946, told that New York had only five days to come up with a site, Nelson Rockefeller managed to convince his father, John D Rockefeller Junior, to give the money for the land, Willam Zeckendorf to sell the land and Robert Moses to push through permits to allow the project – all on the site of a former coalyard and slaughterhouse known as 'bloody alley'. The secular Vatican of the 20th century, whose parti if not its whole character derived from Le Corbusier, was antithetical to the 'Dead End' of a decade before.

And yet, in the same period, Jules Dassin filmed *Naked City* (1948). At the Williamsburg Bridge, 3 miles south of the United Nations, he presented a very different world. There were sunny public spaces, like the pedestrian boulevard atop the bridge which, filmed on location, appears as perhaps the most powerful public space New York has ever known, and at first as benign, a place for children on roller skates. Down below, at the docks, it was dangerous – the film even begins with a body being dumped in the East River. Yet by the end of the film, with a spectacular shoot-out on the bridge, no place is safe from the tough streets. *Naked City*, like the photographer Weegee's work on which it is based, is the flip side of the United Nations. Despite the dreams of Le Corbusier and Moses, 'the street' and its rules survive. As Marshall Berman wrote about the interstate system (not unlike the UN's posturban identity), it may have destroyed neighbourhoods and the town square throughout America, but 'They failed to kill the street'.[3] Berman sees this as a triumph of human spirit, resiliency and New York's uniqueness, but is it also a triumph of 'streetwise' attitude, the kind that the unbourgeois life afforded by the riverfront?

Architect Miriam Gusevich has identified the East River as a place of 'desire and disgust', where the city can't quite decide what it wants – pleasure gardens or garbage-transfer stations, high-income housing or dwellings for the sick and indigent.[4] Yet from the 1970s onwards desire, if not action, has been the ruling principle. That decade saw a major push to transform the river and its public spaces, although there was little interest in the form or character of the street, despite the powerful influence of writings by Jane Jacobs among others. On the Manhattan side, the Waterside Complex (1974) pushed out into the water beyond Bellevue, and was a consummate enclave despite its public walkways (often locked). At its heart, Welfare Island once again had a new name: Roosevelt Island. In 1971, under a state authority, a master plan was developed by Philip Johnson and John Burgee to create an ideal community. Its arcaded pedestrian central street, courtyards and public spaces were an exotic alternative to urban life, although at odds with New York's climate and particular character. In 1974, the original state authority collapsed and Roosevelt Island was able to build out only part of its plan in the 1970s, with another wave of building in the 1980s.

In the same era, most of the shipping and much of the industrial activity on the Queens and Brooklyn side dissolved, finally undone by containerised shipping, the rise of trucking and the shift of manufacturing away from cities to the far, highway-convenient suburbs and other continents. The venerable Brooklyn Navy Yard closed in 1966. In a few years one of the world's greatest shipping and manufacturing centres changed from a site for production to a canvas for artists, film-makers and photographers. Some documented its remains, while others actively intervened, as with Gordon Matta-Clark's pier-cut projects in the 1970s. For the next quarter century, as the dreams of the 1980s real-estate boom came and went with little change, that waterfront scarcely altered. It became a drab view from the mediocre East River walkway or, from the other direction, a rivetting foreground of industrial archaeology for films and photography shoots looking beyond it to the Manhattan skyline.

In the 1990s the East River reached the verge of significant change, although by the end of the decade there was no guarantee that this would be fully realised. On the Manhattan side the city's Economic Development Corporation, enriched by the federal government's transport enhancement programme, was able to push through improvements to the East River walkway, renaming it an esplanade, and also sponsored small design interventions like the new ferry terminal structure at the Wall Street pier by Smith-Miller + Hawkinson Architects. On the Queens waterfront, the huge Queens West park project, first approved in 1984, finally broke ground in 1994. While the first building is disappointing, the Gantry Plaza State Park (Thomas Balsley Associates) has been recognised as one of the few public spaces in New York to address ecological, historical and programmatic complexity, with its hard and soft edges, four public piers and restored gantries.

There are still community groups fighting a rearguard action against the slow-moving Queens West project, attacking its indifference to the scale and character of the existing neighbourhood and finding little to admire in the park. Queens West is burdened by following the megaproject model of Battery Park City, which while it may provide a potent public space on the water is by design an enclave, especially against the low profile of existing Long Island City. To the south, in Brooklyn, intricate private ownership has stalled the transformation of the waterfront and community groups have developed their own plans for the river's edge, most notably to sustain the public access to the piers that they have become used to in the years since the piers' commercial functions ceased. Just south of the Brooklyn Bridge, after the thorough rout of a proposed multistorey development on Piers 1 to 5, a publicly driven group is once again initiating a design process for the piers, while to the north, in the DUMBO district between the Brooklyn and Manhattan bridges, David Walentas' 20-year campaign to gain control of the Civil War era warehouses appears to have fallen through, perhaps for good, despite his success in garnering the zoning changes that allow him to develop the loft buildings that surround the public site. New York rarely entertains proposals for, much less builds, daring architecture and while Walentas sponsored Jean Nouvel's design for a water hotel cantilevered out across the river, and it engaged the *New York Times* architecture critic, the proposal was dead on arrival so far as community activists were concerned.

It is in this context that Van Alen Institute: Projects in Public Architecture sponsored research and discussion on the East River, in a project predating Nouvel's proposal and the design project for Piers 1 to 5, led by Kenneth Greenberg, which was begun in late 1999. For the institute, the city's commitment to public access to the waterfront was the starting point; the questions that followed were what sort of public realm was imagined, and what sort would be realised by the policy, planning and design initiatives either under way, planned or under discussion.

The process of the study included a workshop, web site, a series of exhibitions, an international design competition, lectures, panels and the remarkable entries to the competition. In addition, the Van Alen Fellowship in Public Architecture sponsored Jesse Reiser and Nanako Umemoto and their team in developing a widely published and exhibited East River Corridor project. Conventional notions of park, edge, waterfront, street and urban, and ultimately, public space were all put into question.

Most entrants in the competition, no matter that they swore

217

218

their commitment to 'urban space', were focused on reclaiming the East River as a natural environment, however pointedly artificial they might make that nature. Kevin Bone of Bone/Levine Architects and his team proposed 'Transfiguration' that would 'reintroduce fragments of a more complex network of water-based natural systems'. The Hunters Point Community Coalition advocated an entire system of 'habitat restoration' sites along both sides of the strait, while Alan Berger's 'Landscape Strai(gh)ts' project, which buried the FDR Drive, provided a complex natural habitat to the waterfront and insisted that it become a colossal straight line, one which could be read as a man-made intervention on the scale of the city. Jens Brickmann and Fabien Gantois, with the freedom that an ideas competition allows, proposed '(this is not Manhattan)' in which the entire edge of Brooklyn and Queens becomes a beach to further intensify the divide between the towers of Manhattan on one side and the low profile of Brooklyn and Queens on the other.

For Victoria Thompson and Steven Tupu, whose 'Till' won first prize in the competition, the chief issue was again creating a natural (though highly unnaturalistic) landscape. They identified the city's greatest physical problem as coping with waste and poisoned lands, and designed a new waterfront for Brooklyn and Queens with a vigorous topography of ramps and dales, coupled with an ambitious schedule of strategies for leaching out, growing out and putting out the toxins in the waste and earth. At the same time, through their images, they indicated that the most valuable public space was space for recreation. Not that the ardour of work is absent: the images are of mountain biking and demanding play, a vision common to many of the entrants including Philippe Baumann and Karl Jensen and the Office for Global Architecture (Leslie Neblett, John Herrera), who presented a packet of postcards from the year 2048, when the East River would be known as Middle Park.

For the sponsored design research of Reiser + Umemoto, the challenge was to take the apparently 'destructive' entity of the FDR Drive and transform it into a generator of valid contemporary urban form and public space. Reviewing the community boards' wish lists for their waterfronts, first compiled by the Department of City Planning's reach studies and updated by the Van Alen Institute study, they construed a supple, self-regulating frame that integrated the FDR into multiple systems of slow and fast vehicular traffic, pedestrian territories and millions of square feet of commercial, civic and service space. Drawing on the concepts of 'infrastructural urbanism' that Reiser, as well as Stan Allen and others have helped to develop, Reiser + Umemoto's project recalled the complex section of the Brooklyn–Queens expressway, where the highway stacks up beneath the Brooklyn Heights promenade.

The Reiser + Umemoto project, while agile in connecting the systems of its project to local streets, is hardly a celebration of the street. Instead, it looks to the interaction between pedestrian, vehicular and waterborne transport systems, together with the programming of the recreational and commercial space, to create an authentic contemporary public realm. Rather than romanticise an historic urban street as the generator of public experience, it finds the 'energy' – some might even find in it a kind of menace – through the scale, traffic and complexity of its form.

Given the authorised and speculative designs for the future of the East River, is there a specific, as opposed to generic, future for New York's public realm? Will it manage to encourage not only 'face to face' encounters in the darker New York vein that some crave – the 'in your face' encounters that Andrew Shapiro, theorist and practitioner on the future of the Internet, insists are the necessary essence of public space online or off?[5] Or is the 'in your face' city just a negative world of squeegee men at the Lincoln Tunnel, as you try to drive under the East River?

A contemporary position could start with recognising that whatever the site – street, square, park, waterfront – New Yorkers crave a 'shared satisfaction' that is not all sweetness and light, but very urban and in its own way civil. The 'ballet' may have a great deal more to do with recreation than in the past, but that is the nature of cities today, no matter how much we yearn for the city of Louis Kahn where, to paraphrase, a six-year-old could walk through the city and learn what he wanted to do for the rest of his life. Today, most of the work happens inside, beyond the street, and it is recreation more than anything that is left to animate public environments. Given that condition, it is critical to be resolute in demanding recreation and multiples scales, for multiple publics. In this context, a New Yorker can continue to be a demanding audience and, when called on, an actor in this urban theatre.

Notes

1 Jane Jacobs, *The Death and Life of Great American Cities*, (New York), 1961; Modern Library Edition (New York), 1993, pp65–71.

2 Fred Siegel, 'Reclaiming our Public Spaces: Strategies to restore civility to our streets and parks', *City Journal* Vol 2, Spring 1992, pp35–46, citations p35.

3 Marshall Berman, 'The Lonely Crowd: New York after the War' in *New York: an Illustrated History*, editors and co-authors Ric Burns and James Sanders with Lisa Ades, Knof (New York), 1999, pp536–41, citation p538.

4 Miriam Gusevich, unpublished presentation, Van Alen Institute, 1997.

5 Andrew Shapiro, unpublished presentation, Van Alen Institute, 1999; see also Shapiro, *The Control Revolution: How the Internet is Putting Individuals in Charge and Changing the World We Know*, Century Foundation, 1999.

It'll Be a Great Place If It Ever Gets Finished

Malcolm Holtzman

New Yorkers, no matter what they know of their city's history – facts or familiar stories – are sure of one thing: the only constant in New York is change. As its physical features are transformed the city's identity as America's foremost urban centre remains unaffected.

Known for its big buildings and big population, New York changes in big ways. This has been the case ever since the grid pattern was superimposed, in 1811, on the substantial undeveloped portions of mid and Upper Manhattan. In almost every era since then, large-scale development projects have been the criterion, many of them realised in the 20th century: Rockefeller Center, Sunnyside, Robert Moses' parkways, the United Nations headquarters, Peter Cooper Village, Lefrak City, Lincoln Center, the World Trade Center, Battery Park City and, most recently, the reconstruction of 42nd Street and Times Square, the 'crossroads of the world'.

Despite the inevitability of change in New York its denizens have, within the last 30 years, taken it upon themselves to protect some of the city's heritage. To preserve the past and stabilise the present, however, can be a quixotic endeavour. Although architects can physically turn back the clock by invisibly repointing brick walls, reweaving fabrics and insulating old windows, it is the life within and around buildings that propels the city forward. Buildings can be preserved, but the activities within them change constantly. They metamorphose every day, sometimes imperceptibly. New Yorkers demand the latest 'necessities': cell phones, t-lines, palm pilots, personal trainers, astrologists, feng shui counsellors, yoga instructors and more. While we now know how to maintain structures, there is no desire to limit their usage.

Preservation and renewal issues are not confined to buildings. Since the early 1990s, the members of at least three Gramercy Park associations have been wrangling over the park's landscape. Trees planted many decades ago appeared old and tired. Should they be taken down or left to die on their own? Acrimony reigned. The battle appeared to have been won by the 'leave it alone' faction until a big storm ripped through New York, felling the trees on the park's western side. This previously canopied mid-Manhattan oasis is now almost totally open. Sometimes doing nothing causes greater change than a Supreme Court judge's ruling. (I note this paradoxical event because I live and work in this section of the city.)

New York's inhabitants, too, are in perpetual motion. 'Odd yet typical' are the only words that, in retrospect, can describe my own peregrinations of the last 30 years in this area of Manhattan. I have resided at 22nd Street and Second Avenue, the north side of Gramercy Park, 17th Street and Fifth Avenue and 24th Street and Park Avenue. During this same period my architectural practice has moved from 25th Street and Lexington Avenue to 21st Street and Park Avenue South, and finally to 21st Street and Broadway. My locus of activities may be more tightly focused, but the frequency of my moves is probably not very different from that of many other New Yorkers.

Small, unrecognised alterations can be significant modifiers of the city environment. Unplanned by government agencies, developers or banks they happen spontaneously, individually, incrementally and, most frequently, invisibly, until enough of them accumulate in a given location to become apparent as a larger whole. For example, the street-level retail spaces in my section of the city, along 23rd Street and Park Avenue, Fifth Avenue and Broadway number close to 150. Since 1970 all but two of them – a novelty store and an optician – have been recast. There were three full-service bank branches. Two have closed and one is now an ATM. Restaurants, bookstores, dry cleaners, florists, delis and drugstores are still present but in new locations managed by new operators. Starbucks, chi-chi restaurants, supermarkets, discos, topless bars and children's clothing stores have arrived along with other new inhabitants. A vacant storefront is hard to find. The demand for these spaces and the services they provide is constant but changing.

For most of the 20th century in this area, when large-scale commercial endeavours were centralised in the city, spaces above street level were devoted to manufacturing or second-class office use. (The only exceptions were the insurance companies that constructed buildings for their own use on Lower Madison Avenue and 23rd Street.) Everything from umbrellas to pool-table felt was made here. The changes to these upper-floor spaces are even more radical, though unheralded when they initially occurred, than those at street level. In the last two decades, the automobile and the expanding digital economy have further contributed to dispersing commercial activities beyond the edges of the city. Residential lofts appeared first in these newly emptied spaces; then architects, designers and photographers turned manufacturing spaces into studios and specialised office space. On a larger scale, publishing and advertising firms succeeded them. The two latest arrivals are at opposite ends of the space-needs spectrum. A large international bank has occupied half of the 2.2 million square feet in one of the insurance company buildings on Madison Avenue. The other influx has been tiny e-commerce companies that occupy side-street lofts in the area now christened 'Silicon Alley'.

Another form of change, the renaming of districts, plays a

prominent role in legitimising increasing real-estate costs and confirming that an area has been gentrified. It was not long ago that 'Hell's Hundred Acres' became 'SoHo', 'Hell's Kitchen' was dubbed 'Clinton' (prior to the president's election) and the area adjoining Gramercy Park was labelled the 'Flatiron District' after the renowned building. At about the same time there was an attempt to revive 'Ladies' Mile' for the area on Broadway below 23rd Street, even though no ladies' department stores exist there today.

The make-up of New York's population is yet another way to gauge change. Traditionally, waves of immigrants to the city provided an inexpensive workforce. Considerable attention was focused on this aspect of city life when, in 1990, the Ellis Island Immigration Museum was opened by the federal government. Immigrants from all over the world continue to flow into the city in great numbers. Today, New York's population is 35 per cent foreign-born; some predict this percentage will increase. Equally noteworthy has been the departure of blue- and white-collar jobs. Manufacturing and business administration can be accomplished less expensively outside New York City. No one wants to assemble machinery or manufacture pocketbooks here. Large banks, insurance companies and other businesses may keep executive functions in the city, but clerical operations have been decentralised and located elsewhere. The spaces vacated as a result of this migration are most often being converted into residences. With the absence of manufacturing and commerce, which leaves only support services, public transport, schools and cultural facilities, New York City is in danger of becoming the ultimate suburb.

In the wake of the departure of businesses the population has undergone another subtle metamorphosis: the arrival of NIMBYs, a suburban phenomenon if there ever was one. In recent years neighbourhood organisations, community groups and individuals have been remarkably successful at stopping or significantly altering large-scale development. There have always been nay-sayers in our midst, but now there seem to be more of them. 'Not in my back yard' is a call that can be heard from Columbus Circle to First Avenue and the United Nations to Canarsie. People want to preserve landmarks, but many others want to protect their real-estate investments, their views, their way of life or their sense of what the city used to be.

These days, it may be easier to stymie big projects than keep track of small ones. Having neither advocates nor adversaries, the latter are seldom challenged because they are not publicly put forth for discussion. We may have reached a time when the grand changes that have always sustained the city must become modest ones. If that is the case, these small transformations must be encouraged because, without any change at all, New York will no longer be the place everyone thinks will be 'great' if it 'ever gets finished'.

Looking down Broadway to Union Square

© Cervin Robinson

220

Computer rendering by pixelbypixel, NY

PROJECTS 8

©Solomon R Guggenheim Museum. Photo by David Heald

KOHN PEDERSEN FOX

ROCKEFELLER PLAZA WEST

Facing Seventh Avenue at Rockefeller Center's western edge, this 55-storey office building responds to strict zoning requirements for both New York City and the Times Square Theater District. The 1.6-million square foot building also houses performing arts rehearsal studios and is linked to the underground concourse network of the centre.

The contrasting models of corporate and public Modernism set the stage for the project and inform its design. A central vertical core pins the building to the site and defines it on the skyline, joining the axis of the GE and Exxon buildings. The building is clad in limestone and clear glass with stainless-steel ornamentation placed on the surface of the stone to articulate building setbacks and shimmer in the sunlight.

A two-tiered podium, slid towards the west, adds to Seventh Avenue's street wall. Its surface is covered by electronic signage, and a building entrance is indicated by a tower of light. An irregular configuration created at the Exxon plaza provides the main entrance to the building. A portion of the building facing Times Square is disengaged and transformed into a metal and glass sign. Lit at night, it brings the building into the bright ambience of Times Square.

222

© Jock Pottle/Esto

© Jock Pottle/Esto

Above: project 1, 1.6 million square feet;
Left: the crown.

Kohn Pederson Fox

After the financial setbacks of the early 1990s, the project re-emerged with a different developer and different parameters.

The primarily glass and metal building rises to a height of approximately 600 feet through a series of alternating setbacks. The setbacks are a product of the necessity to maximise the bulk of every floor and comply with the stringent zoning requirements. The gross building area is approximately 1.1 million square feet. There are one and a half floors below grade.

The Times Square sub-district has stringent requirements for signage provision along Seventh Avenue. The requirements are met by creating a rear illuminated curtain wall along Seventh Avenue above the ground floor for the first and second setbacks. The setbacks generally correspond to the heights of the surrounding buildings, and in this way, the project responds to its context. The setbacks help reduce the mass and scale of the building. Because the structure is part of the Morgan Stanley Dean Witter campus and because of its close proximity to Times Square, the southwest corner is architecturally developed to gesture towards 1585 Broadway and to the 'bow tie'.

© Jock Pottle/Esto

Top left: project 2, 1.1 million square feet, signage studies for 7th Avenue;
Above: pocket park;
Left: project 2, massing study with the GE building and Rockefeller Center in the background.

SKIDMORE, OWINGS & MERRILL
COLUMBUS CENTER

Columbus Center is a 55-storey building massed in a tripartite composition, with a base rising to 100 feet above curb level, a mid-section which reaches 290 feet, two high-rise residential towers located on the western portion of the site extending to a height of 720 feet, and a third mid-rise residential tower, located at the south east corner of the site on Columbus Circle.

The retail portion of the project extends for five storeys, including a two-storey high Harrods style food court on the Concourse level and is approximately 300,000 square feet. The shops are served by a four-storey curved Galleria – the common public circulation space for retail, cinema and studios. An 18-cinema multiplex occurs on the third and fourth floors of the Galleria. Levels 5 and 6 house twelve column-free, state-of-the-art television and recording studios ranging in size from 6,000 square feet to 15,000 square feet.

The large glass Globe, the icon for this project, houses a public restaurant. Located on the sixth floor, the Globe commands views of Central Park and the surrounding streetscape.

A 300 key luxury hotel and 750 condominium and rental apartments complete the scheme and form the cluster of three towers that rise above the retail and studio component. The residents and hotel guests have access to a deluxe health club at the base of the residential towers located on the seventh floor.

224

Above: computer study of the multiple elements;
Left: computer view above Columbus Circle;
Opposite page: Central Park, 57th Street, Broadway and Columbus Circle.

Model looking south across Central Park to Columbus Circle

© Jock Pottle/Esto

© Jock Pottle/Esto

Above: night view from 57th Street;
Left: computer study of the central passage between the towers of the site for Jazz@Lincoln Center.

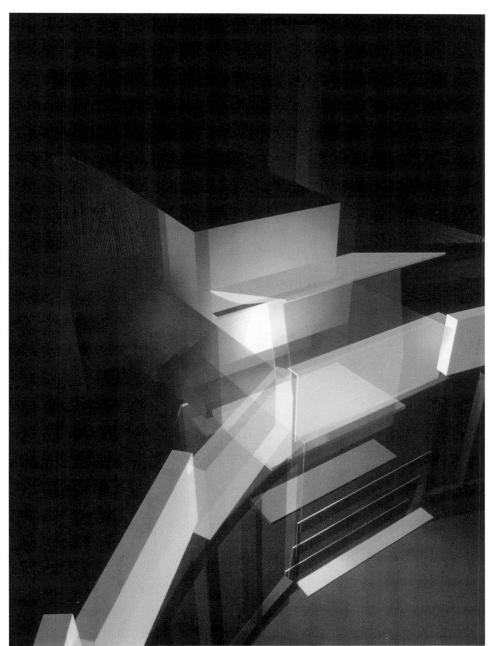

RAFAEL VIÑOLY
JAZZ@LINCOLN CENTER

Jazz musicians have always played on the street, in a club or in places that were primarily designed for classical music but there has never been a place built just for jazz. Therefore, building a place for jazz is about capturing a certain feeling.

Viñoly's response to this begins with multiplicity. Rather than having one space adapt to all of the possible functions, he has created a series of places throughout the whole facility for music to occur in different situations, combinations and settings.

One arrives at the concert theatre through a series of more informal spaces. One of these is the jazz café, a space that is open to various readings and uses. It can be interpreted as a nightclub but also as a place to relax, a classroom, a cabaret or a lobby. The plan of the whole place works to provide that flexibility.

The performance atrium situates the performers in the city, creating a place of diversity and excitement. The space also puts the audience in a situation that is interactive with the musicians, in which the dance floor is part of the stage and the seats wrap around in tiers. The intention is to blur the distinction between front-of-house and back-of-house which is so much part of classical notions of music and theatre. The seats are disposed so that they are related and interact with one another in multiple balconies and the floor doubles as a dance floor, creating another layer of intimacy and communication between the performers and the audience.

228

Above: occupying the central space between the towers of Columbus Circle (computer model of the performance Hall); Left: in performance with views to Central Park and 57th Street.

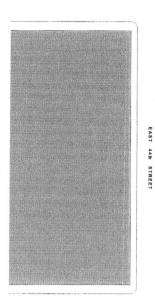
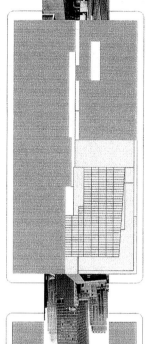

FIFTH AVENUE

EAST 44th STREET

EAST 45th STREET

MADISON AVENUE

SKIDMORE, OWINGS & MERRILL
350 MADISON AVENUE

The proposed renovation and addition to 350 Madison Avenue calls for changes at both the street level and the rooftop of the existing structure. The two-storey lobby, located in a zone between 350 Madison Avenue and the adjacent building, is open to the sky from the roof. This entry zone is lit from below, creating a volume of light between the buildings. New retail spaces are enclosed by glass panels that wrap around into the lobby, tying the two together and reinforcing the pedestrian scale of these spaces. The dramatic lighting of the entrance is intended to identify the building as a destination at both street level and above.

The elements of the addition are enfolded in a continuous metal mesh surface at the lobby level and over the existing structure, unifying them with each other, while distinguishing them from the existing building. The glass curtain wall of the rooftop addition is echoed in the fenestration of the storefronts at street level. The rooftop addition of 110,000 square feet of office space enlarges the existing floor plates. Terraces provide views of several New York City landmarks, including the Empire State and Chrysler buildings, while the cantilevered top portion creates panoramic views from many points within.

229

Above: site plan; right: computer model of the building envelope; Opposite page: physical model of the building envelope.

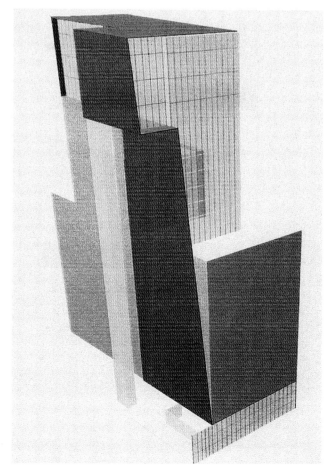

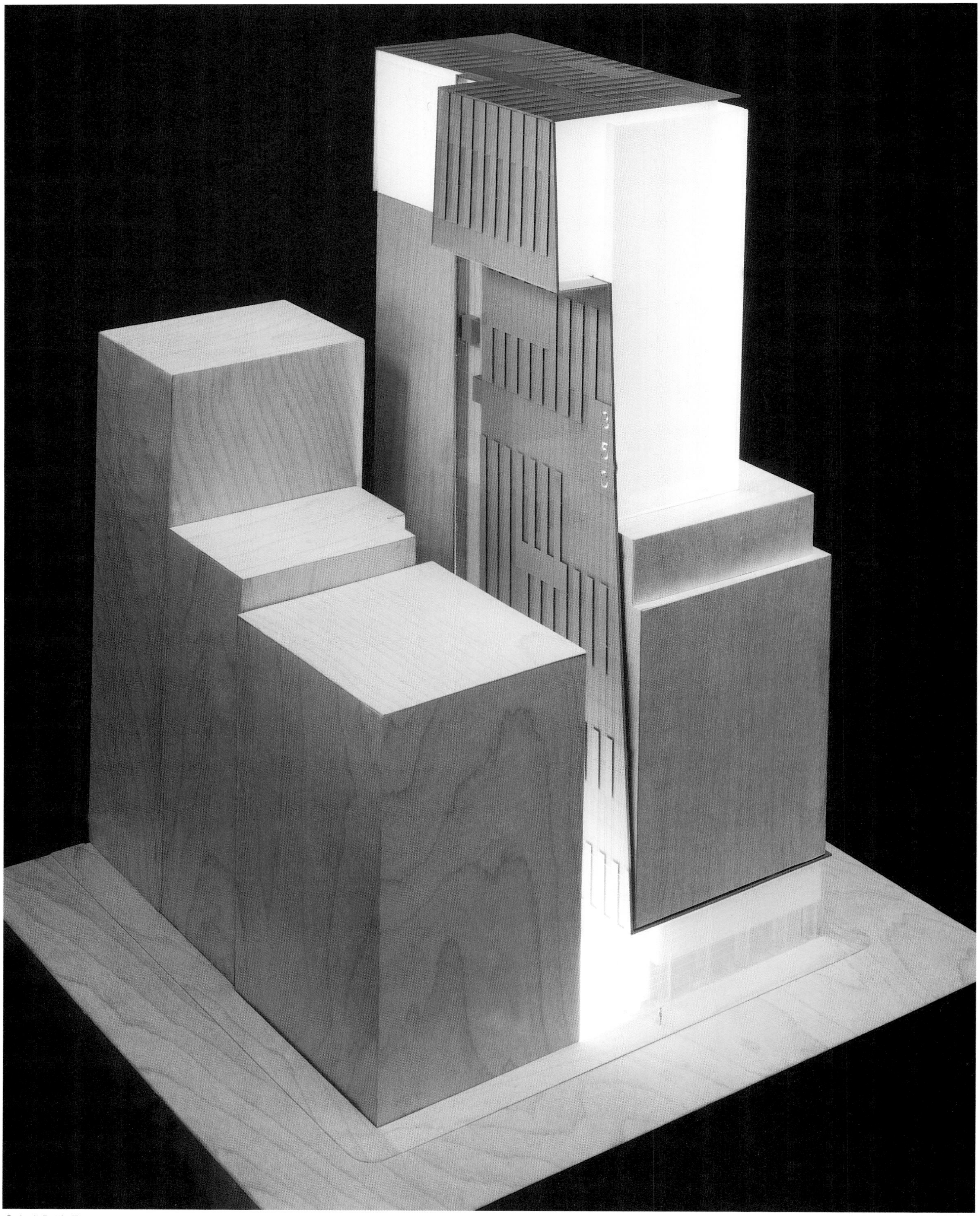

© Jock Pottle/Esto

© Jock Pottle/Esto

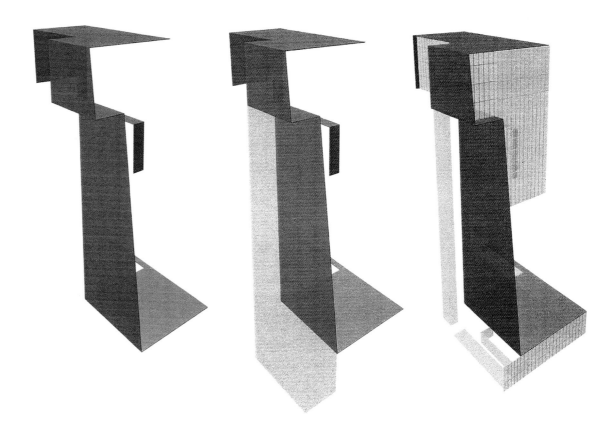

SKIDMORE, OWINGS & MERRILL
TIMES SQUARE SITE 2

The architects for this project researched the history of 42nd Street to create a building that belonged in the context of the Entertainment District. The basic rectangular prism is metaphorically sliced by a curving beam of light. This effect creates 'two buildings' each with its own sculptural profile. The easterly volume is firmly anchored to the ground and is clad in horizontal bands of earth-coloured bronze glass. Bands of black-painted glass in gold and rust emphasise the horizontality of its patterning. The westerly volume rises above the ground, levitating five storeys above the corner of 43rd Street and Eighth Avenue in defiance of gravity. An atrium lobby in clear glass ends in an angled ceiling that becomes the underside of this suspended building. In contrast to the easterly building, its thin volume broadens as it reaches toward to sky. It is clad in vertical bands of space-age steel and blue-grey glass. This 52-storey volume rises above the 45-storey side, revealing its lit up curved inner surface to Times Square.

On 42nd Street, the tower appears to rise from a 'rock'. This rock actually houses the suites of the hotel and is shaped like a jagged rocklike form approximately 10 storeys high. It is clad in mosaic and its irregularly shaped collage is punctuated by a checkerboard of glass squares – the windows of the guest rooms.

Opposite page and left: computer renderings of the building in performance.

Computer rendering by pixelbypixel, NY

Computer rendering by pixelbypixel, NY

Institutional Arts

PETER EISENMAN
STATEN ISLAND LIGHTHOUSE MUSEUM

Bringing together the contemporary experiences of theme park, museum and cultural centre, the Center for Electronic Culture (CEC) proposes itself as an entirely new type of urban institution.

The centre's programme is conceived in three layers: a main 'infotainment' or extravaganza hall comprised of displays, games, stations, projections and films; a museum component with five multimedia exhibition tracks with complementary lectures, a library, bookshops and a publications programme; and a commercial/industrial component that functions as a clearing house documenting developments in all aspects of high-technology research.

Like the undulating forms that characterise its physical design, the Center for Electronic Culture should be conceived as a kind of perpetual documentary film unfolding in four dimensions. The structure and presentation of data is at once didactic and as seamlessly compelling as mass entertainment programming, yet with uncompromising integrity with respect to the depth and breadth of its subject matter. It transcends the traditional custodial idea of a museum altogether: it is a new type of living institution, capturing and deploying in real time a living history in motion.

234

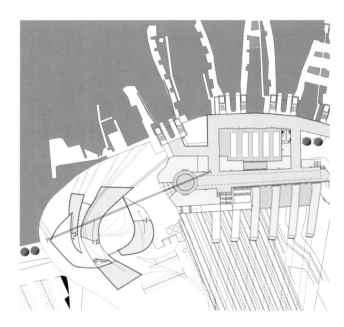

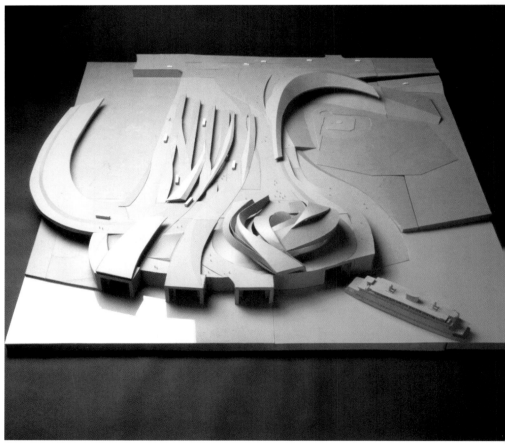

Above: early study model showing museum integrated with the ferry terminal on Staten Island;
Left: the site plan showing the museum in relation to the terminal.

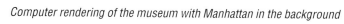

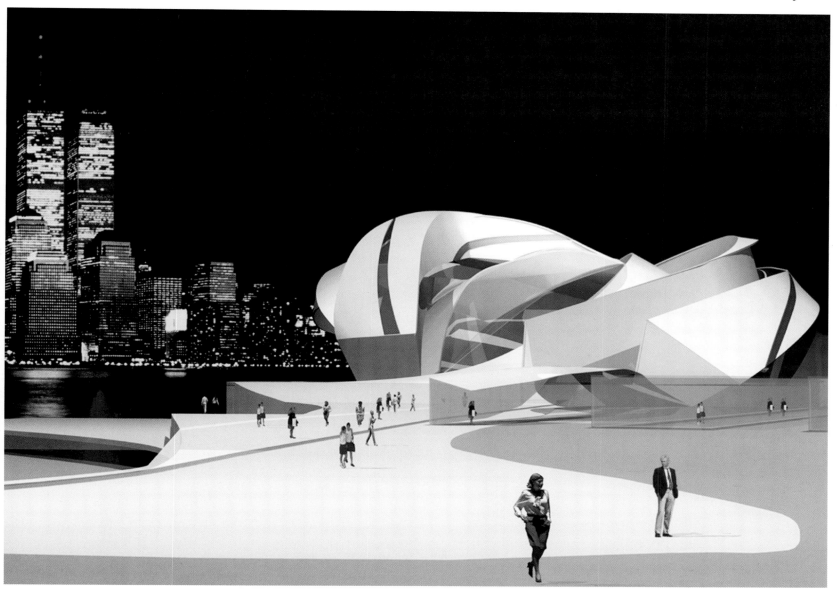

Computer rendering of the museum with Manhattan in the background

SHARPLES HOLDEN PASQUARELLI
MUSEUM OF SEX

SHoP began the Museum of Sex project by first asking some questions. Is there a relationship between form and performance that could aid in the design of a space for human sexuality? Is there a relationship that does not utilise a bifurcating model of male/female, straight/gay, spectator/participant, but rather a resilient and ambiguous correlation between desires and an architecture that allows a museum of sex to re-evaluate ideas and concepts?

The site of the Museum of Sex is a narrow corner lot on Fifth Avenue with views of the Empire State building. The extremely narrow floor plan suggested the use of a layered organisational device, and the generative concepts of organic form, tactile expression, exposure and concealment led to thinking of this device as 'skin'. This skin is made up of layered surfaces with specific functions, defining the physical and conceptual parts of the building. The particular placement and curvature of the walls are designed for optimal performance as dictated by requirements such as circulation, exhibition, flexibility or lighting.

The innermost wall conceals necessary building infrastructure within a continuous sculptural shape. The exterior envelope is a play of several translucent layers of steel and glass. With variations of transparency, the facade becomes part of a flirtatious game played between the building and the city. The street level is transparent, inviting entry with nothing to hide. The public is invited to peek behind the veil and become part of the architecture and exhibition.

Right: study model of the facade;
Below: topological study of surface form.

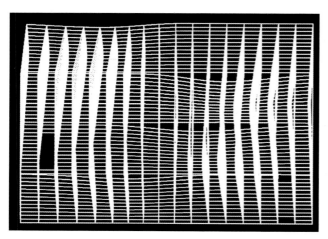

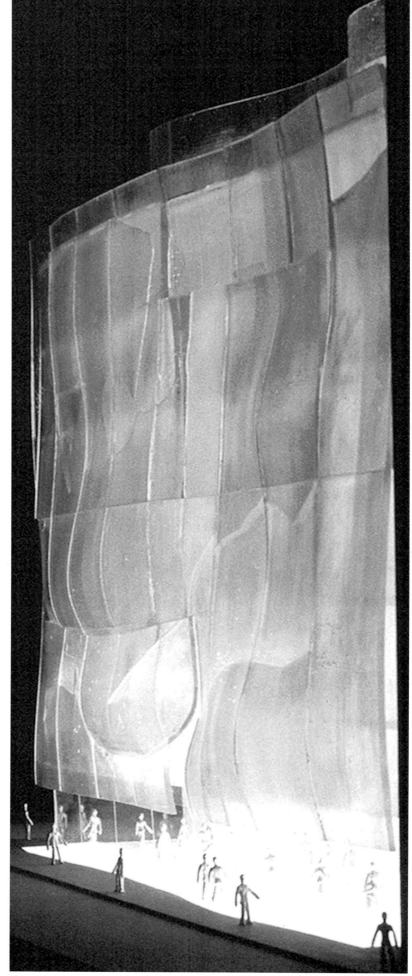

236

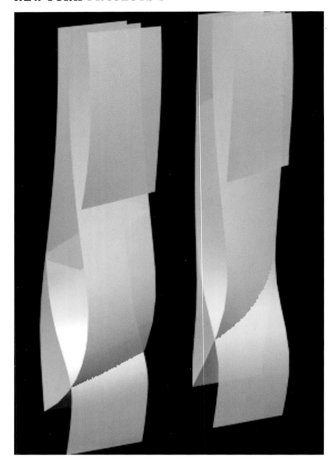

Opposite page: computer study in perspective;
Above: studies of the double skin of the facade;
Right: detailed rendering of the space between the skins;
Lower right: studies of the human body as a source
for the form of the building's skin.

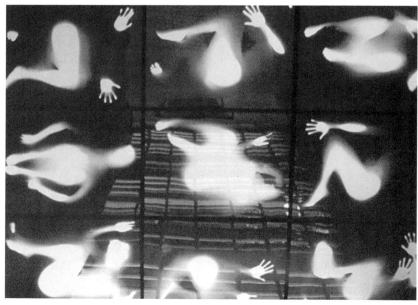

Right: developing the structure to support the undulating skin;
Below: the skin.

239

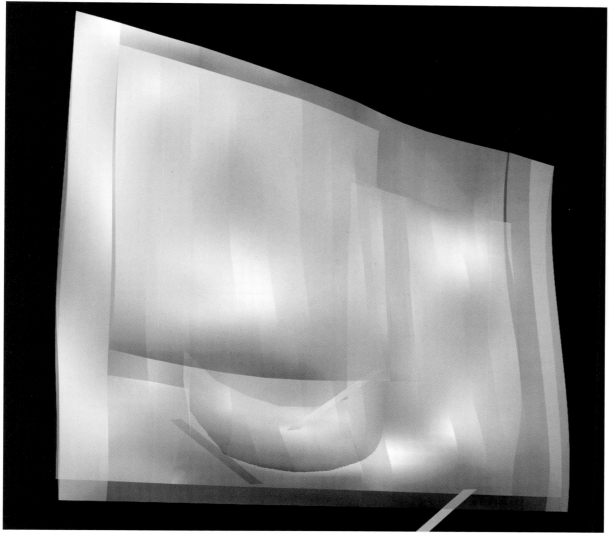

YOSHIO TANIGUCHI
MUSEUM OF MODERN ART

The winning competition entry for the expansion of the Museum of Modern Art was from the Japanese architect Yoshio Tanaguchi. The two other entries on the final short list of three were by the Swiss team of Herzog and de Meuron and Bernard Tschumi of New York.

Taniguchi's scheme displays skill in relating the prevailing cornice height of the 53rd Street and 54th Street frontages to a single existing high-rise structure in the centre of the block, in effect the 29-storey museum tower which was completed to the designs of Cesar Pelli in 1978. A balance is achieved in terms of overall mass between this curtainwalled residential high-rise and the adjacent brownstone-scale to either side.

Of equal importance on both the 53rd Street and the 54th Street elevations are the 80-foot high marble-clad blank facades fronting the expanded museum facilities, aligning on the 53rd Street front with the cornice of both the original Philip Goodwin building and the Philip Johnson addition. While on 53rd Street the single blank facade will enclose a bookstore on the first floor with windowless galleries above, on 54th Street one of the blank facades will house the new education wing comprising offices, study centres, libraries and archives. This blank block is lit from its glazed north-west return facade facing the garden. A similar side-lighting strategy is adopted in the case of the second blank face of 54th Street which houses the temporary and permanent collections on the site of the former Dorset Hotel.

240

© 1997 The Museum of Modern Art, New York

Above: the grand foyer;
Left: model photomontaged into New York.

©Kotaro Hinaro

The view down 53rd Street

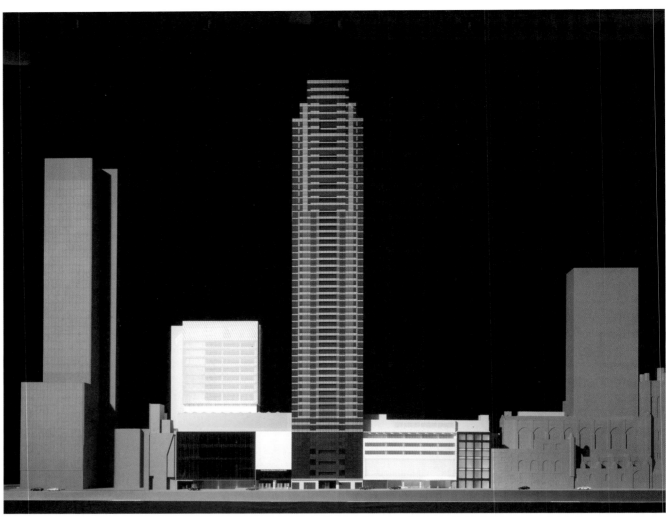

53rd Street elevations

*Left: view along 54th Street;
Below: looking into the new
garden of the museum.*

FRANK GEHRY

GUGGENHEIM

The architectural plans for a new Guggenheim Museum were designed by Frank Gehry who won acclaim for his design of the Guggenheim Museum in Bilbao, Spain. 'Despite the 1992 renovation of its landmark Frank Lloyd Wright building on Fifth Avenue and the opening of an addition designed by Charles Gwathmey, the museum does not have adequate space in New York to show major portions of its collection,' states Thomas Krens, Director of the Solomon R Guggenheim Foundation.

As designed, the new museum building would occupy a total of approximately 520,000 square feet, augmented by a significant public park and outdoor sculpture area and would have more than 200,000 square feet for exhibitions. The entire museum would be built on connecting platforms resting on piers at water level. In order to preserve the openness of the platform and to create a sense of space, light and views from South Street through to the East River, the overwhelming majority of the museum building would be raised above the platforms. This design creates both a view corridor of the waterfront below the level of the FDR Drive, as well as a public waterfront promenade, sculpture garden, fountain and an expansive public park on the platform with access to the water for ferry service and possible other boating activities.

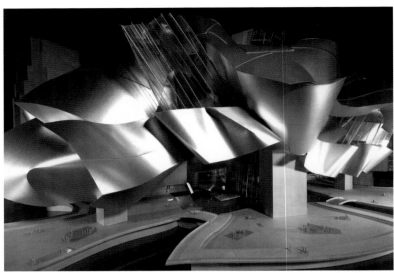

© Solomon R Guggenheim Museum. Photo by David Heald

Above: the view from the East River without the backdrop of Manhattan;
Below: promenades on the public waterfront.

© Solomon R Guggenheim Museum. Photo by David Heald

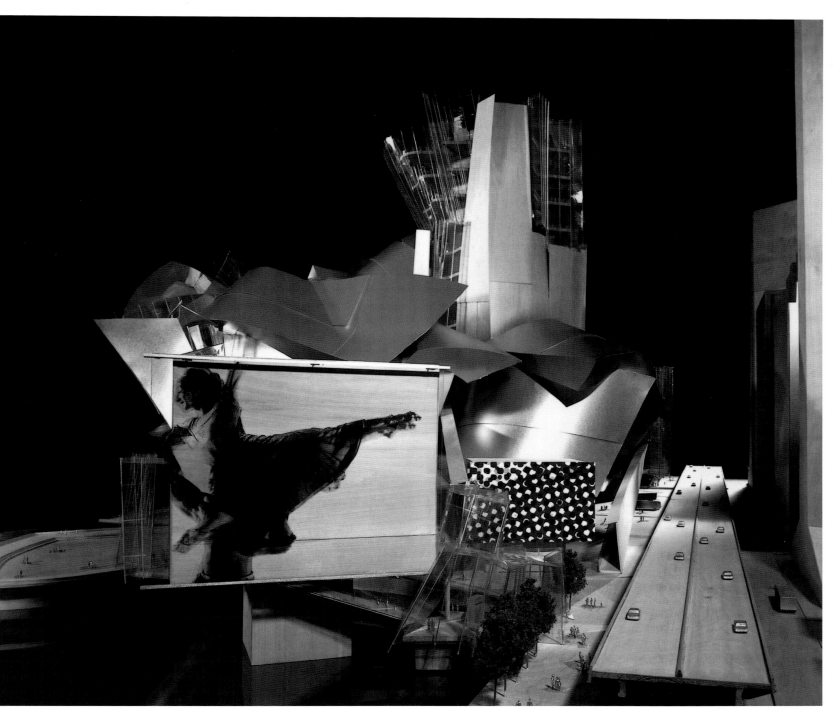

Below and opposite page: views up and down east River Drive;
Over the page (247): public promenades and the central atrium.

© Solomon R Guggenheim Museum. Photo by David Heald

Institutional Public

AGREST & GANDELSONAS

BRONX SOUTH COMMUNITY CENTER AT MELROSE HOUSES

The Bronx South Community Center is geared primarily towards teenagers and provides them with facilities for activities of interest, such as athletics, arts and crafts, videos, and computing. The design of the centre reflects a desire to avoid a fortress-like solution and instead provide the community with a building that conveys a sense of openness and accessibility. The project calls for a strong formal solution to play a symbolic role in the community.

The various social, physical and contextual conditions are very important to the form of the solution. The gymnasium, oval in plan, presents a strong image suggesting movement when seen from the road. The oval rests in unstable equilibrium near a bar-like building which contains the remainder of the programme. The bar and the oval are linked by a thin neck which serves as a common entrance and an exhibition space.

By separating the gymnasium from the other programmatic elements – administrative offices, classrooms, etc. – building use is compartmentalised relative to scheduling and security. Thus, when an event is under way in the gymnasium, the centre's other facilities can be closed, or vice versa. The entry hall can also serve as a public exhibition space for the various works produced at the community centre.

The building is made to look as transparent as possible. Curtain wall glazing along the length of the bar exposes the interior to public view in both directions. Additionally, an exterior video screen linked directly to the centre's audio/visual facility provides a venue for public showings of videos produced at the centre.

248

Above: in construction;
Left: computer rendering.

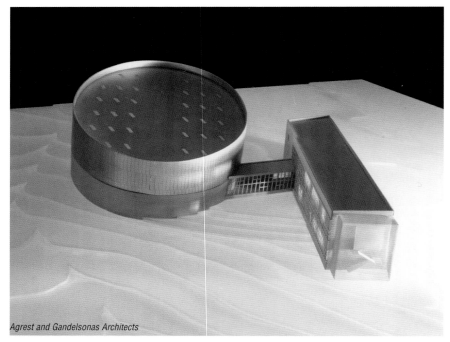

Agrest and Gandelsonas Architects

View from the garden

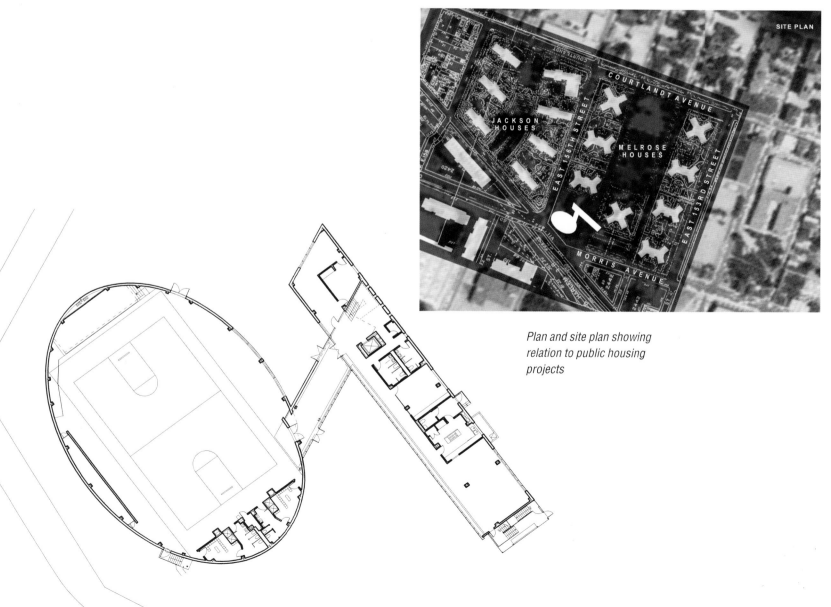

Plan and site plan showing relation to public housing projects

HARDY HOLTZMAN PFEIFFER ASSOCIATES

CENTRAL SYNAGOGUE

Central Synagogue, constructed in 1872, is the oldest building in continuous use as a synagogue in New York. Remarkable for its Moorish design and ornate interior, it is both a New York City and a National Historic landmark. Severely damaged by fire in August 1998, comprehensive restoration was undertaken to preserve its historic character and allow it better to serve contemporary needs.

The multitude of materials which comprise the exotic motifs of the sanctuary and its foyer have been refinished, replaced or repaired. One of the most significant restoration efforts was the repainting of the extensive geometrical, multicoloured stencil patterns on walls and ceilings. The sanctuary's 12 double-storey stained-glass windows, ornate rose window and stained-glass laylights were also restored.

On the exterior, ornamental details missing for decades were recreated. Visible from the street, HHPA returned the black and red slate geometric pattern to the gabled roof, accenting the crenellations along the roof and the twin minarets with gold leaf.

Alterations to enhance the use of the synagogue respect historic design elements. A new section of movable pews, which permit a range of seating configurations, is fabricated in a style evocative of the original's detailed millwork. The main entrance was reconfigured to create a grand entryway for comfort and ease of flow of congregants. Below, a multipurpose space was redesigned to better accommodate a variety of public functions. Completed, the restored synagogue brings back to life an architectural treasure that has played a significant role both in the history of American Judaism and the history of New York City.

250

©Chris Lovi/HHPA

Above: interior;
Left: exterior.

MARGARET HELFAND

THE CHILD DEVELOPMENT CENTER AT BRONX COMMUNITY COLLEGE

The repetitive module of the classroom made this early-childhood education centre at a New York City community college a good candidate for preassembled construction. Perched on a steeply sloping site at the edge of the campus next to a wooded area, the two-storey structure could be entered at grade at the upper level while the classrooms at the lower level could also open on to an outdoor activity area.

The architecture of the project embodies the essential duality of the educational process: the simultaneous needs for order, logic and predictability and for creativity, intuition and surprise.

The three blocks of classrooms at the lower level organise the building and create a square void at the centre. This space, with its translucent, panelised, field-installed roof, becomes an indoor activity area for the children and a meeting space for the school. Each classroom consists of two factory-assembled units that fall within the dimensions allowable for transport. On site, the units are interconnected and stacked. All interior and exterior finishes are installed in the factory except along the joints between the units.

The brick veneer on the exterior of the building is enlivened by using two slightly different shades of brick. Within each colour zone there are also sections of contrasting joint patterns. The brick installed in the field at the construction joints is given its own identity by shifting the pattern as well as by shifting the plane to projecting (at vertical joints) or recessed (at horizontal joints and parapets).

251

Above: the entrance showing the translucent roof;
Below: section through the central meeting area.

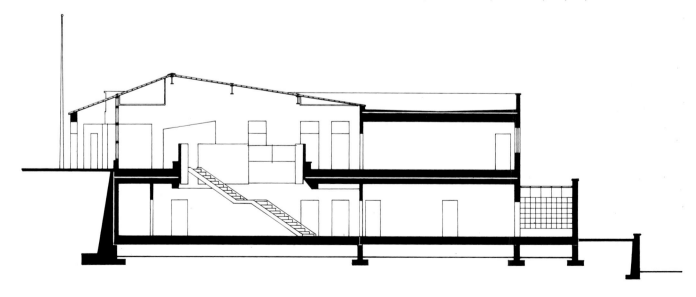

RAFAEL VIÑOLY
BRONX CRIMINAL COURT COMPLEX

The new Court Complex is located on a three-block site on East 161st Street near Grand Concourse Boulevard. The new court facilities will work with the existing Supreme and Criminal/Family Courts located near the site. The project goal is to integrate the 1.1 million square foot court complex within the existing community formed by low and mid-rise residential buildings to the north, elementary and high school structures to the east, and retail and commercial activity along 161st Street. This is achieved by massing the building along the perimeter of the site, creating on open civic space that will act as a transition between the Criminal Court and the residential and school neighbours. The building responds contextually to the surrounding and adjacent neighbourhood structures in its massing height and scale.

The civic plaza that covers an underground parking structure will be landscaped and occupied by recreational and community uses. Above the plaza, a system of cantilevered stairs will connect different public circulation levels, reducing the demand on vertical transportation and enhancing the movement of the public within the courthouse.

Above: model of the private circulation areas;
Below: model view of the civic plaza and the cantilevered stairs connecting the public circulation.

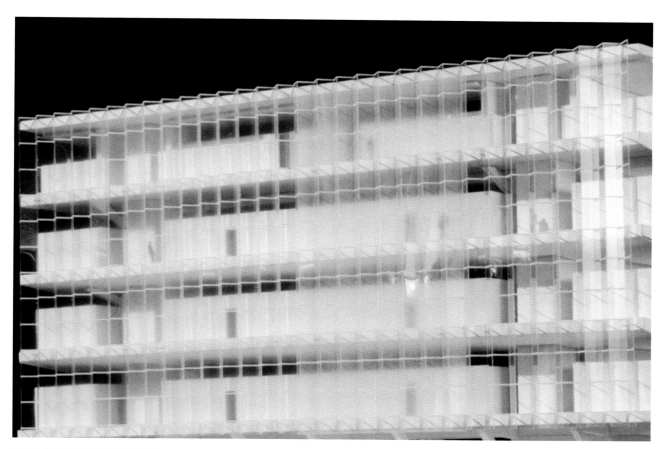

Above: model of the perimeter elevations;
Right: section through the perimeter wall diagramming the penetration of natural light at various times of day.

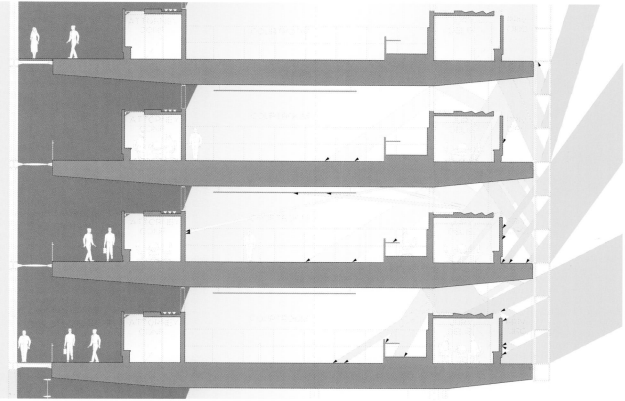

Transportation

DI DOMENICO JOHN
ATLANTIC AVENUE TERMINAL COMPLEX

The Metropolitan Transportation Authority has undertaken an ambitious plan to redevelop a significant site in Brooklyn. Located in an area of downtown Brooklyn once bustling with activity, at the crossroads of Flatbush and Atlantic Avenue, the Atlantic terminal project is part of a larger redevelopment plan which includes a 500,000-square foot retail centre. The terminal serves the arrival and departure of commuters on the Long Island Rail Road and three NYC transit stations. The most prominent element of the terminal is an entry pavilion connected to a planned adjacent retail complex and the transportation centre below ground.

The new terminal entry pavilion is entered from two locations on the street. From these 'pylons' commuters descend to the main train concourse below or pass through an entry vestibule to the retail centre.

The site called for an urban intervention that would re-establish it as the gateway to downtown Brooklyn. The gently curving wall of the entry pavilion shapes a noble entry hall that is the main waiting room for commuter trains and the subway. Shaped by mass and revealed by light, the space becomes a stage whose walls serve as the backdrop for a theatre of commuter ritual – a space to collect one's thoughts, and shelter for a musical interlude, as sounds fill the void until boarding time. The exterior glazed wall and skylight above the main concourse area are shaped to allow for the dance of light and shadow across the walls of the entry pavilion.

254

Above: entry pavilion at the crossing of Flatbush and Atlantic Avenues;
Left: section showing the pavilion in relation to the transportation centre.

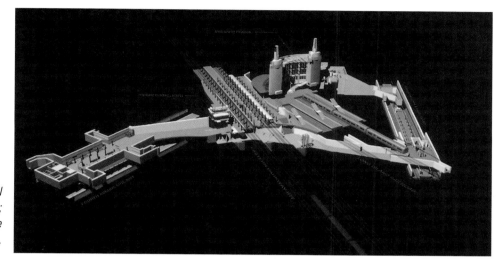

Right: computer model of all the interconnecting stations; Below: computer studies of the interior of the pavilion.

SKIDMORE, OWINGS & MERRILL

PENNSYLVANIA STATION REDEVELOPMENT PROJECT/POST OFFICE RENOVATION

SOM is the designer for the conversion of the landmark McKim, Mead and White Farley Post Office building, which will expand the facilities of the adjacent New York Pennsylvania Station. The work includes creating a new departure hall, a ticketing hall, and retail and operational areas within the landmark building. These new facilities will serve as the hub station for Amtrak's Northeast Corridor high-speed rail service introduced at the end of 1999. The station will also serve the new train services to John F Kennedy and Newark International Airports. The project is due to be completed at the end of 2002.

256

Opposite page: the entrance in the new ticketing hall occupying the service passage in the centre of the Farley post office;
Above: inside the departure hall;
Left: the platforms below the departure hall.

Computer rendering by pixelbypixel, NY

Computer rendering by pixelbypixel, NY

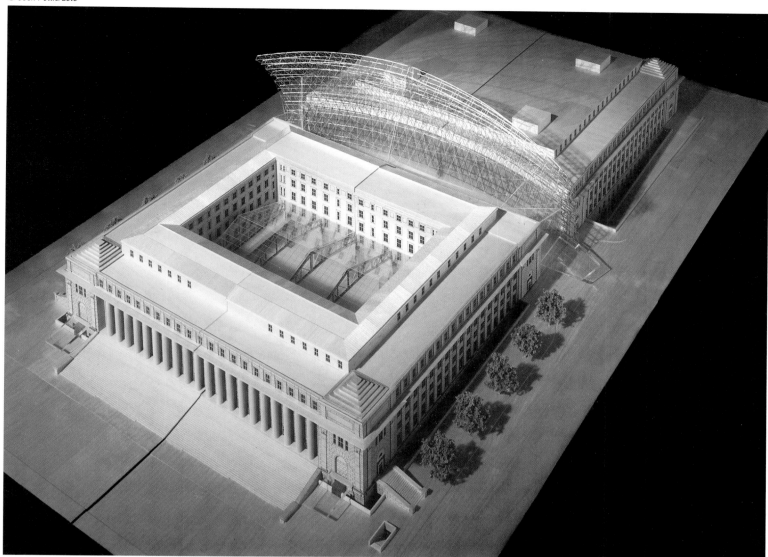

Above and right: model showing the 8th Avenue elevation of the post office, the new roof over the departure hall and the symbolic structure above the ticketing hall.

Opposite page: Computer rendering by pixelbypixel, NY

SKIDMORE, OWINGS & MERRILL

JOHN F KENNEDY INTERNATIONAL AIRPORT, INTERNATIONAL ARRIVALS BUILDING

SOM, in conjunction with TAMS and Ove Arup & Partners, is completing plans for the redevelopment of the International Arrivals Building at John F Kennedy International Airport. The existing terminal designed by SOM in 1957 is being completely replaced by a 1.5-million square foot state-of-the-art terminal that will reassert JFK's place as an international gateway to North America. Being built in phases, the airport will provide uninterrupted service throughout construction. The new terminal will initially have 20 gates and be capable of processing approximately 4,000 passengers per hour. Capacity is provided to allow the new terminal to expand to twice its first phase size without construction disruption to future operations. Dual-level roadways will serve arrivals on the ground level and departures on the third level. The second level will incorporate all of the mechanical and baggage systems serving both departures and arrivals, as well as the station for the new airport-mover system connecting to other terminals and regional transportation hubs.

Above: the end of the terminal showing the proposed airport-mover system.

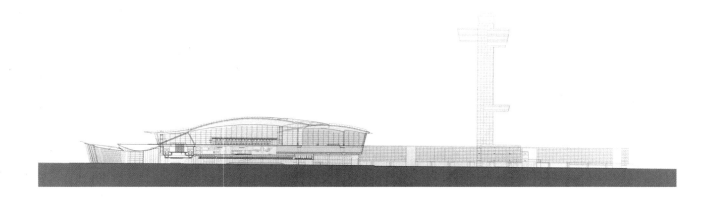

Above: perspective inside the terminal;
Left: the terminal showing transport connections.

Landscape

MARGARET HELFAND

PETROSINO PARK

Petrosino Park is located in SoHo in lower Manhattan. Centred among diverse ethnic and economic communities, the park is bordered by two major travel arteries bringing traffic into the city. The park area measures approximately 160 feet in length and 40 feet at its widest.

Construction lines for this project are generated by the passage of the sun through the seasons and people through the park. Shadows cast by surrounding buildings on four significant dates mark the pattern of ground plane fragmentation. Several modes of human transportation regularly occurring in, along or under the park are defined by textural transitions on the ground plane.

Edges of the triangular park are allowed to extend beyond the immediate site. Approaching streets and sidewalks are embossed with the softly knurled texture and fractured pattern of the park, mediating thresholds. The fast moving traffic relents to the rough texture of cobblestone. A glass prism allows shared light to pass through to the subway platform below, connecting the subterranean and surface layers of activity.

Right and below: the ground plan disturbed by the figures based on the shadows from surrounding buildings and the prismatic light well to the subway platform.

262

In planning an end of the millennium series on the city, the publishers developed a clear structure: Paris was the consummate city of the 19th century, New York fulfilled all the desires of the 20th century but had nothing to offer the future. The city of the 21st century would be either Tokyo or Berlin. In this proposition they failed to acknowledge the essential difference between New York and all other major cities – those of Europe and Asia are the products of public calculation; New York is, and will always be, a city of continuous private speculation.

What are the many futures that will be desired for New York, and how will they coexist? Unlike the remaking of Berlin, the future of New York lies more in the actions of those seeking gain than in any public vision. And though Manhattan is one of the world's most powerful fields of speculation the grid forces remarkable conformity. And whereas there is in Berlin a shared and relatively common vision of what constitutes the public realm, New York is formed from many realities, all with very different values, held within the frame of the grid. In examining the diverse desires these produce the experience of space and place must be combined with all the other sensations that establish the reality of the city.

All made realities are fictions formed out of need or desire. The need to grid Manhattan becomes hard and clear when one confronts the myriad desires that had to be accommodated and reconciled in the fabric of the city. Manhattan and the oldest parts of Brooklyn continue to be held within this grid whose intent was to ensure a republican public order. However, as the culture of speculation has driven the continual redevelopment of the city, this generalised republican constraint has given way to the local demands of developers and neighbourhoods. Despite a culture that espouses personal freedom and takes pleasure in speculation, the architecture that results from this process, driven by short-term gain, is not just conformist but dismal. New York's may be a culture of infinitely rich and varied desires but these are seldom expressed in an architecture of any significance. The certainty implicit in the gridding of the island is absent elsewhere in the city, making the task of imagining the future much more uncertain.

Beyond physical order, the politics of the city increases its unpredictability. Compare the process by which New York is continually renewing itself with the reconstruction of Berlin. In Berlin renewal is managed through highly centralised committees elected to represent the public good. These have the power to legislate, precisely, the form of the streets, buildings and public places. The process presents a unified vision for rebuilding the city. During the most intense period of rebuilding, the city *Baumeister* publicly declared his intention to return the city to what he termed traditional European models of urban planning – in effect, to the structures and

orders of the 18th century. The commissioner for planning New York has no such power, nor would he wish it. There are areas in which the city has to exert its influence, transport for example, but in most respects it remains a vast field of enterprise and multiple desires. Multiple desires that are held in check by an elaborate set of zoning regulations, which attempt to be as even-handed and neutral in maintaining public order as was the grid.

Consider attempts by architects to project the future form of the city:

The IFCCA Competition

The first action by the newly formed International Foundation of the Canadian Center for Architecture was an ideas competition for the development of a large site in the centre of Manhattan's Eighth Avenue and the river between 30th and 34th Streets. The five entrants selected by Phyllis Lambert, the creator of the IFCCA, were Ben van Berkel, Peter Eisenman, Cedric Price, Tom Mayne and Reiser + Umemoto . Ms Lambert sponsored each of them to prepare lavish presentations of their visions and a jury led by Frank Gehry selected Peter Eisenman as the winner. The unrealised dreams of architects take one into a giddy and disturbed world and these presentations are splendid demonstrations of the euphoria that still drives the desire for prophecy; all the architects save Price are active players in the pseudo *avant-garde*, the promotion of which has been Peter Eisenman's most creative achievement. The presentations included many computer-generated images of a richness and complexity only possible within this medium, some displayed on screens, some in full colour on large-scale panels. Perhaps the brilliance of the computer imagery increased the impression that these were utopian projections wholly disinterested in the forces that shape the city. All the projects, except for the pleasantly nutty field of pictorial moments from Price, indulge in heroic displays of spectacular form, utterly convinced of the autonomous power of architecture. Though each architect describes his vision as taking decades to achieve, they all seem to desire a fabric created at one time and under their total command. The viewer is made to feel like Superman, able to soar above these vast intricate structures that are more like acts of mechanical nature than fields of selfish speculation. These are passionate examples of architecture's continual search for a new paradigm, the forms for a new condition of architecture that would act not just as a mirror, but be formed in such a way as to clarify and intensify the spirit of the age. These are objects wilfully disconnected from history that stretch materials and technologies to effect a seemingly effortless complexity. These are places formed from an exchange of ideas between a handful of individuals, some theorists and many architects, who seek this new paradigm in vague notions of complexity seasoned with a touch of philosophy without much reference to specific activities or places. Mayne is the most scenographic of the entrants, but he shares with the others procedures for developing complex forms through highly inventive conceptual strategies.

This activity has been greatly legitimised by the huge popularity of the Guggenheim Museum in Bilbao, designed by Frank Gehry, and Bilbao must have been in the minds of the IFCCA competitors. Gehry is the most successful practitioner of what can be called 'art practice' works in which the architecture is allowed to be a wholly poetic confection, utterly personal, and sensational. He has single-handedly created acceptance of a new freedom for architecture. Those returning from a visit to Bilbao describe the museum as the cathedral for the new age. This brilliant burst of energy seems concerned only with itself, resisting interpretation, resisting connection to any sources but the creator's imagination. This building will seed the desire not only for more like it, but for spiritual and religious explanations for its sensational presence. A dangerous possibility: it is an object capable of spectacular corruption.

Such desire for complex effect is both the strength and weakness of the IFCCA submissions. These are thrilling objects, and all save one are totally unrelated to the process of land speculation that shaped Manhattan. Eisenman's proposal is the exception: it conceals beneath its gratuitous heaving roof a very careful development strategy, guided by expert real-estate advice. He took the competition seriously, suffusing or suppressing his theoretical urges and taking instructions from experts: engineers, transport engineers, and real-estate consultants. The jury selected Eisenman, because of the work of this expert team. The power of his proposal lies much more in real-estate consultant Michael Rishman's revenue-generating stadium, and the careful management of traffic, than in the waving roofs and walls of Eisenman's fading vision of architecture.

Clients looking for a new paradigm for architecture will find more spectacle with less pain in Gehry's imagination. In this period of giddy trends and fashions, the desire of the architectural avant-garde to generate thrilling and strange complexity is a reflection of architecture's need to compete with all the new mediated realities.

It is disappointing that the entries represented such a narrow set of ideas, both on architecture and urbanism. None appears to find interest in the commissioners' grid. Even though the development is on the 'air rights' over the multiple tracks entering Penn Station, some grid-like framework could have been formed to sustain the neutral field of enterprise that is the essence of the city. The architecture of Manhattan is the grid. Buildings are merely transient moments in its eternal prospect. This is too impersonal an idea for these architects.

In the end, the influential forces in the culture buy what they want, not what architects offer, and architects and architecture adapt. According to this view the architect, captivated by poetic vision, arrogant and self-sufficient through a warped sense of superiority, fails to see him/herself as merely the agent of society, and society benefits in avoiding past confusion between architects' dreams and social reality. The architect, in this interpretation, is the scribe and the aspirations of society provide the text. Architecture may have a coherent language; the architect is the person least able to understand it.

Other competitions: The IFCCA competition can be seen as the most generous investment in cultivating visions for the future of the city. Almost all the other unbuilt works are unsuccessful entries into much more commercial competitions: Columbus Center, 42nd Street and MoMA. The most interesting exceptions are products of the ideas competitions sponsored by the Van Alen Institute under the direction of Raymond Gastil. Both in scale and choice of subject – Pier 40, the shores of the East River and the Tickettron kiosk for Times Square – they have drawn the imagination of the world to New York. In many ways the city is a more romantic idea and stimulus for the world's imagination than it is for that of New Yorkers. Gastil's potentially most notable achievement may be in encouraging designers to give form to the development of continuous parks along major stretches of the water's edge both on Manhattan and in Brooklyn, postindustrial land that has lain derelict for a decade and more. Such parks could rival Central Park and provide a renewed relationship between the city and nature, demonstrating the worth of a civil society and the pettiness of politicians.

It is surprising, given the power of the idea of New York in the world's imagination, that very few architects make it the subject of their work. An exception is Michael Sorkin, a gifted writer who has also over the years created a succession of visions, speculations of possible futures for fragments of the city. Intricate, almost baroque in their complexity, they challenge the conservatism produced by the market and the grid.

The necessary structures of buildings are manipulated by architects to affect both the body and the senses. The major architectures that occupy the five boroughs of the city convey meanings including bourgeois refinement, imperial power, civic generosity, corporate identity and more. Architecture throughout its history has always been a public art, conveying in its forms the symbols and values that are shared by the community at large: the power of the king, security in God, shared pleasures of civic life. The recent rise in public pleasure in eccentric and personal architecture suggests the potential for infinite freedom within the definition of future realities. A society that no longer accepts the lessons in civics, no longer needs symbols of authority, no longer needs reminders of the power of God, will allow the producers of life styles free play in the production of spectacles that continually recycle the promise of the new.

Consider the key elements in the structure of the city that will frame the future.

Order

Among the many definitions of order, those that apply most aptly to the city are a state of peaceful harmony under a constituted authority or, perhaps better, under a particular sphere or aspect of a sociopolitical system. A barely examined aspect of sociopolitical systems worldwide sees the merging of what is desired in middle-class cultures. New bourgeois suburbs from Ahmadabad to Sao Paulo, Shanghai to Jakarta, are more similar than different. All these places share the same picturesque groupings of pitched-roof houses and crudely decorated apartments. The constantly expanding mass affluence in the emerging middle class is creating a new world order of consumerism, dedicated to cultivating desire for an increasingly narrow set of lifestyle products. The United States is the source of much of the imagination that drives this. Within the American city such products, from fashion to freezers, have replaced any need for large unifying public landscapes, for manifestations of civic culture. Consumer culture has displaced civic culture in the maintenance of order. Selfishness masked as self-realisation has displaced communal sensibility as the culture's motivating force. The order of consumerism allows for continual manipulation of the desire for goods and services, and self-serving illusions of reality, whose unifying effect on the worldwide order of things is far greater, for those who can afford it and many who can't, than was ever achieved through politics or religion.

Time

There was a time when one could ask, 'What time is this place?', when architects believed their work should be of their time. Some sought to build to deny the effects of time, some to accelerate it, but from the 20th century on the relativism of multiple times and speeds of experience has less and less use for an architecture of permanence except in the home. The home will continue to be what it has been throughout the history of the nation: the most stable, the least changing reality. Producers and markets grow in other aspects of reality, energised by continual change, continual claims for newness, by the creation of the new. New is always better even if this newness is based on looking old. Timelessness and permanence will become a rare curiosity used only to enhance the 'theological whim of goods', to quote Marx. Changing fashions draw reality into a continual process of recycling to maintain desire for the new, or the renewal of the old. The rise of public pleasure in architecture of private fantasy may be of

our time, but only as it appeals to individual sensation. The history of architecture is a history of the powerful, whose palaces and cathedrals were public objects that symbolised and generalised that power. It is surprising but not inappropriate that, within a culture that promotes the illusion of power residing in the individual, public architecture should be shaped by private fantasies, which at their most ambitious- such as the work of Eisenman - make claims to any larger truth. All actions are inescapably caught in time, but at the start of a new century there are only the private fantasies of art practitioners to sustain the exploration of being in time.

Memory

For those who remember, memory was one of the most charming elements of that random array of ideas briefly entertained under the title Postmodernism. In its embodiment of desire, architecture creates the structures of memory. Memories revisited are always places revisited. Smells and sounds may be more poignant, but the mind carries dense memories of place. The recreation industries both trade on such memories and create artificial destinations to exaggerate them. The promotion of goods and services also commodifies the world's significant places and where necessary recreates them, led by that most formative condition-of-reality building – the Las Vegas casino. The reproduction of memorable places leads to an expansion in serialising desire. Memorable places need not be historical or powerful places. In many ways the serialisation of the world's fast-food vendors, retailers, motels and hotels trades on memory of place to give security and confidence to the retail experience. This process of creating satisfying illusions of place to strengthen commerce is becoming more and more artful. Through this process the world is creating its own versions of Manhattan and Manhattan, to stay ahead of the competition, has already begun to recreate a hyper-reality version of itself on 42nd Street.

Symbol

The signs and symbols of the world's trademarks offer an authority and comfort equalled in history only by the heraldic devices of clans and nations. The confidence inspired by the brand images of McDonald's, or Coca-Cola, or Marlboro, or Reebok far surpasses the limited range of ideas conveyed by the signs and symbols of architecture. The billions of pounds the major lifestyle industries spend to maintain our attention and remain fresh in our minds consumes more creative energy than was ever employed by nations or religions. Hitler's Germany and quattrocento Italy held populations enthralled with much less effort than any one of the major corporations expends. Perhaps it is the overwhelming authority of trademarked and serialised realities that has reduced so much architecture to a subsidiary effect in corporate identity. This has both diminished the conventional languages of architecture and encouraged the search for extremes of difference, prescient in works such as the Guggenheim in Bilbao, just to reassert the idea of architecture. Apart from a limited group of what might be called 'trophy buildings', its future will focus on providing rapidly built, efficiently organised boxes, whose distinct identity and character will be represented by the trademark on the walls. The buildings lining 42nd Street demonstrate the dissolution of the language of architecture into the texts and signs of corporate symbolism.

Progress

At the start of the 21st century it seems as though the notion of progress has become irrelevant in this once most progressive of cities. There is extensive poverty and desolate slums, yet little evidence from politicians of a belief in improving the quality of life for all. Loss of interest in the idea of progress is paralleled by a decline in public compassion. Mario Cuomo said the most lasting achievement of the Reagan years was to make not having compassion acceptable. There may still be a desire to use architecture for the public good, but there are few opportunities to do so. There was a grandeur to many aspects of the Robert Moses vision for the city, from the parks he created to the highways and bridges he built. Grandeur, above all, in that most significant element of progressive thought: belief in the beneficial effects of plans that may take decades to be realised. The good news was that Moses and his agencies were able to look 30 years and more into the future. The bad news was that his programmes were so abusive to race and poverty that they have left a legacy of division and ghettoisation. However, a political climate of localism and pettiness means that few in any part of the city's administration are today able to see beyond the re-election cycle – at the most three years.

Deception

The needs and desires that form the structures of New York's five boroughs produce a complex of fictions that are more confused than deceptive. The desires that drove a civic dream of culture have left a legacy of gracious and monumental works: city halls, museums, synagogues, banks and libraries, railway stations, all reminders of how much has changed. The desire to restore such works does little to restore the civic consciousness that formed them. What were once objects that helped form a shared civility, are now the trophies of patronage. The complex deceptions from the Moses years that used architecture for social engineering have left a legacy of public housing, public schools and hospitals that are poorly constructed and devoid of promise. These structures from a cold detached authority are the most telling residues of a

political system that, while loving freedom, lacks compassion for those unable to compete. More recently, the cold, grey awkward structures that contort the housing on Roosevelt Island into the form of a European town are lies told with the best intentions. Postcivil society is devoid of the visions of the past. Nowhere are there realities of promise. The culture of consumption gives immediate satisfaction. On Manhattan the presence of personal electronic devices creates a network in which every individual is in some way monitored and controlled. In this world bathed in radiation, electronic media drive, instrument and complement almost every desire, every illusion.

Speed

Changes in speed have been the major impetus for major changes in the scale and form of the city. The commissioners' plan could never have been influenced by the technologies that were available when it was conceived. It would have taken a day and more to walk the length of Manhattan and the horse and carriage was painstakingly slow. It is as if the commissioners were confident that a means of transport would emerge that would be of sufficient speed to encourage development of this vast field. Irrespective of the type of transport, the grain of the grid has imposed a rhythm and pace to the city that has remained constant over the years. With every shift in modes of transport, horses to trolleys to steam-driven railways, to elevated railways, to subways and then to automobiles, the fabric of the city has been stretched and pulled and perhaps become weaker and thinner.

The subway system was almost fully extended across four of the five boroughs when Robert Moses initiated his far-reaching plans to open the city to the automobile. His decision to drive highways, bridges and tunnels through the centre and around almost every edge of all five boroughs, allowing fast fluid movement into the city from Long Island New Jersey and Connecticut, was devastating to both rail and subway systems but particularly to the latter. The neglect of the subway system during the Moses years has created a problem of crisis proportions that may destroy the city. Because of this neglect, the cost of restoring and expanding the system is vastly more than either political agendas or funding programmes can begin to address. It is arguably the most important public facility in the city, the most useful instrument in civic life. Of those travelling to Manhattan, 70 per cent use it. Yet for over half a century it has been chronically under-maintained and undercapitalised. Since the 1930s only the most modest extensions have been made to the system and current plans for a light rail link into the system from both major airports are long overdue and not ambitious enough. In all areas of civic infrastructure New York has much less distinction, and much less clarity of purpose, than Paris, London or Tokyo; but

268

nowhere is the weakness in the civil life of the city more evident than in its decrepit subway system.

The problems facing the system are many. The extensive stretches of elevated structures are falling down. The tunnels throughout Manhattan were built by cut and fill and form shallow trenches which surface water continually penetrates, eroding the structures and causing extreme structural deterioration. Much of the physical infrastructure is nearing the end of its life. New lines promised for many years – the Second Avenue line on Manhattan for example – are still uncertain. After almost 100 years this most crucial element in the city's operation shows no ability whatsoever to transform itself for the needs of the 21st century. The economy of the city depends on the effective operation of its transport systems. After education, they are its most important public responsibility and could be a splendid demonstration of the intelligence of civil society. Restoring them is a project that will take billions of dollars, and determined political will and leadership. Every element of the city, from politics to business to communities should be combining to drive the programme for the complete renewal and expansion of the transport system. By such decisions, or lack of decisions, are cities judged. By such failure to reinvest, cities fail.

Two scenarios

In the first, a commission is established early in the 21st century to propose a master plan for the total reconstruction and renovation of the city's systems of transport and communication. All technologies are considered and careful thought is given to future changes in patterns of population growth. The plan has two major recommendations: First, tax incentives will be used to encourage the formation of satellite centres of population, relieving the pressure on Manhattan. Second, all new development on Manhattan can only be justified in terms of least impact on the transit systems, and limits are placed on the number of automobiles allowed on the island. A 20-year plan is developed for the complete renovation and extension of the rail and subway systems. All tunnels are rebuilt and new deeper one are dug. The elevated system is replaced and extended by a system of magnetic levitation ('mag-lev') vehicles, automated, silent, fast. Private companies are given permission to develop new transport systems along the water's edge leading to intense development of all the waterfronts. The enormous cost is to be shared by federal, city, state and private interests. It is a painfully slow process, endlessly beset by financial, political and community problems, but by mid-century all systems are renewed. Although imperceptible at first, what has been achieved is a massive regeneration of all the vital arteries, like a vast transplant. This not only maintains the city as the world's leading financial power, but also forges among all the towns and

neighbourhoods and communities throughout the five boroughs a renewed commitment to the idea of New York as the most tolerant and fertile destination for ambitious people throughout the world.

In the second scenario, the plan to renew the systems fails. It meets violent opposition from all those parties, particularly politicians from upstate New York, who had been taught to hate the city. It is weakened by foot dragging, compromise and failure to reach agreement, during which time the inadequate transport systems seriously damage the city's economy and reputation, threatening its status as a world financial centre. In response, the city administration begins to campaign actively to discourage people from working in Manhattan, and corporations swiftly move to equip large numbers of workers with remote electronic offices. Corporations find that all they need in Manhattan is a front office. The island becomes a frenzy of real-estate speculation, and out of this comes a powerful political lobby calling for the deconsolidation of the city – let the other boroughs be independent, they get in the way of Manhattan's ambition. Manhattan concentrates on maintaining its dominance in world financial markets. A complex hierarchy develops within the corporations between proximity workers who are encouraged to develop social skills and come to the office every day, and electronic workers who have the freedom to work where they like and when they like. The island actively gets rid of low-paying jobs and invests heavily in mechanising much of the service activity: food service, cleaning, and couriers. Satellite towns begin to develop, mostly within the old centres like Brooklyn and Flushing and around areas with strong ethnic communities – West Indians in central Brooklyn, Russians in Brighton Beach where ethnicity is the basis of the economy. These specialise in ethnic services: tourism, food preparation and distribution, cabs and cultural theme parks. As the communities evolve, many of them develop hard borders, controlling entry, controlling behaviour, controlling politics.

Production of difference

The difference between rich and poor is what most threatens the future of the city. Wealth brings freedom, allows the fulfilment of desire and dreams beyond this lifetime. The majority construct their worlds from what is available. The poor take what they can get or what is given. The desires of the wealthy are seen as public-minded, as good for the city; they built the great public institutions: the Metropolitan Opera House, the Metropolitan Museum of Art and the Museum of Modern Art. They purchased the art of the world, first for their own pleasure, then as a gift to the city. It was philanthropy that restored the great reading room of the public library, financed the extension to the Museum of Natural Science and the restoration of Carnegie Hall. Into the future major cultural institutions will continue to be formed by such patronage; and it may be only the actions of the wealthy that can continue to reform and sustain unifying civic projects. Yet such actions, while enriching the Eurocentric heart of the city for a small segment of the population, may only serve to exaggerate the distance and difference between the cultural elite and the majority. The distances between, say, Sutton Place and Long Island City, its neighbour across the East River, or between Park Slope and Red Hook less than a mile away, are exaggerated by highways, by the selective routes of transport systems and simply by disinterest. The realities of the rich rarely touch and influence the realities of the poor. And neither out of compassion nor curiosity are the realities of the poor addressed. At least Moses did something. There are exceptions to this attitude, however. White Manhattan would be surprised to see the numerous tour groups from Germany or Scandinavia being guided along Lenox Avenue on a Sunday morning to attend services at one of the great black churches in Harlem. The difference created by poverty poses a continual threat to the future of the city. The attraction of New York City as the entry point for immigrants from around the world will mean that the majority of the city's communities will remain in a state of flux for the foreseeable future. And from the evidence of the last decade, the gap between rich and poor will remain, as will neighbourhoods of extreme poverty and desolation.

In whose imagination is there concern for the future of the poorest in the city? Architecture has ceased to trust in social causes. Though the problems of inadequate housing and poverty are still very much with us, they no longer stimulate architects' imaginations. Schools of architecture no longer cultivate dreams of solving the ills of society. This is due as much to the crude utopianism that willingly provided the architecture for the disastrous attempts at social engineering in the 1950s and 1960s, as it is to a re-emphasis on individual invention in this essentially fashionable discipline. We will very soon face the consequences of a culture that no longer cultivates, in the dreams of architects and policy makers, solutions to the problems caused by poverty. To a great extent the future of the poor in the city will be shaped from within. The dreams from poverty are hard and practical. How to pay the bills, how to feed the family, where to find work. Place is of concern only in relation to survival. The family of the young boy portrayed on American television as desperately trying to find a safe way home from school – avoiding certain streets, climbing through backyards, all to avoid the drug pushers – wants, above all, to feel safe. The poor are susceptible to the same mass-produced desires for fashion, food and music as the rest of us. Escaping from the ugliness and brutality of place into fancy dress, or music, or dope, or religion is for many the most available way out. No part of the city avoids some kind of speculation; even in the poorest communities billboards push

cigarettes, beer and shampoo. Gangs map and defend territory and the business of drug distribution requires careful planning, positioning and surveillance. Even the meanest streets are of strategic interest to someone. Some solution to the problems of poverty are being formed within the neighbourhoods themselves and energised by the ambitions of newly arrived immigrants.

The production of life style

The continual ascendance of social control through consumerism has put increasing emphasis on the production of objects of desire. The catalogues of the leading producers of life style – K Mart, Wall Mart, Target Pottery Barn, Crate and Barrel, et al – stimulate desire in ways that increasingly impact larger realities. The start of the 21st century sees taste-makers to the middle classes cultivating pleasure in late 19th-century comforts, in wood, leather and brass, in homespun, muted colours and things natural, encouraging a nostalgic return to an age of privilege. Did they make this up, or did we want it? In the continually responsive relationship between seller and buyer both sides have influence. Are we searching for realities that have substance, character? Just as the early cinemas compensated for the lack of sound by exaggerating the fantasy of the buildings, the uncertainty of most lives and careers leads us to seek reassurance in store-bought fantasies. This same reassurance is present in the interiors of shops and department stores that carry the accessories of life style; Victoria's Secret provides accessories for and advice on, the performance of mainstream sexual activity. Life style retailers not only dress and feed us. They also give us in the movies and television and advertising, the moves and stage management for our daily performance. They are reinforced by the music industry which harmonises intimately with our experiences. The retailers who choreograph and colour our daily lives produce an excess of objects and sensations in their attempt to match our desires. The 20th century ended with the triumph of popular culture. No matter that its origins are manufactured, there has to be a clear and powerful resonance between producer and consumer for the system to work. At no time in history have the lives of the vast majority of people been so shaped and stimulated by art, by poetry, by design in the service of consumption. In a commercial world that gains power by anticipating our most intimate needs, architecture is significant only to the degree that it contributes to fashionable desire.

Production of spectacle

Twenty five years hence the glow of Manhattan can be seen from 100 miles away. Emerging from the soft, seemingly infinite, carpet of street lamps is one brilliant eruption of light. The streaming walls of advertising that surround Times Square form a base of colour from which soaring columns of laser light disturb the heavens. These are products of ferocious competition between manufacturers who continually stretch the bounds of technology in their need to attract attention. The temperature on the square is at least five degrees warmer than elsewhere in the city and attracts hundreds of thousands of tourists nightly. Traffic has long since been rooted around the area and advertising is spread across all surfaces. Benches at street level have personal sound and movement systems built into them, and high above 42nd Street arcing screens on a great vaulted roof carry the promotion of goods and services into three dimensions of the city. The square has become the favourite launching pad for new music and new stars, mainly Asian. Down the centre of the street are elaborate rides, carousels, Ferris wheels, free-fall machines all in some way arranged to confront the spectator with the pleasures of products: free fall within a can of Coca-Cola, soar through space on the Swatch wheel. The imagery that fills the constraining walls consumes most of the artistic talent of the nation. As the most powerful commercial display in the world it demands continual change, continual re-orchestration; new products, new spectacular sensations.

There is in the hyper-reality of 42nd Street a thrilling fusion between electronic and physical experience. Everyone on the street is equipped to receive multiple bands of data tuned to respond to their every need and causing the physical world to slip from the imagination. The all-embracing responsiveness of personal electronic equipment allows every individual to be continually part of a world network that offers an unceasing supply of information, connection, image, service – anything and everything one might need. The failure of education to prepare for such an overload means that the majority use it for immediate gratification. The exaggerated reality of the display in and around Times Square is a direct response to the disappearance of an architecture that speaks of itself. Much money is made out of structures that illustrate and radiate the messages of others. These intimate networks liberate but they also make everyone captive to the world's commercial will, now the major force for maintaining public order worldwide. These machines allow the promoters of goods and services to control the collective consciousness of the society, to directly fabricate reality. Relationships are formed between the media walls in Times Square and each individual's personal video equipment: the transmitters know where you are and engage you in conversations with the images on the screens. Even rival advertisers speak to each other seemingly on your behalf.

In the future of the commercial city there is a lingering interest in the objects of history. Here and there, portions of the historic city which advertising has helped make mythic are reconstructed, themed places where the interest is in being transported back in time to a re-created way of life. Rockefeller Center, 42nd Street, the United Nations Headquarters, Grand Central Station all need to be experienced in the flesh. Parts of Harlem have been remade to represent the creativity of the Harlem renaissance of the 1920s; Greenwich Village in the 1960s, and SoHo in the 1990s. There is even an extensive reconstruction of British New York in 1760. All are products of the corporate theming of New York – its histories, myths and dreams packaged for a world audience.

The need for a satisfying quality of life has led to extensive and brilliant residential and recreational development. People work much more from home, combining work with recreation and family life. The city land is so valuable that useless structures and roads are quickly removed. The new buildings, vast and tall, flow and change and have the intricacy of natural landforms. Within their undulations, natural landscapes of trees and streams imperceptibly shift into cascading terraces of housing, infrequently exploding into vast glazed courts of entertainment and exchange.

And there are the survivors of past ages, buildings that, through use or attraction or historical association, have been spared. The public library, now within its glass enclosures, looks more like a plaster model than a crusty old survivor from tougher times. With its flashing marquees and its street life, 42nd Street is retained as a memory of urban experience. Although the Met Life building has gone, Grand Central Station remains a pantheon to industrial heroes. Sutton Place remains, as does some vestige of the old financial district: anachronisms of old capitalism and old capitalists, uncomfortably reactionary and unrepentant.

St Patrick's Cathedral and Rockefeller Center, once competing in celebrations of God and mammon, are now conjoined in an urban centrepiece for all ideals. Visitors are guided through the music hall, where masterpieces from the golden age of cinema are shown along with a meticulous reconstruction of the Roxy stage show. The NBC buildings have been restored to their original form and reproduce for visitors the first radio and television productions; all the actors and producers wear period costume and the effect is similar to colonial Williamsburg. And after much debate and concern over what JD Rockefeller Junior would have done 100 years previously, his writings have been used to justify the decision to restore the concourse to its exact original form, and to replace the Sert murals with the infinitely more distinguished Rivera painting purchased from the Palace of Fine Arts in Mexico.

The fragmentation of order

The great debates that had so troubled the founders of the American republic about how to maintain social order in a democracy – by force, by law, by the cultivation of civil sensibility – have long since been forgotten. Only vague memories survive of the political philosophising that gave order and performance to the new republic, of the conceptualising that laid the grid on the surface of Manhattan. Many communities in New York will be categorised as 'postcivil' societies, societies without even labour as a unifying bond. Societies without allegiance to any unifying order save to an ethnic group and, despite extremes of cultural difference, remarkable uniformity in the consumption of manufactured goods and services. This is evident in the almost complete absence of any civic institutions except the uneasy survivors from the 19th and 20th centuries. Do the citizens in the many separate communities claim any allegiance to the ideals of the United States or is their relationship merely selfish opportunism? Would they claim a deeper commitment to the idea of the republic than to their own culture or religion? How, within this dispersed field of enterprise, can unifying civil projects ever again emerge? The only elements that unify cultures are mass subscription to the proliferation of lifestyle goods and services that conform the world. The international retailers formed their own cities in the margins between the dense mosaic of communities, long snaking structures that enclose extravagant fantasies as they rival each other for attention. The surrounding communities react to their spectacular artificiality by seeking some authenticity in structures – churches, mosques, synagogues – that mark the centres of their neighbourhoods.

At least two-thirds of the communities that form the boroughs of New York City proclaim and defend the differences between them. Legislation now gives local control of banks, real estate and business and allows the imposition of religious laws within the enclaves. Schools are either run by religious or ethnic groups or are contracted out to private vendors. In the most extreme cases communities have walled themselves off from their neighbours, helped by the barriers of water and highways and by patrolled borders. Gates control exit and entry into these communities. Opposition has been weakened by recent legislation that encourages segregated subdivision development within areas of clear racial and ethnic difference. This was pioneered by the Orthodox Jewish communities in Crown Heights who sought to impose the laws of the Sabbath throughout the neighbourhood. This Hassidic community has been the most aggressive in moving to gain complete control there, driving out non-Jews and gradually imposing religious law on all activities within the neighbourhood. There is fear that this control will expand; not unlike the struggle to regain the land of Israel, this would increasingly colonise the surrounding areas. Legal authority to close roads on Saturdays is used to invade surrounding neighbourhoods and drive wedges into their communities. These actions are fuelled by the millions of dollars that flow into Crown Heights from across the world. The community's success has become a model for other ethnic and religious communities.

The Hassidic dominance of the consumer electronics business has become a model for other groups; many of these have specific agendas and moral constraints and are forming coordinated opposition to certain practices of multinational corporations. Just as there is Jewish control of entertainment and consumer electronics, so Indian and Chinese businesses control food distribution, and Hispanic and Afro-American ones control music delivery. This creates cultural biases that affect production worldwide. The conflict between free trade and the private agendas of minority businesses corrupts trading practice. The Greeks and Italians have been forced to become aggressively ethnic-centred, subcontracting and hiring within their own cultures and developing exclusive trading arrangements with Greece and Italy. The city divides evenly between three distinct forms of communities: the fully integrated; those integrated within broad racial and ethnic groups, such as the Hispanics, Afro-Caribbeans, Afro-Americans and Asians; and those separated into narrow ethnic and racial communities, such as the Russians, the Hassidim, some Afro-American groups and some Hispanic groups. It is members of the last community who build walls and oppose any notion of integration. The most fruitful is the second community. The great Asian city of Flushing blends Chinese, Indian and Korean cultures to create not just a pleasurable fusion, but business enterprises that are having worldwide influence. Equally significant are the new Afro-American centres led by Caribbean immigrants, where much of the new business is based on exploiting the natural resources of Africa. It is the first business activity in this century that is capable of changing the ghettoised character of the poorest, traditionally black, neighbourhoods.

And the wastelands remain, the residue of devastated communities that decades of public investment failed to save. Some have been declared non-places by the state: hundreds of acres imprisoned behind high barbed-wire fences, cut off from all services with roads, foundations and even some buildings slowly disappearing beneath grass and trees like some ancient archaeological site. Perhaps unavoidably, these abandoned places have attracted the abandoned population who manage, in some way, to sustain life in the refuse of the city.

The most unsettling areas are those where poverty and lack of influence have allowed the exploitation of the least skilled workforce, where noxious industries are able to pollute without interference. The most curious sight in the wastelands is the conversion of majestic abandoned public buildings – former night courts, synagogues, churches – that have been converted to casinos; outlined in neon during the day and floodlit at night, they offer a kind of promise. They have sprung up everywhere, in the way Pachinko parlours litter the landscape of Japan. The only problem is one of oversupply. Not even such a peculiarly venal instrument has halted the process by which the city continues to harden the boundaries between wealth and poverty, between races, between religions. The loss of any sense of unified culture, of allegiance to anything beyond tribe and sensual pleasure, has collapsed the democratic process. The factionalism that now dominates New York is part of a world condition in which resistance to control by a larger authority has led to the emergence of aggressively separate communities based on nationality, race and religion.

Grand illusions

272

The new order in the world will be governed by the global industries, whose products will range from the essential, to the stimulating, to the destructive. They will assume authority over nations and divide the earth into several realities. Among these will be the reserve lands, abandoned regions whose small populations and insufficient resources are of no interest to world banks or producers except as dumps for the corrosive wastes of industry. They are excluded from the consumption programme except to be used and abused. The resource lands are rich in natural resources, but poorly developed. Consequently they are dominated by the global industries who unsparingly strip them of their mineral and vegetable assets, particularly where there are docile populations and accommodating governments.

Populations large and small will be kept powerless and become essentially the property of industry, within which there will be little chance for individuals to prosper. The ambitious will leave, as they always have, for the great cities. Irrespective of cultural and productive history, uncontrolled population growth and consumption will demand a balance. Stability is essential to consumption. Governments and religions old and new will construct vast artificial destinations, for the flesh and for the spirit which will become the reality engines of the new millennium. In this New York, once again, compels the imagination of the world. In New York vast cathedrals are constructed to satisfy the mass imagination, but as much to deceive and pacify as to inspire and entertain.

The future of New York will be a product of a complex of fictions. In an imagined discussion with a very old Chinese politician who had been in Tiananmen Square 60 years earlier it became clear that his concern was to share a vision that had haunted and frustrated him since his youth. It was a dream. A dream that somewhere in China a community of people, thousands upon thousands, would come together and begin to build a great cathedral. The vision was specific in his imagination. It would be like the Empire State building. He had read about it in his history books and had subsequently visited New York and been awestruck by this immense pile of harmonically ordered stone, shaped by innumerable hands to become a perpetual symbol of enterprise. He said he believed

that in both the act of building through several generations and the eventual realisation of such an epic structure, a spiritual and political path would emerge that would confirm and secure a meaningful future. It was clear that he was not religious, for his vision was all to do with politics and his love of people, and had little to do with notions of salvation or the life hereafter.

Vast and awesome structures gained a power in New York because of the need to overwhelm the force of trademarked realities and all-pervasive industrial manipulation. Architecture has always been the premier instrument for establishing order and authority. It is capable of the grandest illusions, monstrous deceptions and fictional creations of vast portentous dimensions, conceived as the cosmic palliative to address what must be a future of intolerable insecurity for many. They are structures that combine the communal ritual commitments of the new religions with all the elaborate machines of illusion that are now the most fruitful products of the world's industries. Their construction is conceived to give meaning to meaningless existence, subtly tempting and gratifying all the desires of the flesh as being necessary indulgences through which salvation will be achieved. New York will lead the production of these vast and intricate spiritual engines, present a reality so satisfying that even those who know it is corrupting will be seduced and silenced. And for most it will seem like a golden age; the building of these structures will be compared with the building of cathedrals.

The dilemma for architects lies in the ability of architecture to deceive. When there are no longer any shared tangible values all reality can be deceiving. The greatest strength that New York City brings to the new millennium is the continual redefinition of its reality within the rational frame that grids Manhattan.

DREAMS 10

Commercial High Rise

MURPHY/JAHN
COLISEUM SITE AT COLUMBUS CIRCLE

The new construction of the Coliseum site consists of four levels of retail and hotel services up to 85 feet covering most of the site and focusing on a skylit atrium that provides access to all the lobbies and streets. Above the retail base and surrounding the atrium on two sides is an 18-storey L-shaped office slab that rises to the height of, and abuts a portion of, the existing office building. On top of the new office slab are two hexagonal towers. The taller one consists of 50 floors of residential accommodation and the shorter one is a 30-floor hotel. Both towers have setbacks at 560 feet, relating to the top of the adjacent Gulf & Western Tower.

The exterior of the existing office building is reclad in a manner compatible to the new development. At the lobby level, alterations are made to architecturally integrate it with the new construction and public atrium. From 75 feet upwards, the building continues to be utilised as office space. The levels below are rehabilitated and utilised as part of the new retail construction. At street level, four loading bays are kept to serve the office floors above. The two levels of parking and building services below grade are kept throughout the site.

Above: computer model viewed from Columbus Circle;
Left: plan showing the two triangular towers divided by a continuation of the path of 57th Street.

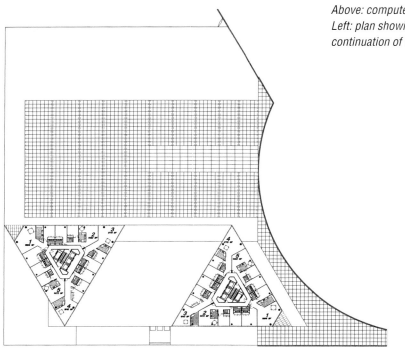

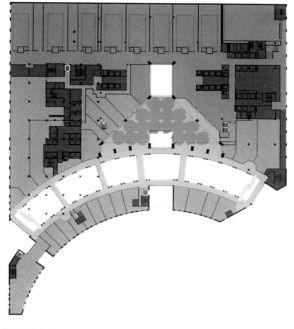

Retail ■ Galleria ■ Cinema ■ Garden
■ Mechanical ■ Passenger Elevator ■ Service Elevator

Third Level

MOSHE SAFDIE & ASSOCIATES
WITH EMERY ROTH AND SONS
COLISEUM SITE AT COLUMBUS CIRCLE

Columbus Center, a winning proposal for the redevelopment of the New York Coliseum site, is situated on four acres at Columbus Circle adjacent to Central Park. The project incorporates offices, residences, a hotel, a major retail centre, and a cinema complex. The offices include the world headquarters of Solomon Brothers and its state-of-the-art trading centre. The organisation of the complex, the network of public areas and the placement of public spaces are designed to reinforce the civic image of Columbus Circle and to enhance the public life of the street.

Two towers set back in a V-shape surround a 190-foot-high garden atrium. A great galleria follows the curve of Columbus Circle. Secondary tower-like facets, comparable in scale to the apartment towers along Central Park to the north, form a transition between the urban scale of the Upper West Side and Midtown. Setbacks in the two main towers accommodate five-storey greenhouses, which provide an amenity for the office workers and create a strong visual connection with Central Park. The crests of the towers combine arrays of smaller greenhouse and duplex residential units.

Work on the project was suspended due to the withdrawal of Solomon Brothers in October 1987.

275

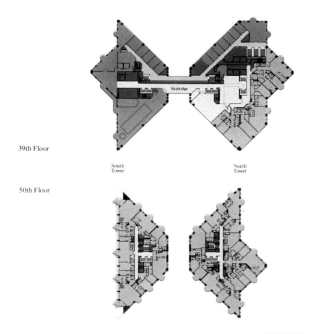

39th Floor

South Tower

North Tower

50th Floor

■ ■ ■ Apartments ■ Atrium ■ Health Club
■ Support ■ Mechanical
■ Passenger Elevator ■ Service Elevator

Tower Residential Floors

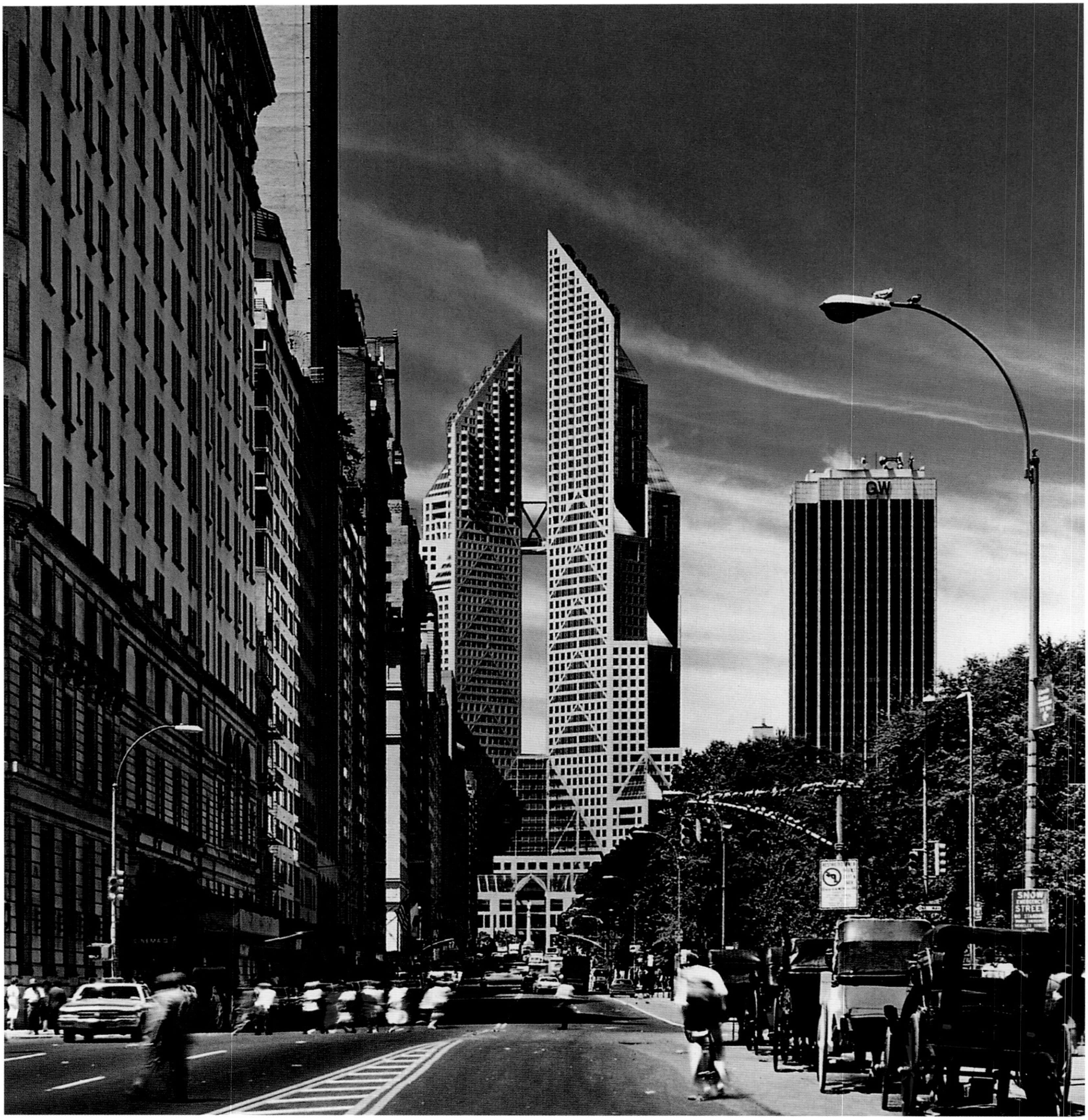
GW
SNOW
EMERGENCY
STREET

© Robert AM Stern Architects

Perspective from high above 57th Street

ROBERT AM STERN
COLISEUM SITE AT COLUMBUS CIRCLE

The proposed design is for a 2.1-million square foot mixed-use project on the site of the existing New York Coliseum. Approximately 600,000 square feet of retail space will be developed in the existing exhibition hall, and renovated for its retail occupants. The current 640-space parking garage will be retained and rehabilitated. The existing office building will be fully demolished to grade and will be replaced with a 1.5-million square foot multi-purpose structure composed of various elements: a 750,000-square foot condominium/hotel and a 750,000-square foot luxury residential condominium split between units for sale and for rent.

The building includes a new tower with a 750-foot high facade towards Central Park, and a western wing which lowers in a series of steps towards the west. Chevronlike setbacks at the top of the tower accentuate the reflective quality of its glass construction. The base of the building, rising to a height of approximately 100 feet, follows the curve of the Circle.

The condominium/hotel is composed of 900 units while the residential condominium will be composed of 660 units. The condominiums for sale occupy the uppermost sections of the tower with the rental units below. The retail component is developed within the current exhibition hall which will be refurbished. Its location above five major subway lines and its large parking garage makes it ideal for a major retail/entertainment complex. Large public open spaces are created within the shopping complex to include a series of open landscaped areas and a rooftop garden.

277

ROBERT AM STERN
42ND STREET SIGNAGE

The core of this urban redevelopment project consists partially of four sites at the intersection of 42nd Street and Times Square that were slated to be developed for office buildings in the 1980s. After the existing buildings had been vacated, the office real estate market collapsed in Manhattan, leaving the developer and the city with the prospect of a large group of buildings that could remain empty for years until recovery of the office market. What had only 10 years before been a primary, if seedy, place of popular entertainment, had now become a depressing and dangerous ghost town. An interim plan and guidelines were developed with the help of the New York State Urban Development Corporation, the City of New York and the developer. A new image for these sites and for the rest of the street extending to Eighth Avenue had to be created, bringing back to life what was once the most famous entertainment street in the world.

The design includes proposed uses for the lower floors of currently vacated or under-utilised sites, and on a critical step towards getting things moving, the development of a forward looking image for the street that is based on, but not sentimentally tied to, 42nd Street's great history. The proposal adds a few key iconic buildings as well as a myriad of new signs and lights all of which will be added on to what is already an almost archeological record of 20th century architectural and stylistic history.

278

© Robert A M Stern Architects

© Robert AM Stern Architects

Above and left: idea drawings suggesting a new image for 42nd Street. Done in conjunction with graphic designer Tabor Kaman, these drawings served as guidelines in shaping the theatrical vision for the street.

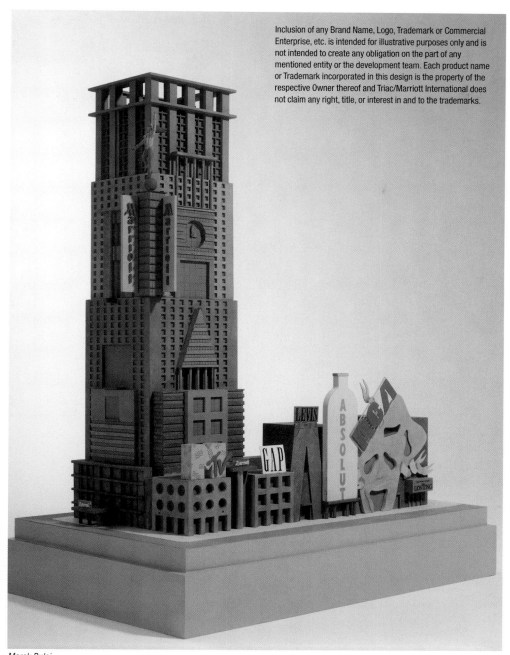

Marek Bulaj

MICHAEL GRAVES
42ND STREET HOTEL AND MIXED-USE DEVELOPMENT

Following the design recommendations and building envelope of Robert AM Stern's 42nd Street Now! guidelines, this project consists of a Marriott Hotel tower on top of a base of retail and entertainment facilities that form the street wall along 42nd Street and Eighth Avenue. The base of the building includes a 2,000-seat, state-of-the-art Broadway theatre located midblock on 42nd Street. This design illustrates a variety of possible retail, restaurant and entertainment tenants. The storefronts are varied in scale and are designed as a series of independent establishments consistent with the traditional patterns of use in this area. Each has its own identity signage incorporated into the storefront, creating a dynamic collage of signage and illumination techniques.

Several grand-scale iconic elements identify this project and the district: the Big Apple, a multi-storeyed figurative construction at the corner of 42nd Street and Eighth Avenue, a pair of large-scale dramatic theatre masks that mark the location of the new theatre, and the large square clocks and crown that top the hotel tower. Within this diverse ensemble, the architecture of the building base acts as a framework for the kinetic life of 42nd Street, while the hotel tower represents the traditional nature of the city and acts as a beacon for the activity of the district.

279

Above: at the corner of 42nd Street showing the tower of towers rising above the continuous public zone on the lower level with its hyper streets and trapezoidal glass boxes; Right: the view down 42nd Street.

ZAHA HADID
42ND STREET HOTEL AND MIXED-USE DEVELOPMENT

The complex is comprised of two commercial podia and two hotel towers, linked through physical form as well as a visible circulation system, a kinetic signage and lighting system, and through the synergy of related entertainment and retail use.

The hotel tower of Site 7 is a vertical street – a tower of towers. Buildings and towers are stacked in the geometric plan configuration of the square. Each 'building' or 'tower' contains slightly different room and facade configurations. Another vertical tower exists in the north-west corner containing support programmes for the hotel such as a beauty salon, a lounge and a library.

As the Site 7 hotel tower connects to the commercial podium, the vertical street spreads out into the horizontal plane and spills out a network of retail shops and restaurants which brings the tower through the space and into the integrated complex of the city plan. This transition begins with the roofscape at the fourth level of the commercial podium, and continues down below grade into the subway concourse level. The roofscape is a direct result of the configuration of the third floor, seen as a continuous public zone between the two sites. Vertical connections from this level down are made through a series of hyper streets – trapezoidal glass boxes contained within projected sign environments.

The concourse level houses programmes of cultural significance which do not require natural light such as museums, cinemas and a nightclub. At street level, pedestrians are met by transparent glass retail facades. The third and fourth floors of both podia form a continuous carpet of public facilities as a partially enclosed urban plaza.

Above: model showing the tower formed from many separate elements;
Left: Hadid's conceptual drawing of the dynamic interaction of parts.

Above: model of 42nd Street development;
Right: at the corner of 42nd Street.

RICHARD MEIER & PARTNERS

MADISON SQUARE GARDEN SITE REDEVELOPMENT

The programme for this competition called for the redevelopment of the existing Madison Square Garden site into 4.4 million square feet of office space including trading floors.

The influences on the site include the future growth of this part of the city that will occur to the west, beyond the Post Office covering an entire block. The physical location of One Penn Plaza and the way in which people move under and through this development to enter the site, and the overriding grid of Manhattan are factors that exercised an influence on the organisation of the project and on the basic decision to subdivide the required development into three interrelated towers. By aligning each of these towers with the outer boundaries of the block, the fundamental street grid of the city is respected.

The entire structure is placed on a raised podium with the large trading floors beneath. The resultant elevated plaza is lined along its perimeter with shops and restaurants. Access is provided through a series of stairs and ramps while the major approach in an east–west direction is provided by a gradual slope in the podium down to Eighth Avenue.

Metal panels with punched windows are used on the rectilinear edges of the building expressing the core and structure, while glass and glass-panel banding is used along with projecting balconies and *brises soleil* to articulate the more freely expressive sides of the buildings.

The view from the roof of the old Farley post office

Ezra Stoller © Esto

Left: aerial view showing the new public plaza and the old post office on the right;
Below left: plan of the elevated plaza;
Below right: the view from 34th Street showing the corner of the post office on the right.

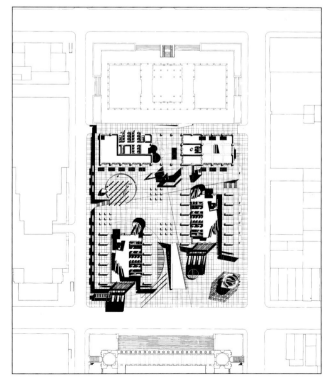

ARCHITECTURES JEAN NOUVEL
THE RIVER HOTEL

The River Hotel's panoramic views stretch for miles through large, clear sheets of glass. Images distend and duplicate in these glass panels, in a constant interplay between the real and the virtual.

The hotel rooms are designed as spacious balconies boasting panoramic views of Brooklyn Bridge, the downtown skyline or the Manhattan and Williamsburg Bridges. Views stretch from the Statue of Liberty to the skyscrapers beyond the South Street shoreline all the way uptown to the Empire State building. Other rooms have low angle perspectives of Manhattan Bridge and play on its impressive size. The river hotel is a bridge between two bridges: a place for looking at the city's landscape the way you would see it from a ship. It stretches its front to the utmost, extending on to the riverfront as if to reach over to the other side – a symbolic gesture of a pier that belongs to Manhattan as much as to Brooklyn.

The west deck of the hotel's lobby takes the shape of a bay window over a 100 metres long. Cinema goers can also take advantage of the panorama: during intermission the screen lifts up to reveal the world famous New York skyline. A selection of shops coast the pier's riverside promenade.

284

Left: photomontage of the proposed hotel in the shadow of the Manhattan Bridge, with the Brooklyn Bridge in the foreground (also known as the Dumbo Hotel);
Opposite page (top): the west deck of the hotel lobby looking towards Manhattan
Opposite page (bottom): the River Hotel from the East River.

Residential

MICHAEL SORKIN STUDIO

THE NEW LOFT, MANHATTAN

SoHo and TriBeCa are comprised for the most part of loft buildings. Dating largely from the 19th century, these lofts were originally built as generic warehousing and manufacturing space. Later, as the result of economic shifts, they became redundant, having outlived their original uses. The rest of the story is familiar: discovered by artists, followed by galleries, SoHo (and now TriBeCa) became everybody's favourite examples of gentrification, an economic bonanza.

But the reinhabitation was problematic. While the vast high-ceilinged spaces of these lofts were great for studios, problems often arose as to their subdivisibility when the room plan ran up against the raumplan. Partly-walled buildings usually admitting light only at the front and back, make them ultimately inflexible. They did, however, have the aura of a particularly Modernist fantasy of flexibility, the so-called equipotentiality of emptiness. Like Beaubourg, the dream was of infinite accommodation, of insertion rather than fit. Such perfect flexibility can run to money.

A certain shift is required. The new loft – like the old – should offer a certain amount of resistance, the kind of difficulty that is entailed by the reinhabitation of an old city by a new use, a new sensibility. The resistance Sorkin has in mind for lofts would lie in the particularity of the construction, in the idea of an architecture that formally exceeds a precise sense of its own requirements, including the requirement for flexibility. Instead of uniform open space, they would provide a wide variety of sizes and configurations, a resource susceptible to combination and recombination. These spaces would take careful note of view, of solar access, of ventilation, and of neighbours' needs.

These two early specimens, designed in 1991-3, are located on opposite sides of Canal Street in SoHo and TriBeCa. Both stand in spaces presently relegated to the car, a parking lot and a piece of street that might be easily removed from the automobile system.

286

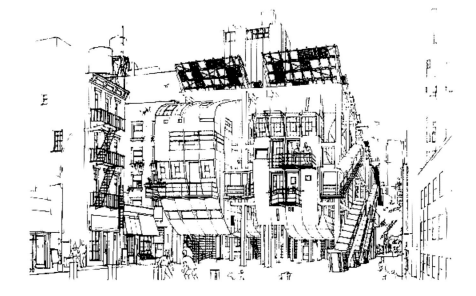

Michael Sorkin Studio

MICHAEL SORKIN STUDIO
WATERFRONT BROOKLYN

An earlier scheme for a smaller set of abandoned piers on the Brooklyn waterfront is even more intense. The intention is to create a kind of park-bazaar that offers a range of recreational uses for its visitors. Included are a conference centre and hotel on a decommissioned aircraft carrier, a barge-building and fitting yard. The idea is that barges – fitted out as playing fields, swimming pools, gardens, etc – will be built in the yard and floated into position to form the texture of the park.

Michael Sorkin Studio

Top left: development around the piers and warehouses of Red Hook in Brooklyn;
Left: plan;
Above: Sorkin's drawing of the existing Brooklyn waterfront.

Michael Sorkin Studio

Institutional Arts

TADAO ANDO
PENTHOUSE IN MANHATTAN

This project consists of the addition of a penthouse to a 1920s 32-storey high building in Manhattan which is designed to serve as the owner's residence as well as a guesthouse. The penthouse is mounted on the top of the structure and appears to be floating in the air, resembling a box of concrete covered with a glass membrane.

Five floors down from the top and stuck into this 70 year-old classic American Beaux Arts style building, is a geometrical box made of glass, metal and concrete. The objective of using these contemporary materials is to revitalise the building as a whole. The addition of a floating glass box, an atmospheric pool and undressed concrete walls contribute towards creating a state-of-the-art penthouse.

288

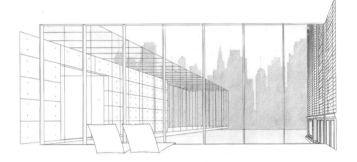

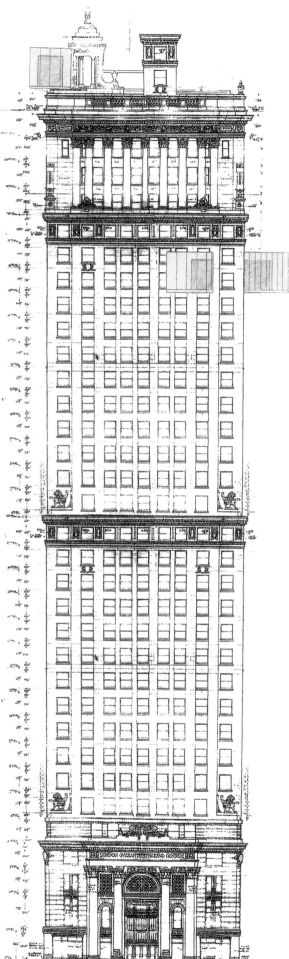

Above: the sensation from within;
Right: the original elevation with the insertion
on the 27th and 28th floors;
Opposite page: photomontage.

HERZOG & DE MEURON

MUSEUM OF MODERN ART

The new museum complex will need to focus on the encounter between works of art and people. An art museum is a place for art and people. It is a place where the world of art can express itself in the most direct and radical way – in spaces that find the approval not only of architects and critics but of artists and visitors, spaces that stimulate people to concentrate on the perception of art.

Unlike other great Manhattan museums, MoMA does not border on an avenue. Urban strategies for the new MoMA site will therefore need to enhance the fact that the complex is located between two streets. Public space could be one space or a suite of open and closed spaces. Open courtyards could alternate with covered or enclosed lobby spaces.

Flatness means to accept the allowable street wall height of 85 feet and to turn this height into an overall horizon of the new building complex. This continuous facade height helps to integrate existing buildings along 53rd Street. This landscape-like building with courtyards and gardens inside and on top of the roof would have a very complex spatial structure with different transparencies generated by the layering of spaces, courtyards and surfaces.

The flatness of the building could be interrupted and accentuated by some individual buildings which could stick out from roof gardens. These buildings could be a group of roof galleries, perhaps the library or the restaurant. The MoMA roof garden fitted out with modern and contemporary art will be a thoroughly genuine Manhattan experience. An artificial natural space will extend between 53rd and 54th Streets in courtyards at street level, in patios on higher levels and all over the roof of the new building complex.

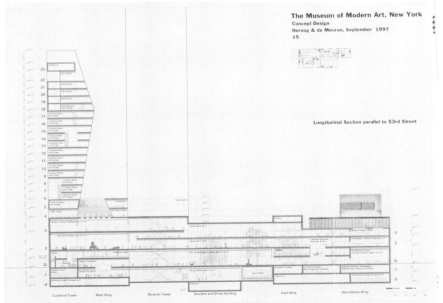

The Museum of Modern Art, New York
Concept Design
Herzog & de Meuron, September 1997
15

Longitudinal Section parallel to 53rd Street

BERNARD TSCHUMI
MUSEUM OF MODERN ART

In 1997 Bernard Tschumi Architects was selected as one of three finalists for the expansion and renovation of the Museum of Modern Art. The constraints of the site, marked by a collage of existing buildings and by complex zoning regulations, presented considerable challenges. The existing site conditions ruled against starting from the outside and in favour of starting from the inside, carving a series of interior spaces that would function somewhat like an outside, but inside.

The 'solid' would be made out of the existing buildings and notional envelopes defined by zoning regulations. The carved spaces would trace an urban route with 'streets', 'squares' or 'plazas' linking the exhibition spaces and functions. The building would be like a city carved out into a mass of solid matter, with careful filtering and distribution of light into the core.

The new MoMA combines three distinct types on one site: a received type, the 25-foot square column grid and double bay of the historical MoMa for its departments; a borrowed type, the columnless factory type for its temporary exhibitions; and a new type, fixed, variable and 'inter' spaces for the permanent collection.

The museum garden was rethought according to its little-acknowledged dimension as a programmatically flexible social space, and extended through the Museum in a series of interior 'courts'. These courts alternate between art space and social space, presenting locations for special museum events and providing artists with exhibition venues that mediate between the museum's more public spaces and the private experience of its galleries.

292

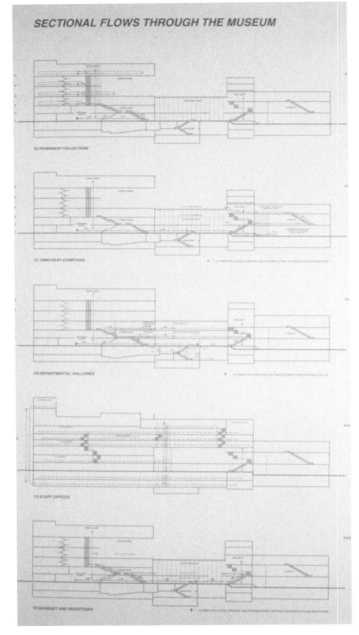

SECTIONAL FLOWS THROUGH THE MUSEUM

Above: studies of the passage through the museum;
Left: the neutral quality of the galleries.

Above: the view west on 54th Street;
Right: model presenting the major
themes of the proposal.

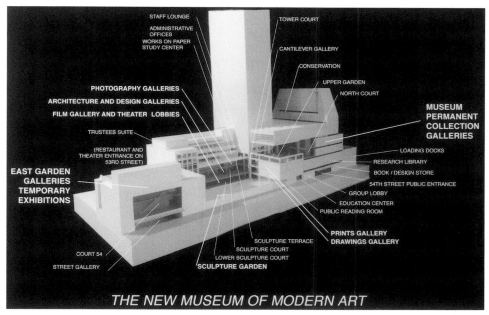

THE NEW MUSEUM OF MODERN ART

TOYO ITO
MUSEUM OF MODERN ART

Toyo Ito has three main concepts for the expansion of MoMA.

MoMA is another tower (lying skyscraper): many historical places where art and space coexist are scattered around MoMA. The new MoMA must integrate these fragmented places and create a strong image as a whole through the expansion. His proposal is to design a skyscraper that lies horizontally on 54th Street, connecting the Abby Aldrich Rockefeller Sculpture Garden and the expansion site.

MoMA conceived as a bar(r) code: town houses in Manhattan are laid out in a bar code manner along the streets. MoMA, which has been expanded over time, also conforms to this bar code spatial structure through the expansion. Specifically, Ito proposes to enhance the bar code of time (history) along 53rd Street, and the bar code of space along 54th Street. The bar code system juxtaposes all the components as parallel, without any centre and creates a kind of abstract space which enables free expansion.

MoMA embodies another Manhattan within Manhattan: these two parallel bar codes create a rather ambiguous space between them, and that is where a junction-like traffic space is provided, connecting the two bar codes. This space is not to be a simple linear route but rather a kind of changeover, instrument-like space that enables visitors to choose their own different routes. This space enables visitors to develop a poetic sensibility by making their own free choices.

Conceptual drawing by Ito of the contrast between the parallel bar codes and the ambiguous space between. Waving lines indicate the path of free choice.

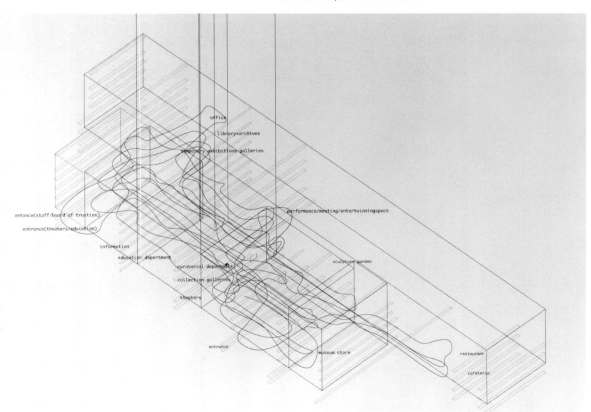

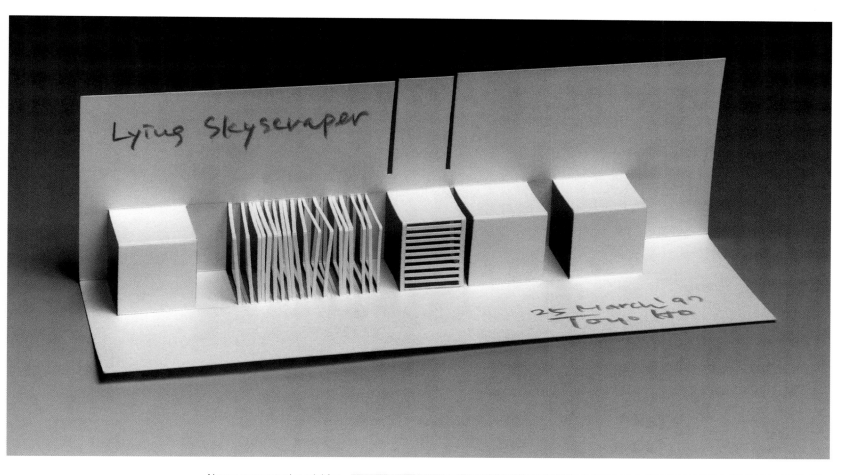

Above: conceptual model for the skyscraper that lies horizontally;
Right: conceptual studies to explore using distinct materials for the disparate elements that make the 'lying skyscraper'.

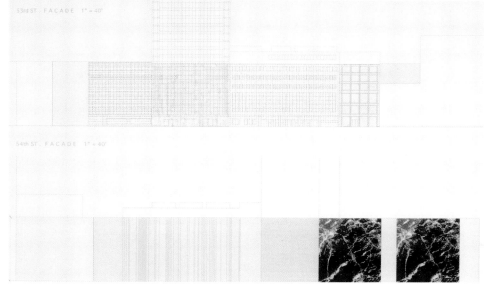

STEVEN HOLL
MUSEUM OF MODERN ART

Bottom: the 53rd Street elevation showing the mass of the building envelope;
Below left: creating galleries by cutting into the building envelope;
Below right: study drawing on the character of the galleries.

The origin of museum as a room of the muse, a place to think and consider deeply and at length, is an idea to contemplate as we are faced with a major transformation of the Museum of Modern Art. Steven Holl proposed two concepts to enable a better understanding of the potentials for MoMA's expansion. These are outlined below

Concept A: Cutting

The new site's zoning envelope is taken as a ready-made form, which is cut for natural light. A major cut is made for the main lobby, connecting 53rd and 54th Streets and the garden. This is a large public space with a ramp down to the cinemas and up to the galleries. In raising the issue of the evolutional nature of MoMA's campus, this concept accepts each building phase as evolution expressed. The zoning envelope, itself a consequence of building density and light, is incised, creating internal light.

Concept B: Bracketing

A maximum of connectivity of gallery circuits is envisioned within an outer bracket, with the garden as the main focus at its centre. This horizontally organised concept proposes lifting the garden 11 feet and shifting it 70 feet west. This affords a more central position for the original 1939 building as well as two new below-garden experimental exhibition areas of 21,000 square feet each. Access is enhanced from all sides. The garden is perfectly rebuilt with the addition of glass bottoms in the pools and water year-round.

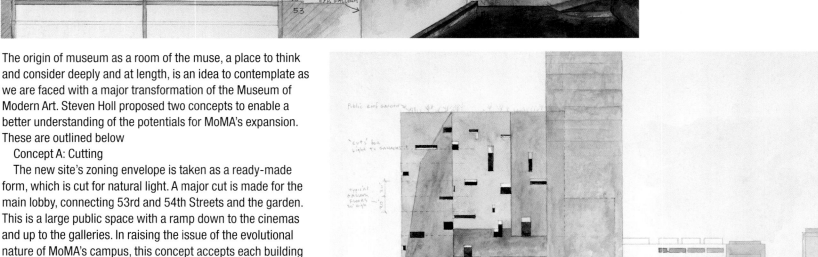

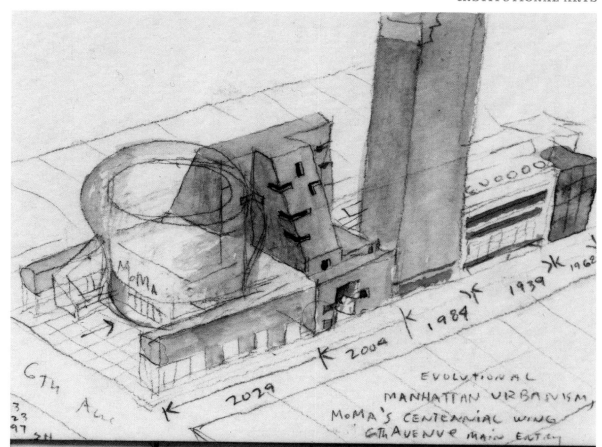

Drawings from Holl's sketch books
Right: the exploring the intersecting masses;
Below: examining the qualities of space.

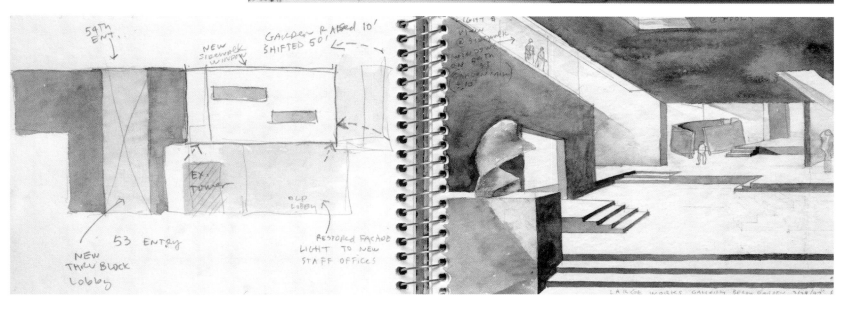

RAFAEL VIÑOLY
MUSEUM OF MODERN ART

Viñoly expresses interest in two particular issues: one, the idea that the experience of art should be decelerated; and, two, the complex layers of this midblock midtown urban condition are rich with potential. Deceleration is generated by friction, and in this case that friction should be produced by increasing attention. An assemblage of disparate functions and identifiable spaces could provide the opportunities for multiple arrests in the journey through the museum. As far as the second, the site's uniqueness, its sense of openness in this dense urban fabric, promotes an architecture of exposure, a building which could relate to the uniformity of the zoning envelope by establishing a dialogue between itself and the city, creating a place from which to contemplate the city, also as a work of art.

For Viñoly, the primary challenge is how to make the building public while maintaining its various degrees of privacy, that is, how to make the transition between the social act of participation and the private act of contemplation without going from monumentality to alienation. The key is in the legibility of the choices and the curiosity that could be generated by the articulation of the spaces. The gallery is the place of resolution between the collective and the individual; the procession to it should simultaneously expose and orient the viewer.

*From the Viñoly sketch book
Top: the view down 54th Street;
Middle: study of the passage through space;
Below: sketch notes on the broad physical elements.*

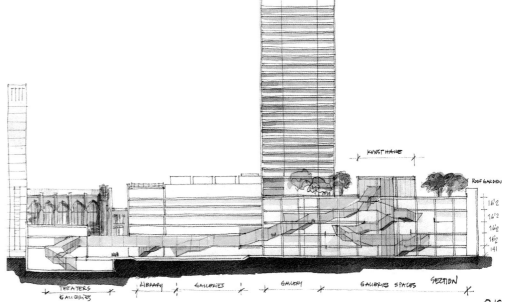

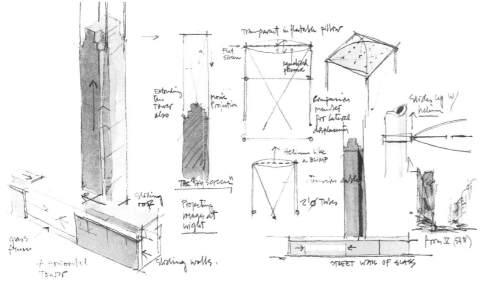

298

Above: the concept model;
Below: photomontage from the north
showing the sunken sculpture garden.

REM KOOLHAAS
MUSEUM OF MODERN ART

Koolhaas' view on the renovation of MoMA is that the city should be admitted to the museum. The ground floor is reconsidered as a single urban surface. The sculpture garden is lowered, so that its perimeter can inject daylight into the former basement. Because the sculpture garden is sunken, the wall that now surrounds it disappears. This creates a direct visual transparency between 53rd and 54th Streets. The two streets acquire a potential equivalence that allows a large variety of entry and exit points and the orchestration of the different flows of visitors. The new level of the sculpture garden is extended as a garden/moat around the entire perimeter of the ground floor which becomes in its entirety a metropolitan island. This islands becomes the new lobby. Technically, these spaces could even be entirely open air in the summer. Daylight now surrounds the former basement on all sides. This new garden level becomes the formal entrance and previously difficult-to-locate elements such as the theatres, benefit from a new exposure.

The site of the present restaurant is liberated. As an interior extension of the sculpture garden Koolhaas projects a MoMA forum: a space designed to enable MoMA to organise a wide variety of events from conferences to parties. A large balcony – partly inside, partly outside – hovers on street level to create a potential autonomy. It has an independent entrance off the revalued 54th Street. Loading bays for both the museum and the tower are organised on the west against the Athletic Club building. The site to the west of the Museum of American Folk Art is used as a temporary MoMA store. Its roof, accessible from the new museum, is used as an outdoor exhibition area.

The programme of MoMA is so enormous that it inevitably organises the public on at least ten levels or more, and the additional site extends the length of MoMA to over 600 feet. This poses a considerable transportation and flow problem, as the escalator cannot deal with such heights or lengths. Koolhaas tackles this problem by using Otis' Odyssey – a small train, platform or large box that is able to move horizontally or vertically. The Odyssey offers hybrid movements up to the challenge: beginning above the sculpture garden, its trajectory perforates the new museum with a diagonal courtyard to ascend to the top of the triangle in a single, fluid movement.

299

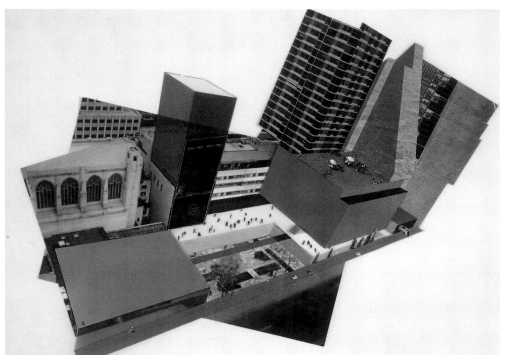

Photo © 1997 The Museum of Modern Art

Above: an image to suggest a multi-media environment;
Below left: within the sunken garden;
Below right: the old MoMA and the possible new one.

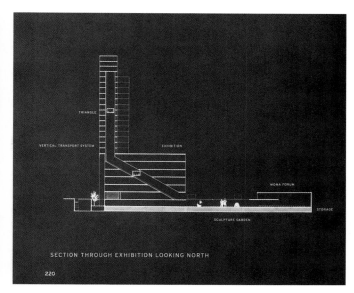

TRIANGLE

VERTICAL TRANSPORT SYSTEM   EXHIBITION

MOMA FORUM

STORAGE

SCULPTURE GARDEN

SECTION THROUGH EXHIBITION LOOKING NORTH

220

Left: section through the exhibition looking north showing the great room elevator moving diagonally through the galleries; Below: the traveling room.

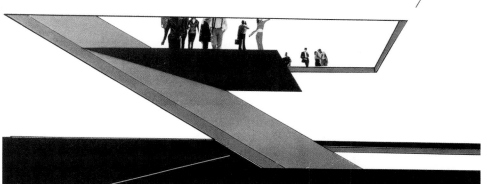

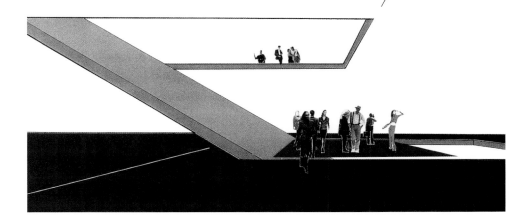

Below: the MoMA forum hovering at street level;
Bottom: the traveling room appears close to the sunken garden.

Studies from the sketchbooks of mood and character.
Above: the view down 53rd Street.

TOD WILLIAMS, BILLIE TSIEN AND ASSOCIATES
MUSEUM OF MODERN ART

TWBTA see the garden as the quiet heart of the museum. The new addition needs to develop other places of quiet focus and delight. They have thought about a great light court, a glass-enclosed space open to the sky that would serve no other purpose than to give the museum a quiet light from top to bottom. Another scheme proposes a large pool of water at the level of the existing lobby, extending the feeling of the garden.

TWBTA propose a vertical excavation of the museum tower's space surrounding its elevator cores. By cutting openings through from floor to floor, this space can be 'mined' to create dramatic vertical shafts of space between the old museum and the addition.

Interior streets moving east–west will structure movement of visitors and staff and these paths will be punctuated by a 'necklace' of large and small light courts and vertical floor-through connections that provide visual orientation and memorable experiences.

All significant structures should be perceived externally and internally and each existing building should stand on its own, its clear expression should come down to the street.

Exhibit galleries should be changed on the ground floor and on the third floor, with 20-foot high ceilings. On the top floor is a temporary gallery for experimental works, with a 40-foot high ceiling. Ceiling lighting grids could raise and lower so that the sense of space can vary from intimate to grand. At the top westernmost portion of the building would be a 30-foot by 30-foot room open to the sky. The ground floor gallery could have a monumental garage type door so that very large pieces of sculpture could be installed with direct access from 54th Street. All new galleries would be structured to be column-free spaces.

303

WIEL ARETS
MUSEUM OF MODERN ART

The history of MoMA is shown literally by the development of
the site and the contributions of different authors. It is this
assemblage of different impressions transforming into a new
idea that Paul Valery based his thoughts upon when he wrote
about the combination of seemingly random impressions into
a new reality. The issue lies not only in the juxtaposition of
different programmatical devices and architects' handwritings
in the building but could also be a strategy to show art.

The double-height entrance hall, connecting 53rd and 54th
Streets, can be seen as a transitional space. It is a space in
which to slow down. One could enter the complex and leave
quickly, yet pass slowly so as to be able to make one's choice
where to go.

MoMA is an urban museum. It is a place to meet people
and to study art. The entrance hall is connected to a café, a
bookshop and design shop and education centre. In the lobby,
one already experiences the galleries through the structural
shaft, through which light from the very top penetrates the
complex. The four theatres are situated directly after ticket
control, where the theatre lobby is a void connecting 53rd
Street with the sculpture garden.

The galleries are positioned between the public entrance
area and the office towers, with their roof garden for the 600
employees. It is the structural void between the towers that
allows filtered natural light to enter the galleries and continue
down to the lobby. These voids visually connect the floors
vertically and create an atmosphere of intimacy. These voids
are sometimes bridged and reading rooms are positioned in
them.

304

© The Museum of Modern Art, NY

Above: an assemblage of different impressions.

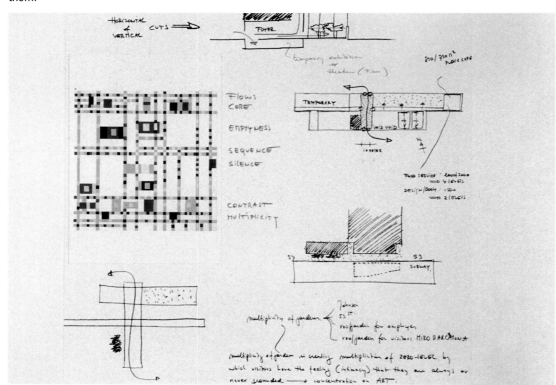

DOMINIQUE PERRAULT
MUSEUM OF MODERN ART

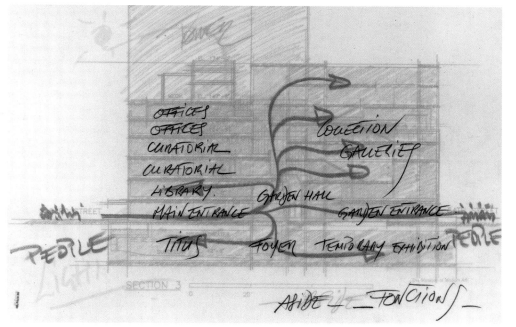

Perrault's design approach eschews aesthetic bias and calls for the intellectual participation of all. Flexibility, interactivity and an open mind put quality at the heart of the architectural work.

Perrault's work is based on a pragmatic approach to working with what exists but without preconceived notions. The new MoMA will germinate, emerge and acquire conviction on the basis of its true situation. Far from rejecting its past, the museum will assimilate its novel geography, constituting both a pole of identity within the neighbourhood and a landmark for the city of New York.

The public or private entrances, like so many addresses along a street, punctuate 53rd Street while preserving the beautiful main entrance which guarantees direct visual access to the garden. The idea of further access on 54th Street, via part of the garden, is in no way incompatible with this. Our transversal configuration opens up the museum to the life of the neighbourhood. The stroller, attracted by the open space of the garden, will be able to enter the museum without having to walk around it.

The entrances situated on either side lead into MoMA itself, whose organisational structure can be compared to that of a tree. It extends into the ground as if in search of 'life force', an elongated main body forms a sturdy 'trunk', while its 'branches' and foliage extend aside, along or above.

305

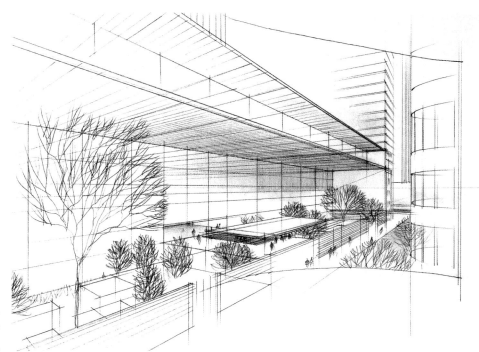

Above: studies of space and operation;
Right: the entrance through the reformed
garden under a great overhanging roof.

ASYMPTOTE
MUSEUM OF TECHNOLOGY CULTURE

The Museum of Technology Culture is part of the city of Manhattan, an urbanism that makes explicit the duality of physical presence and hyper-mediation – creating a condition of perpetual flux.

The museum is a hybrid structure merging a convention centre typology with the utility of a hangar structure, as well as combining the public event programming sports stadia with a museum's ideology. The result is a 300 metre long structure located off piers 9 and 11 in lower Manhattan where the architectural assembly protrudes from Manhattan into the East River. It exemplifies a type of urban intervention perhaps more in keeping with Pacific Rim models of expansion where buildings act as prosthesis to the urban density. An internal space which qualifies as perhaps the largest container of public events and exhibitions in the world is framed by a lightweight steel structure that is designed and constructed using computer modelling and fabrication techniques. The skin is entirely clad in 'video' signals, utilising composite materials that meld LCD technologies with cladding technologies to create a building envelope capable of broadcasting digital signals across the whole surface. The 'liquid' presence of this architecture suggests a structure grafted onto the city's ephemeral and mediated condition.

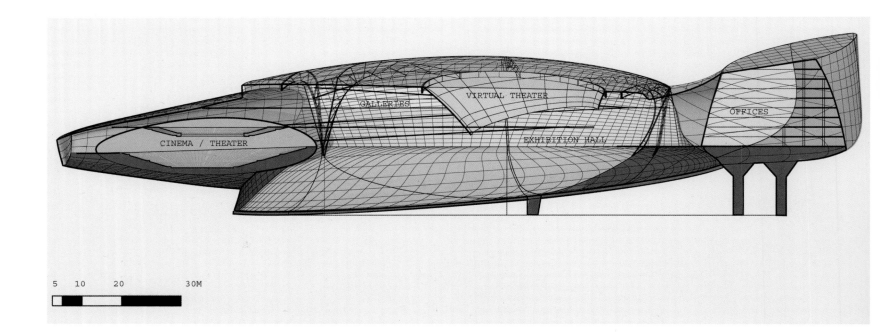

CINEMA / THEATER   GALLERIES   VIRTUAL THEATER   EXHIBITION HALL   OFFICES

5   10   20   30M

OFFICES / ARCHIVE / EDUCATION

GALLERIES

VIRTUAL THEATER

EXHIBITION HALL

RAMPS

CINEMA / THEATER

Above : progressive sections through the project; Opposite page: section.

Institutional Public

SANTIAGO CALATRAVA

CATHEDRAL OF SAINT JOHN THE DIVINE

For the invited competition, Santiago Calatrava was the sole architect (out of a total of 65) not to restrict his contribution to a design for a bio-shelter on the plan of the south transept, as stipulated in the brief. He considers the building as a whole, suggests completion of the north transept by designing new granite and limestone pillars for the existing plinths and develops an entirely new structural system for the south transept. In the rework of the scheme, a slender, filigree spire structure is included.

The original, defined spatial theme of a cathedral is thus transformed into a modern idiom, while the bio-shelter is transferred to the roof space – which opens to the sky, replacing the existing, very poor timber structure with glass and steel – to follow the exact cruciform plan of the cathedral. A lightweight construction is thus created, where each triangular panel can rotate about the longitudinal axis to allow opening of the roof while preserving its overall shape. This raised greenhouse is fundamental to the climate control of the cathedral: warm, fresh air generated in the roof space can be drawn down into the nave and crypt. The bio-shelter, a green garden walkway above the clerical space, offers visitors views of New York City and, at the crossing of nave and transept, a view down into the cathedral as if from the gallery of a dome.

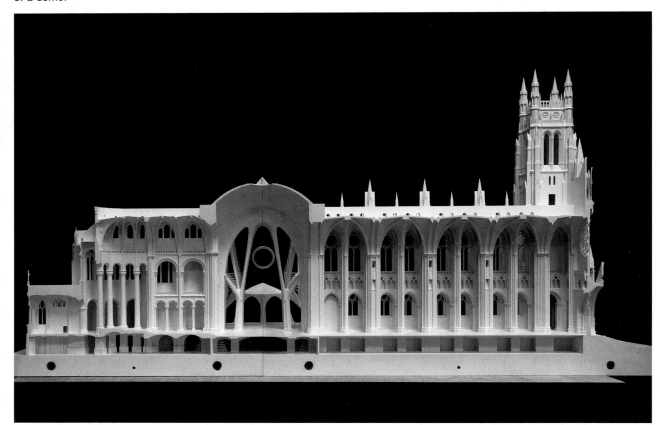

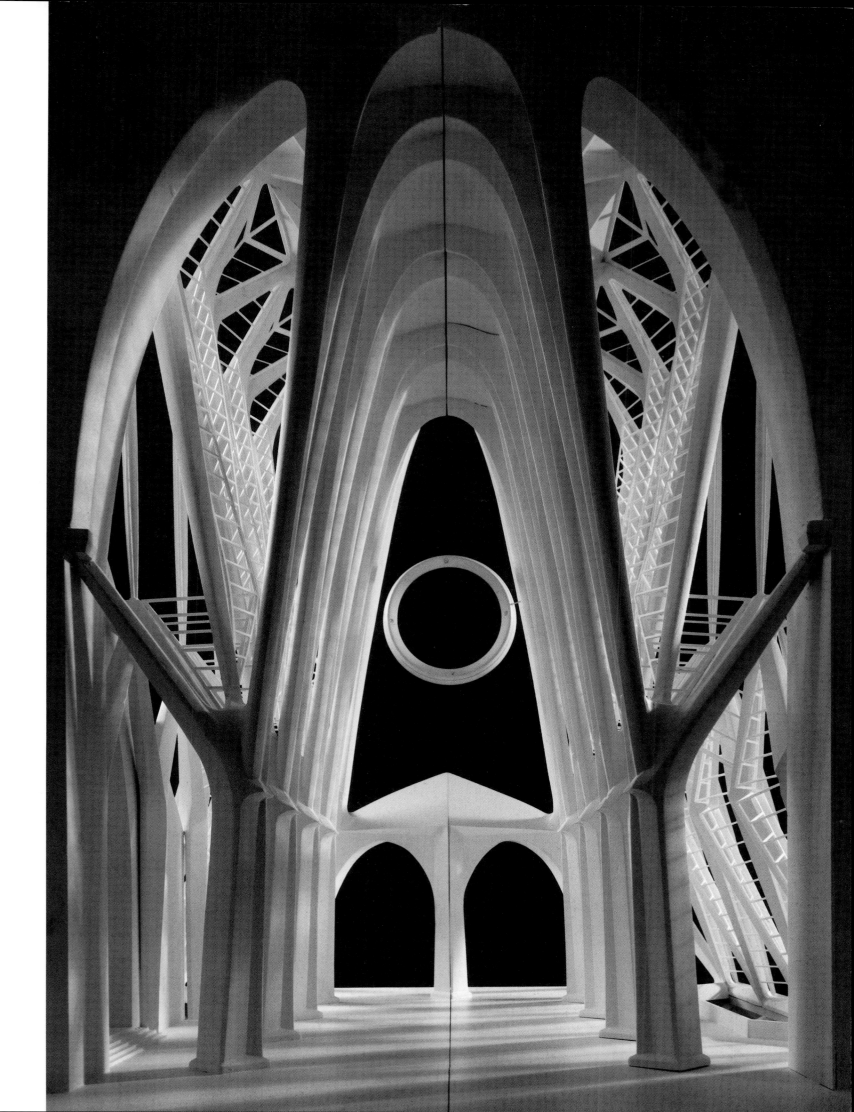

The transept and base of the spire

Left: the lateral section without the spire;
Below: structures old and new.

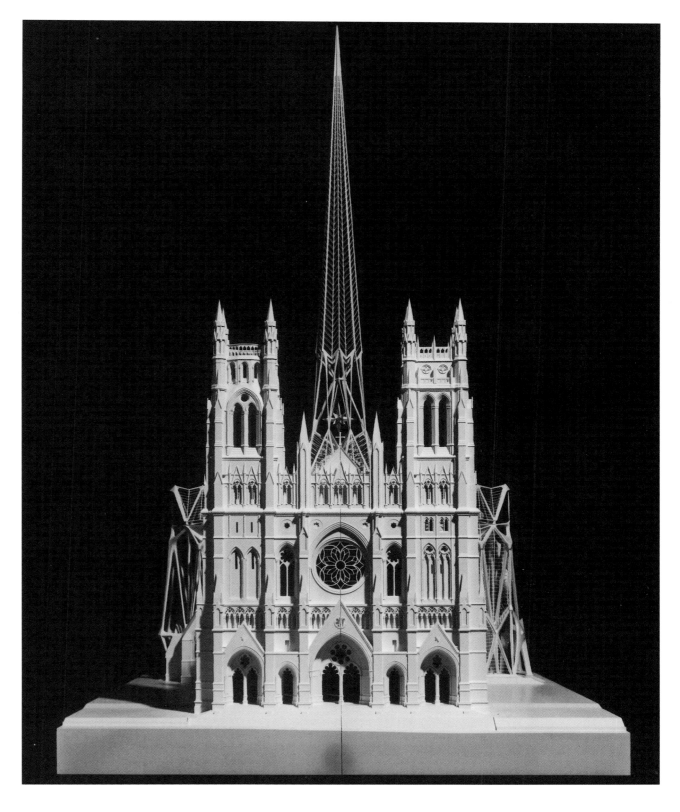

SMITH-MILLER + HAWKINSON
WITH SHEPLEY BULFINCH RICHARDSON AND ABBOTT
MID-MANHATTAN LIBRARY

In conceiving the new mid-Manhattan Branch of the New York public library, Smith-Miller + Hawkinson Architects (SMH), with Shepley Bulfinch Richardson and Abbott (SBRA), have continued an investigation for which both firms are known: explorations of the constant movement of human traffic in public buildings, to create environments that welcome, that encourage community and that allow both stillness and interaction, in all conveying a sense of occasion.

312

Beyond the fundamental attention to the operation of the library, the central concerns in preparing the design were the relationship between structure and sculpture, the effective use of pathways and open spaces, framing views from within and enhancing appearance from without. All to create an architecture that maintains the grandeur of one of New York City's and the nation's most meaningful institutions.

The view across 5th Avenue from the New York public library

Transportation

MURPHY/JAHN

SOUTH FERRY PLAZA

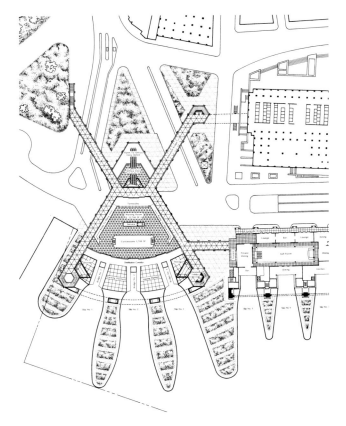

The site is situated at the southern tip of Manhattan along the East River's edge adjacent to both Battery Park and Peter Minuit Plaza formed by the intersection of South Street and Whitehall Street. Its public components include a new ferry terminal operation for the Staten Island Ferry, an observation plaza and the Museum of Maritime History, all gathered beneath the arches of the commercial office tower.

The formal concept of the South Ferry Plaza blends both a poetic vision of a gateway monument heralding symbolic entry to New York with a pragmatic solution to the tangled confluence of vehicular, pedestrian, subway and ferry circulation. Monumental and maritime influences are visible in the form of a lighthouse or harbour beacon that marks Manhattan's prow. A raised observation plaza provides vistas across the water rendering visible the ferry operation.

Approximately 1.2 million square feet of commercial office space is provided over 50 storeys. The 15,000-square foot Maritime Museum hovers above the lobby with views down into that space and out through the arches to the city and sea. Two steel and glass lighthouse towers flank the outside observation plaza illuminating the passage of evening ferries.

Vehicular and pedestrian circulation is vertically separated by pedestrian bridges that link park, terminal and the Battery Maritime Building in an uninterrupted continuation of the Battery Esplanade.

Above: the plan with the old ferry terminal to the right; Left: photomontage from the tip of Manhattan.

KOHN PEDERSEN FOX

SOUTH FERRY PLAZA

This gateway to southern Manhattan is a place of public activity with maritime exhibitions, a public library and a major transportation centre. South Ferry Plaza combines three separate structures into one waterfront centre: Whitehall Ferry Terminal, the Battery Maritime Building and a central office tower which rises between them. The building's design responds directly to the site. The city front is people-orientated with a grand curved colonnade above an arcaded base. Above, a cylindrical tower culminates in an observation deck offering 360 degree views. When seen from the water, the tower appears to become a pair of sentinels, with a ferry slip at the base.

315

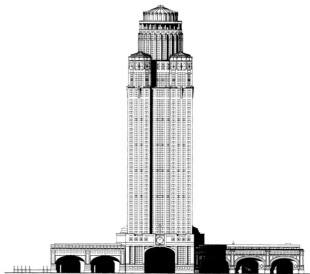

Models, elevations and an atmospheric perspective that could be from the 1920s

VENTURI, SCOTT BROWN AND ASSOCIATES

SOUTH FERRY PLAZA
WHITEHALL FERRY TERMINAL

Because opinions differed over the design for the terminal, the architects ended up creating multiple design schemes for the project. The VSBA competition winning design was publicly condemned by representatives of Staten Island, and soon after the mayoral election of 1993 the city government severely reduced the project. A modified design was drafted based on the new budget and also on a new requirement to accommodate vehicular traffic on to and off the ferries.

The building became lower and simpler, with an upsweep towards the north to frame the immediate view of Lower Manhattan from the inside, and a parapeted, flag-shaped electronic billboard on the water-facing south facade. Its electronic LED images change and move though the predominant image is of a waving fragment of a flag. This scheme was also rejected by the city and VSBA withdrew from the project.

The final design differs from the initial entry design, where VSBA proposed an architectural and symbolic gateway to the city. The design acknowledges the terminal as the first and last building on Manhattan Island. A giant clock was chosen as a classic symbol of civic architecture on the harbour facade (in the second design, the city government required the clock's removal from the initial design). The barrel-vaulted hall extending from the rear of the clock promotes civic monumentality through its scale and symbolises a gateway through its arched elevation. A large-scale programmable video screen spans the wall behind the great clock. The city side of the terminal is an urban transportation place and contrasts with the recreational urban spaces of Battery Park and the river esplanade.

*Above: the giant clock from the first design;
Left: behind the clock a barrel-vaulted hall
whose scale will 'promote civic
monumentality'.*

Panoptic Imaging

*Above: second stage modified design with a flag-shaped
electronic billboard on the water;
Below: the billboard seen from the ferry at night.*

KOHN PEDERSEN FOX
JFK TERMINAL

Upon entering JFK International Airport from the Van Wyck and JFK expressways, the traveller's first impression of the terminal will be made by the inclined drum, housing the airline lounges and the main air intake shaft. This drum is clad in metal bearing all the airline logos at 'supergraphic' scale, identifying the building for its passengers and advertising the airlines to passers-by. At the same time, the air intake location at the structure's highest point assures the highest fresh air quality possible in a terminal environment.

Arriving passengers will disembark at curbside, where a canopy shelters them from inclement weather. The sweep of the departures hall roof, the grille-like quality of its glazed vierendeel truss walls, and its metallic silver cladding establishes formal themes that carry through all the terminal's public spaces.

The departures hall itself could well become one of the late 20th century's best-known transportation spaces. Its large scale and distinct sense of movement evoke at once the train stations of the past and the speed of supersonic aircraft. The five airlines' check-in gates are ranged along a great wall opposite the entry with adequate depth for queuing. A signage band above the counters identifies the airlines and class of service. Above the signs are five very large communications devices that will combine television monitors with departures/arrivals information. These monitors will broadcast a rich collage of images describing each airline's home country, providing impressions for the traveller waiting to check in. The five screens will animate and enrich the departures hall experience, appearing to hover in front of a gently canted metal wall, inset with narrow pieces of stained glass. The terminal's concourse is an airy, light-filled environment from which all the various activities on the runway can be observed. Its enclosing walls are clad in clear glass and fitted out with aluminium sunscreens above a height of ten feet, reducing glare but not transparency.

Above: the plan showing close integration of gates and support functions;
Below: the ticketing hall.

Below: aerial view showing the structural
continuitybetween the various elements;
Bottom: long and lateral sections.

© Jock Pottle/Esto

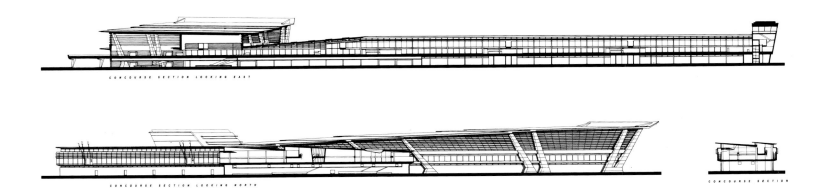

CONCOURSE SECTION LOOKING EAST

CONCOURSE SECTION LOOKING NORTH

CONCOURSE SECTION

Landscape

MARGARET HELFAND ARCHITECTS

OCTAGON RUIN

The ruin of the New York Lunatic Asylum, later known as the Metropolitan Hospital, sits near the north end of Roosevelt Island. The preservation of the structure and the creation of its landscape provide opportunities for physical and metaphoric interpretations of the Octagon Ruin. The former occupation of the site by the ward wings is recalled in land forms overlaying the original building sites. These forms rise to establish the ground scale and presence of the historic wing via a bridge connection into the main level.

These abstracted versions of the ward wings embrace an arc of grass tilting towards the river and Manhattan skyline. From the crest of this outward reaching form, a smaller, steeper, inner sloping form surrounds the Octagon and allows for grass and stone seating facing the south-west facade of the ruin.

Beyond practical restoration, the architectural fabric of the building interior lies in decay and collapse. Following the recommendations of the conservator, the exterior is to be preserved. The window and corridor openings will be glazed at all levels except those providing public access. Access to the building interior is guided by the principle of limited physical access and maximum opportunity to experience the space without actually touching it.

The structure is composed of two octagonal rings, generating an outer ring and an inner rotunda five levels high. At the outer ring, the Octagon's main floor remains open for public use and its upper floor levels removed where necessary due to damage or deterioration. Any new structures to replace damaged or removed floor elements are clearly contemporary.

320

Above: the unrestored interior;
Right: site plan.

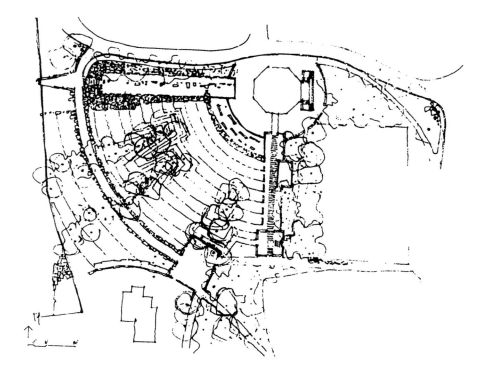

Above: watercolour of the park and Manhattan in the distance;
Left: sectional perspective.

KOLATAN/
MACDONALD STUDIO
WITH ERICH SCHOENENBERGER
5TH AVENUE GIVE & TAKE

In 1997 the Municipal Art Society asked 10 firms comprising architects, artists and landscape architects to submit urban design proposals and strategies for Fifth Avenue. The resulting schemes were presented and discussed with various parties involved in the eventual redevelopment of this portion of Manhattan. Manhattan's horizontal terrain is limited. Aerial views indicate that the mid-air roofscape constitutes a second urban datum. Kolatan/MacDonald's proposal speculates on the potential of this datum to be occupied horizontally.

For example, in the Harlem Block, the spatial structures inhabit the ground. Their co-dependency and co-evolutions are with the streets as horizontal infrastructures rather than with the vertical infrastructures of the elevators in midtown. Therefore their constituencies change radically to driving territories and programme occupations that depend on accessibility of street and sidewalk.

Horizontal expansion at mid-air level allows the development of mid-level neighbourhoods by producing new relations between buildings in the same block and across the blocks, suggesting that the buildings are no longer only related by street locations. Furthermore, it permits the improvement of obsolete office buildings with small floor plates by providing an opportunity to enlarge the floors through horizontal expansion. The new structures tie into existing vertical infrastructures where desirable, but use the opportunity to connect directly to the ground through vertical footholds which come with their own new infrastructure wherever a small building can be replaced.

322

*Above: horizontal expansion at mid-air level seen behind the Empire State building;
Left: modeling forms in the mid-air landscape.*

Top right: the field of play;
Bottom right: ordering strategies.

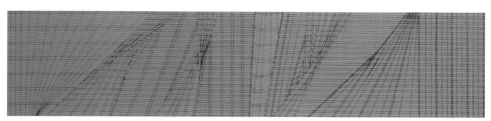

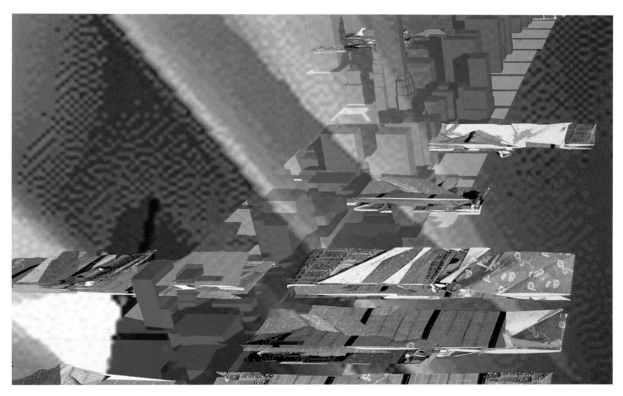

*Left: an evocation of the
rooftop landscapes;
Below: in the new mid-air
landscape.*

ACCONCI STUDIO
WITH DI DOMENICO + PARTNERS
FIFTH AVENUE GIVE & TAKE

Along the line from north to south, Fifth Avenue breathes in and out. The buildings of Fifth Avenue implode and explode, and east and west meet and mingle. The buildings take one step forward, one step backward: one floor recedes away from the street (the building loses face) while another floor advances across the street (the building shows its face).

In each building, the facade is sucked in, making a hole that is available now as a public space. The hole is accessed from the street. For a hole on an upper floor, a transparent elevator lifts you up the building. To replace the private space given up to make public space, the facade on another storey is blown out, making a bulge over the sidewalk and across the street. The side walls, ceiling and floor of the bulge are transparent: the bulge is accessed from inside the building.

The public space gained (the amount of private space lost) is equal to the private space regained (the amount of public air-space lost). The hole is as deep as the building. The bulge extends out as far as the building is deep – when it reaches the opposite sidewalk, it turns up, down or aside. Public space is gained, but inside the building; private space is retained, but exposed outside. The holes and bulges are lit for use at night. They provide, as a by-product, light for Fifth Avenue.

324

Right: the hole in the facade and the transparent elevator.

Many passages forcing public life into the private walls of Manhattan

REISER + UMEMOTO
EAST RIVER CORRIDOR

It must be emphasised that while our present proposal can be seen to fix a certain form or strategy as a finished design it is conceived to be a possible development within a flexible system. The dilemma in a project of this magnitude is that it is necessary to develop the specifics of a proposal to a certain degree in order to understand the systems in operation and the feasibility of propositions to be built. Our working hypothesis that urban proposals of any significance and certainly any attempt at doing something new must arrive out of design and not from generalised planning schemes.

Though thin in the east-west direction, the proposed area's length in the north-south direction coincides with the natural and artificial geography of the edge as opposed to the gridded organisation of the city's interior. As such, it describes a zone that while connected to the city's streets, simultaneously operates as a continuous and somewhat discrete system. Our proposal acknowledges both the unique moments of esplanade development already in place, as well as the long-standing call for a more coherent development of the island's entire eastern edge. We would argue, however, that the occasional and locally accessible segments of esplanade tend to deny the possibility for the very real cultural mixtures, which a continuous public space would provide. Both a park and a path, the esplanade is a unique type of public open space which combines leisure activity and circulation within a single, continuous yet differentiated system. Effectively a public pedestrian infrastructure, this system is itself incomplete without a thorough integration with pre-existing avenues and streets. More important still is the relationship between the esplanade and the FDR Drive.

The continuity we propose is a robust and complex development of structures and programmes. A single path running the length of the island, although desirable, is not sufficient to provide the richness of activity necessary for an intensively-occupied, 24-hour public space, especially one, which is to operate at the urban scale. In light of this, development strategies have been explored which are not exclusively green space, and which will address quite closely the development of new programme and infrastructure elements, as well as the reconditioning of old ones. The programmatic and spatial desires of locales along the edge are incorporated not merely to serve a circumscribed constituency, but rather to produce a variegated pattern of use and structure along the length of the site.

Parks and paths and structures for sports and leisure activities looking south over the Baruch housing project and the Williamsburg Bridge

326

REISER + UMEMOTO
WEST SIDE CONVERGENCE

The natural and artificial geography of the site, dominated by
the railroad cut, the proximity of the Hudson River and the
massive sectional cuts of the surrounding transportation
infrastructures (such as the Lincoln Tunnel and that of
Amtrak's tunnel under the river) produces a vast nexus of
conduits through which the programmatic and organisational
strategy of the project develops. Unlike the rest of the island
grid, the distinction between street and fabric in this area is
less clear; here the very large, open infrastructural elements
which traverse the more architecturally scaled blocks and
buildings of the site create an artificial geography to be
harnessed for its organisational potential. This project
recognises, maintains and improves the existing functions of
these elements and at the same time extends them both
physically and functionally.

    The extreme sectional variation produced by these
infrastructures generates not one ground upon which a
building is built, but rather multiple grounds within which
spaces are developed. This then creates scales of space
larger than would otherwise be possible within the confines of
the street grid, the scales of space necessary for the
production of high density public use.

Above: the roof as landform; Right: the site from the air with the old post office and Madison Square Gardens over Pennsylvania.

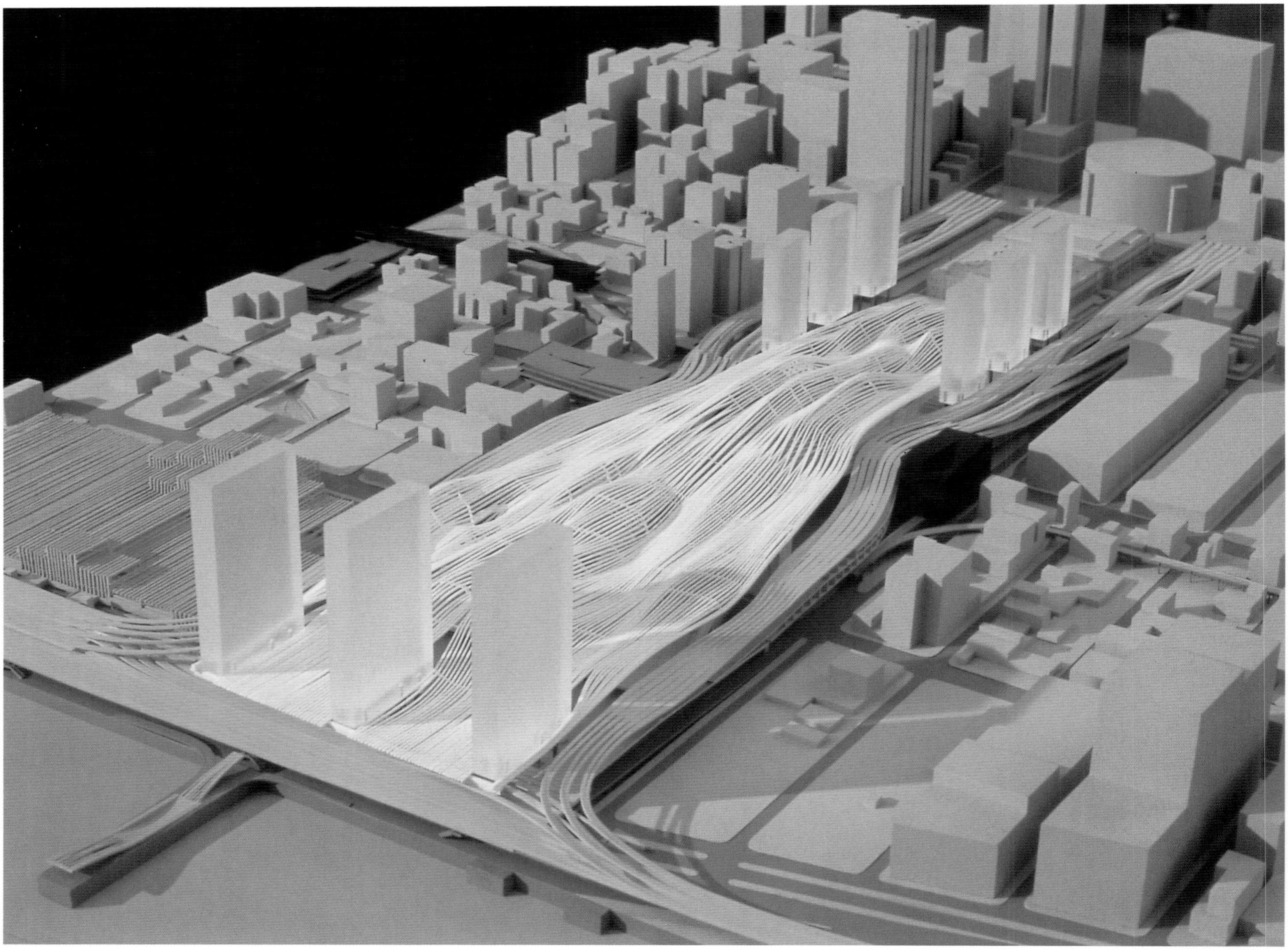

Right: looking towards the river, the roof becomes an occupied landscape;
Below: in the Promised Land.

CEDRIC PRICE
IFCCA

Cedric Price's radical proposal comprises the following elements:

Moving fresh air over the entire site of 100 acres, including the area of the Hudson River (approximately 16 acres); the unenclosed open spaces (railways, rail yards, associated railway properties); streets and avenues, sidewalks, parking lots, etc; structures, including buildings.

Six steel laser transmission towers: these laser beams encompass the entire site at a height of 85 feet from ground level, which will give a rough visual reminder to all, of the former zoning requirements for this area. The laser beams will be obviously affected by the atmospheric conditions – moisture content etc.. Visually, the penumbral interference of the lasers will provide varying definitions of the giant, 'virtual' volume.

The Hudson Sleeve: a continuous enclosed public promenade fronting the Hudson bank. The sleeve extends across the entire site, providing a high-level view for the pedestrian at a height of approximately 20 feet above the river bank. The sleeve's horizontal section acts as a continuous aerofoil, while providing partial shelter to the ground-based pedestrian. The sleeve will be accessible from each end, in respect of the overall design of the Hudson River Park.

IFCCA

*View from within the Hudson Sleeve
looking west towards Hoboken*

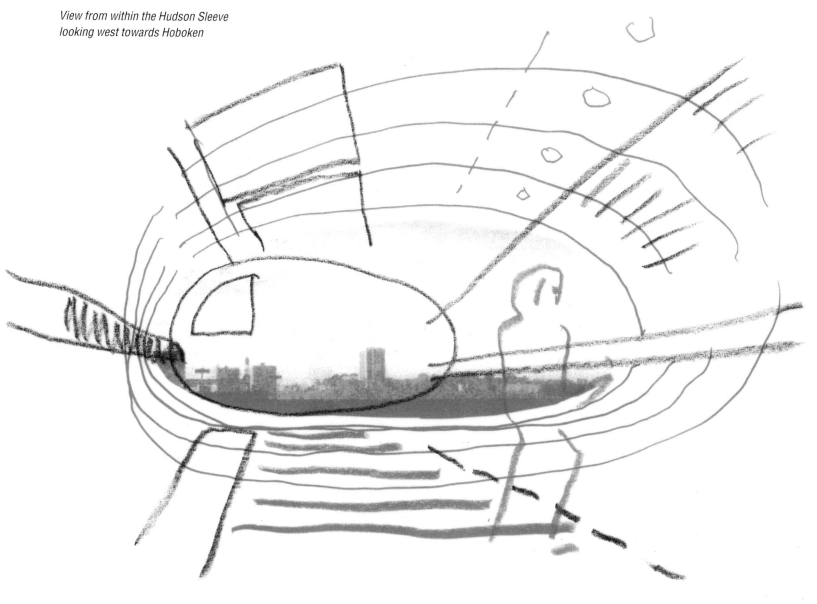

A SLEEVE WITH SIGHTS

The City Sleeve: this sleeve is initially sited along the east side of Tenth Avenue. It enables two-way sheltered pedestrian movement between 31st and 33rd Streets. The City Sleeve thresholds occur at the crossing lights. The double helical spring structure allows the sleeve to adapt to a varied siting and to be repositioned on an equivalent sidewalk.

The Wind Blinkers: the 40-foot-wide wind blinkers, or sails, are sited in the Hudson, standing 70 feet high. The stainless steel structures are supported on stiff, vertical pivots, responding to the prevailing wind.

The Westyard Building: two whole floors are to be removed – floors 9 and 10. This will form an opening in the block creating, at high level, a wind gap in the final tall wall to the rail cutting, and facing the Penn III bulk. This in turn will reinforce the effect of the proposed baffle to the new station. Internally, the multi-purpose westyard building should provide altered floor plans to reflect the need for studio/workshop/office amalgams. Access through this new gap will be confined to elevators and escape stairs only.

Javits Convention Center South Extension: this assembly and storage building is sited to the south of the existing building. The steel structure contains a system of hydraulically powered adjustable floors. Storage capacity is combined with mobile display facilities. Together with an extension to the north, this enlarged Javits Center recognizes the changing demands for conference and display.

Demolition, clearance and control: the cleared land immediately to the south and north of the railway tracks is covered with a cascade of fused blue glass balls the size of canon balls. Cleaned by rain and mist, self-draining, they glisten in the sun while brooding darkly under snow. Further demolition is phased through time, to be determined by others, from the west, eastwards. Throughout the demolition process all sited should be secured with opaque barriers. The extent of such areas should be readily visible. The avenue's vistas must intrigue the pedestrian.

THOM MAYNE/ MORPHOSIS
IFCCA

The issues faced for this project were to examine a new strategy for making public urban space whose formal arrangements provide for the continuous integration of supporting programmatic uses and to use this strategy in designing a proposal for the 16-block project.

The response is the creation of a new kind of public park, running from Penn Station and into the Hudson River, continuously infused with a great variety of public recreational, private, commercial and cultural, social and educational uses. These are positioned in and activate a multi-layered platform supporting and spatially integrated with the park, and also occupy adjacent buildings continuous with the surface and in places canting over the park to create volumetric enclosures open to the sun.

The orientation of the park, the third largest in the city, is on the true solar east-west axis and hence off the alignment of the grid to optimise the penetration of sunlight to one million square feet of public areas and greenery.

Additional private structures for office, commercial, housings, etc are built in the territories flanking the New City Park to the north and south and are connected to the park surface above actual grade and integrated into the surrounding built form of the existing city and its present and proposed transportation infrastructure. The project will be served by its own people mover (free to the public) connecting the new Penn Station to the river, with connections to a proposed fixed rail loop running across 42nd Street along the western edge of the Convention Center. The ferry terminal serving the increasing residential population along the river in New Jersey will be moved south to meet the people mover and fixed rail loop at the beach.

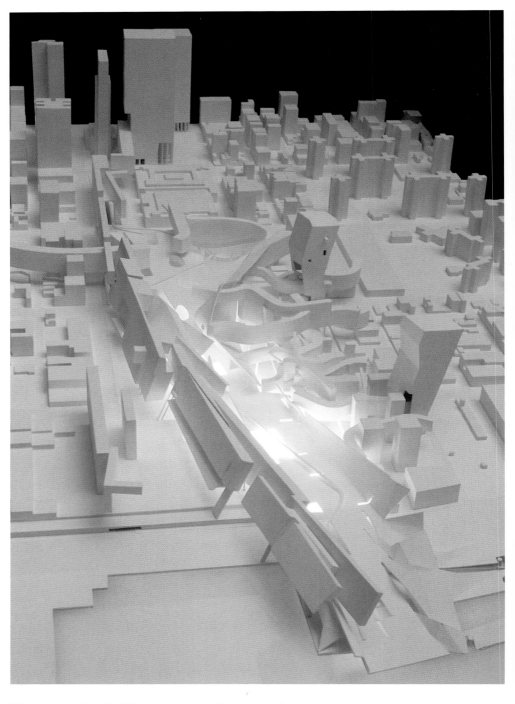

Above: a new kind of public park whose multi-layered enclosures are infused with a vast 'variety of uses';
Opposite page: in the context of Manhattan.

UN STUDIO
VAN BERKEL & BOS
IFCCA

Using combinations of digital techniques, the project integrates infrastructure, urbanism and various programmes by looking for correspondences and overlaps between the locations, parties and functions involved. The procedure of the Deep Plan involves generating a situation-specific, dynamic, organisational structural plan with parameter-based techniques. The combined use of automated design and animation techniques enables a working method that integrates questions of user movement, urban planning, construction and the potential for programme to develop at certain points in this web. The in-depth, interactive nature of the Deep Plan means that it incorporates economics, infrastructure, programme and construction in time.

The fascination of the emerging global city resides to some extent in its qualities of mutability and instability. Absences, deficiencies and deformations carry a transformational potential. In a sense, organisational structures emerging in this way can be likened to performance structures as they operate through living forces at physical and public levels. They are in motion as long as those forces are in motion and contain no hidden meaning independent of those forces. Structures such as these are no longer seen as the representation of homogenous, linear systems, but as process fields of materialisation. They are scaleless, subject to evolution, expansion, inversion and other contortions and manipulations.

336

Left: computer-generated conceptual model;
Below: vision of the Deep Plan
Opposite page: the plan both in action and in context

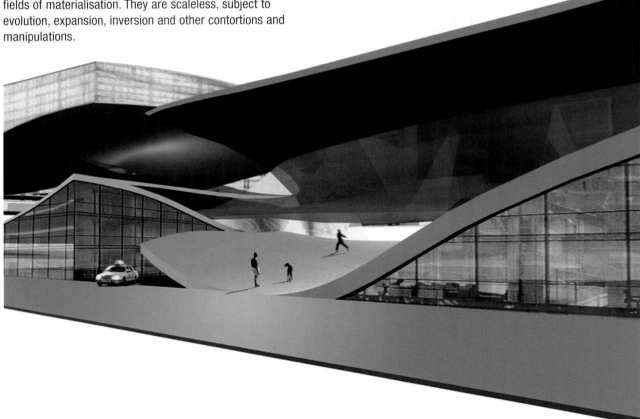

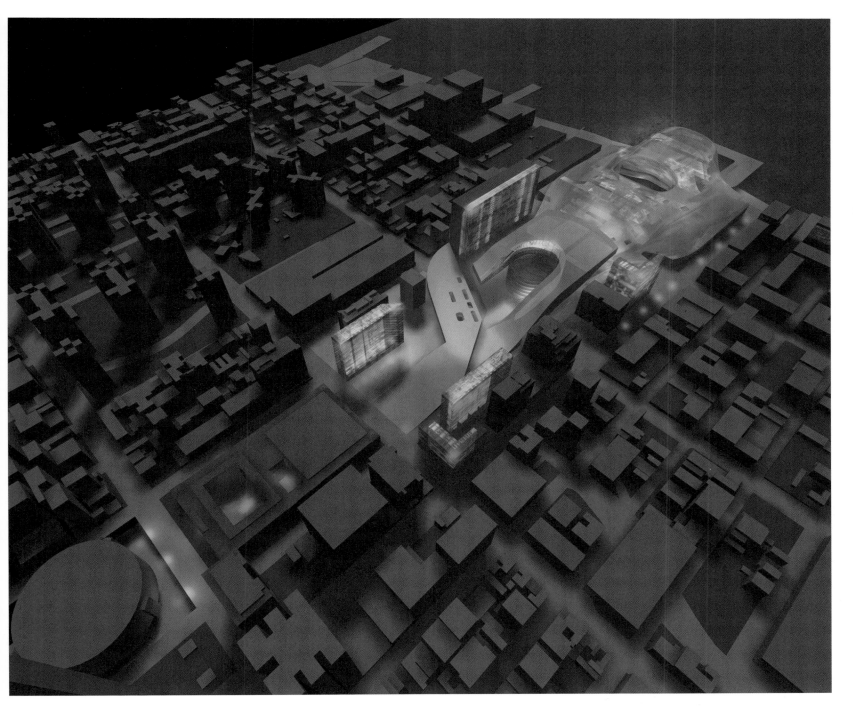

PETER EISENMAN
IFCCA

The West Side project proposes the development of a low-rise, high-density horizontal intervention at an urban scale, and introduces public open space laterally into the city rather than along the river's edge. Such a lateral intervention could be mirrored on the New Jersey side of the Hudson in a kind of reciprocal development. These decisions have implications for economic development and financing, neighbourhood planning, land use and zoning issues, transportation and, ultimately, for architecture.

The architectural consequences of this proposal are:

A way to integrate the old and the new in a new urban whole,

A way to integrate the river edge with the interior of the city,

A way to integrate large-scale public attractions into the city fabric,

A way to integrate low-rise commercial and residential development at a scale and density that marry community needs with economic sense,

A way to integrate regional, citywide and local, public and private transportation systems to provide new and ready access to the far West Side,

To present at different scales a series of public amenities – parkland, shopping, schools, hotels – as an integrated whole.

With the expansion of the Convention Center, the extension of the sub-surface transportation connections and the addition of hotels, shops and media centres, the West Side area will not only become a major magnet for tourism, it will also attract the commercial and residential tenants who make this area a neighbourhood. The proposed texture, density and proximities in the West Side scheme combine economic, social and political advantages with a progressive architectural image to present the first urban icon of the new millennium.

Above and left: views from the river.

A computer rendering in which the river becomes solid and a narrow band of Manhattan appears to be floating

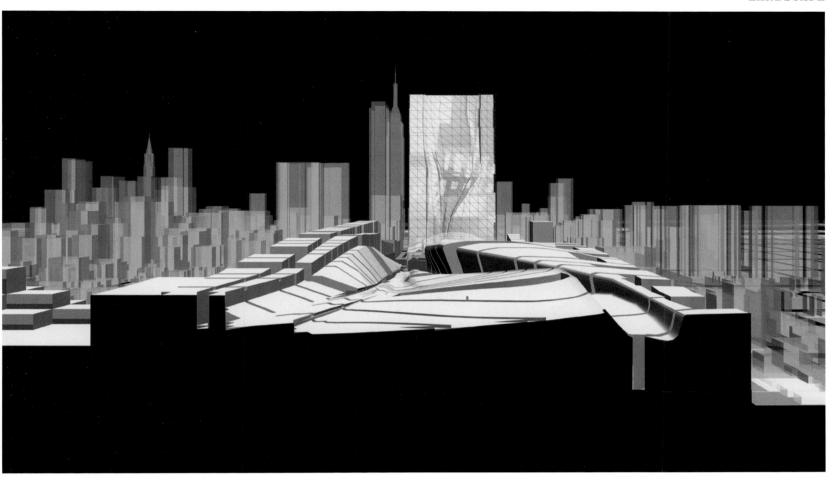

Above: an enigmatic section that appears to be only surface;
Right: the grid of Manhattan and the rail connections east and west – almost
all concentrating on the yards between 30th and 34th Streets.

Points of Interest

NEW YORK CITY AND VICINITY

Facts were up-to-date when prepared for publication but are subject to change.

AMERICAN MUSEUM OF THE MOVING IMAGE (E-3). 35th Ave. at 36th St., Astoria, Queens. The history of motion pictures, television, and video is portrayed through film clips and collections of related memorabilia.

BRONX ZOO (NEW YORK ZOOLOGICAL PARK) (F-2). Access via Fordham Rd., Pelham Pky., Southern Blvd., or Bronx River Pky. Among the world's largest zoos. Thousands of rare mammals, birds, and reptiles are exhibited, most in simulated natural habitats surrounded by moats. Among the many open-air preserves are the African Plains, South America, and Wild Asia. The 38 acres of Wild Asia are traversed by monorail.

BROOKLYN BOTANIC GARDEN (E-4). 1000 Washington Ave., across Flatbush Ave. from Prospect Park. This 50-acre facility is noted for its Japanese Hill-and-Pond Garden, fragrance garden for the blind and the Steinhardt Conservatory.

BROOKLYN MUSEUM (E-4). Eastern Pky. at Washington Ave. near Prospect Park. Collections include art from Egypt, the Pacific Islands and the Americas, and architectural ornaments from demolished New York City buildings.

THE CLOISTERS (E-2). Fort Tryon Park, off Henry Hudson Pky. This complex incorporates original sections from five medieval monasteries and other historic structures. It houses the Metropolitan Museum of Arts medieval collection featuring illuminated manuscripts and the famed Unicorn Tapestries. Gardens overlook the Hudson River.

GUGGENHEIM MUSEUM (E-3). 89th St. and Fifth Ave. Galleries leading off from the huge interior spiral ramp of this Frank Lloyd Wright-designed building display works by leading 20th-century artists.

MUSEUM OF THE CITY OF NEW YORK (E-3). Fifth Ave. at 103rd St. Exhibits present the history and culture of New York from the early days to the present.

NEW YORK AQUARIUM (E-6). W. Eighth St. at Surf Ave., Coney Island. Whales, rare and beautiful fish, sharks, sea anemones, electric eels, penguins, and seals are among the forms of marine life on exhibit. Visitors can watch training sessions.

STATEN ISLAND FERRY (D-5). This five-mile ferry trip between the Battery (the southern tip of Manhattan) and Staten Island provides excellent views of Lower Manhattan.

STATUE OF LIBERTY AND ELLIS ISLAND NATIONAL MONUMENTS (E-4). Circle Line passenger ferries to Liberty and Ellis Islands leave from Battery Park in Manhattan and Liberty State Park in Jersey City, N.J. French sculptor Frederic Auguste Bartholdi's 152-foot-high copper Statue of Liberty stands on a pedestal roughly the same height in New York Harbor. An exhibit in the base tells the story of its construction. An elevator carries visitors to the top of the pedestal, where a 22-story stairway leads to the crown's observation area. The Ellis Island Immigration Museum presents 400 years of American immigration history in the same buildings where millions of immigrants were processed during the peak years 1900-1924.

Index

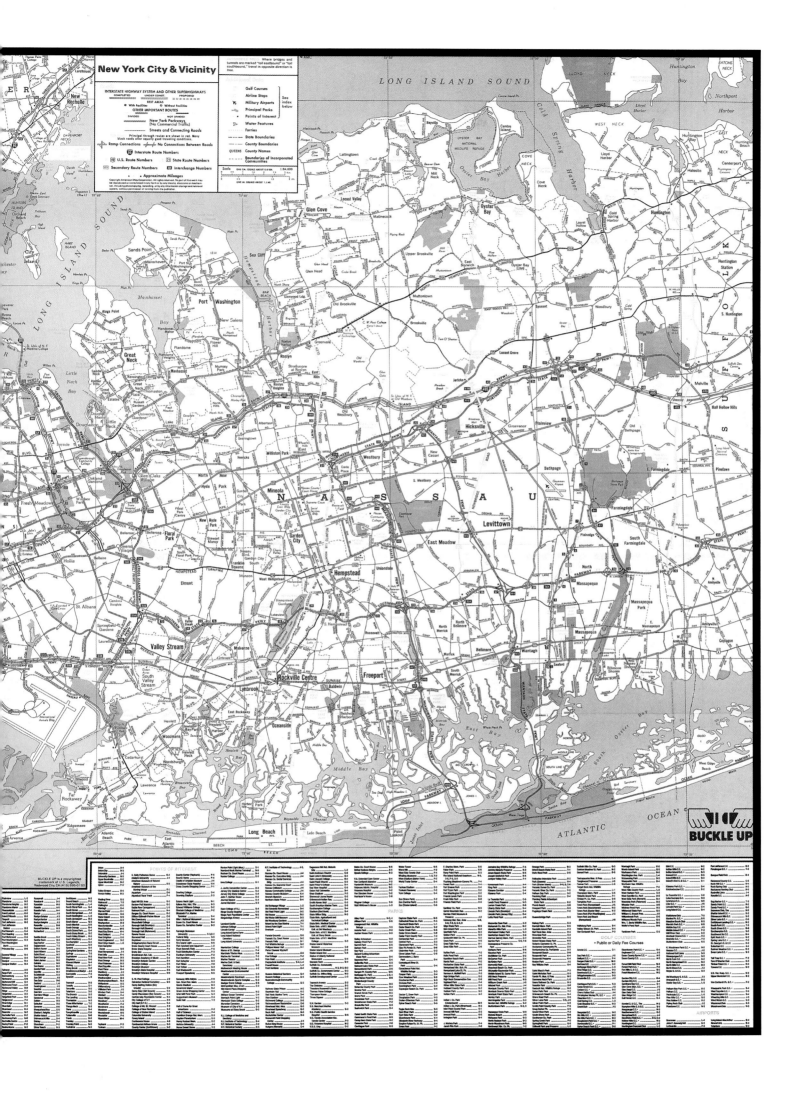

343

Bibliography

The selection of the projects and my essays emerges mostly from the stew of knowledge, memories and experience that great cities force on the consciousness. However, this is a most fortunate time for anyone studying the history and character of New York. Two books published in the last years of the last century offer rich and exhaustive histories of all aspect of the city – *Encyclopedia of New York City* edited by Kenneth Jackson, and Burrows and Wallace's *Gotham*. These are both the fruits of many years of scholarly work – Burrows and Wallace have considered the subject for over 20 years. Kenneth Jackson involved over a thousand people for well over a decade in forming the encyclopedia.

Including the two books mentioned above, the following books offer the richest and most substantial overview of the city's history and growth:

The *Iconography of Manhattan Island 1498–1909* compiled by Isaac Newton Phelps Stokes, published between 1915 and 1928 in six volumes. Republished by New Jersey Legal printers 1999.
The *Columbia Historical Portrait of New York: an Essay in Graphic History,* John A Kouwenhoven, Icon Editions, Harper and Row, New York, 1972
The Power Broker: Robert Moses and the Fall of New York, Robert A Caro, Vintage Books, New York, 1975
The Encyclopedia of New York City edited by Kenneth T Jackson, published by the Yale University Press, Yale & London and the New York historical Society, New York, 1998.
Gotham: a History of New York City to 1898, by Edwin G Burrows and Mike Wallace, published by Oxford University Press (New York Oxford), 1999.
New York: an Illustrated History, Ric Burns and James Sanders with Lisa Aedis.

The most substantial architectural scholarship contribution in the city has come from a series written under the leadership of Robert AM Stern beginning in the early Eighties with *New York 1900 : Metropolitan Architecture and Urbanism 1890–1915*. Since then the series has dealt with *New York 1880: Architecture and Urbanism in the Gilded Age*; *New York 1930: Architecture and Urbanism Between the Two World Wars*; *New York 1960: Architecture and Urbanism Between the Second World War and the Bicentennial* working with Gregory Gilmartin, John Mantague Massengale, Thomas Mellins, David Freedman, Raymond Gastil all published by Rizzoli or more recently the Monacelli Press. Stern's most recent work is *Manhattan Water-Bound: Manhattan's Waterfront from the Seventeenth Century to the Present* with Ann L Buttenwieser, Syracuse University Press, 1999.

Maps:
Manhattan in Maps, 1537–1995, Paul E Cohen and Robert T Augustyn, Rizzoli, New York, 1997.
The Historical Atlas of New York City, Eric Homburger with Alice Hudson Cartographic Consultant.
An Owl Book, Henry Holt and Company, New York, 1994.
Hagstrom Map of New York City: Five Boroughs with Building Numbers. No other document presents so completely the complexity, fragmentation and isolation of the many parts of this vast network. It makes clear the strategic force of the Moses highways, it shows the decline of ideological planning a clearly as it dramatises the power of the Manhattan grid.

Picture books:
Nineteenth Century New York in Rare Photographic Views edited by Frederick Lightfoot, Dover Publications, New York, 1982.
The Thirties by Berenice Abbott and *The Forties* by Andreas Feininger, both by Dover Publications, New York.
Imagining the Future of the Museum of Modern Art, (7 in the series of Studies in Modern Art), published by the Museum and distributed by Harry N Abrams, New York, 1998.

Exhibitions:
City of Ambition: Artists and New York 1900–1960 at the Whitney with a catalogue by Elizabeth Sussman with John G Hanhardt and Corey Keller, (Whitney Museum of Art, New York 1996). No matter the state of the world - the culture, character and health of the city have always been issues of continual importance to the *New York Times*. In the real estate and metro sections all the fine grain frictions that shape a city are continually documented. And in the cultural section a succession of gifted architectural critics have sustained a public engagement with architecture. Herbert Munschamp, the observer for the new millennium, is a wonderfully eccentric writer and is most effective in developing insights and maintaining a sense of the larger forces at work in the city. It is both a tribute to the intelligence of the *Times* and to Munschamp's imagination that he succeeds in maintaining architecture as vital part of the city culture. As with the *Times*, the city, its manners, its style, its moods and foibles, and the physical stage it creates is a perpetual subject in the texts and cartoons and frequently on the wonderful covers of *The New Yorker*. A similar role is played with great subtlety by the newspaper *The New York Observer*.

A final note, the intellectual underpinnings for the essays draws on all the obvious influences from Benjamin to Baudrillard and I find the compelling insights in the writing of geographers such as Edward Soja and Denis Cosgrove, but the book that has touched me most in the last year has been *An Empire Wilderness: Travels into America's Future* by Robert Kaplan (Random House, New York 1998). This offers evidence of deep shifts in the idea of the culture that needs to be recognised.